For Neil

First published by
Atrium
Atrium is an imprint of Cork University Press
Youngline Industrial Estate
Pouladuff Road
Togher
Cork
Ireland

© 2008

Author   Eleanor Heffernan
Photography & food design   Orla Keeshan   www.orlakeeshan.com
Design & illustration   Orlagh Murphy   www.orlaghmurphy.com

Watercolour of Cornucopia restaurant on contents page   Matt Grogan
Photographs on pages 11 (2 images on left), 17 (2 images, top left and bottom left),
   21 (1 image, bottom right) and 182 (1 image, centre)   Angela Marini   www.angelamarini.com
Contributions to staff collage pages 16 and 17   Lenka Valdova
Additional design   Eamon Whyte

British Library Cataloguing in Publication Data
A CIP catalogue record for this book is available from the British Library.

ISBN 978-0-9552261-4-4

Cornucopia
at home
The Cookbook

A collection of recipes from
Dublin's Cornucopia restaurant

Contents

Introduction

neil and deirdre on o'connell bridge, c.1974

A word from the owner

Cornucopia began when my husband, Neil McCafferty (1952–1993), and I returned to Ireland from Boston, USA, inspired to establish a wholefood shop and restaurant. It was the fulfilment of a long-held dream when, in January 1986, we first opened our doors at 19 Wicklow Street, Dublin.

Our concept was influenced by two of our favourite places in Boston – a small café called Pomme De Terre and a health food store called Erewhon ('Nowhere' backwards, and also the name of Samuel Butler's famous Utopian novel). We chose the name Cornucopia because it means abundance (literally 'horn of plenty' in Latin), and we thought it an excellent and apt name for the innovative and beautiful food-producing shop and restaurant we were planning.

Neil and I met in Dublin at the beginning of the 1970s, drawn to each other by a shared idealism. Ireland at that time was a conservative, troubled and economically challenged country, so we decided to seek adventure, work and further education in America. We set off with high hopes and some trepidation in June 1975, established ourselves in Boston that summer and were married in July in a simple but joyful ceremony.

Life in America

What was planned as a brief adventure turned into a nine-year sojourn. Despite acute bouts of homesickness from time to time, our years in America were full and happy. We made many lifelong friendships as we campaigned for social justice and worked our way through college. Through our part-time jobs, we started the embryonic careers that were to culminate eventually in the creation of Cornucopia. I was teaching fitness classes and developing an interest in nutrition and health, while Neil, working as a waiter in a variety of Boston and New York restaurants, was enjoying the buzz of catering. He spoke often of the hum and pleasure of working in a restaurant when everything starts to flow – delicious food, wonderful service, good ambience and happy customers.

At that time, our awareness centred on human rights and social justice. Neither of us was vegetarian or had awareness of food, animal rights, the environment or any of the green issues that are so central to today's consciousness. Though still motivated by political movements, I was also becoming interested in the idea of personal responsibility and was developing an understanding that change is important both within society and within an individual person.

Hippocrates Health Institute

In 1979, as I cycled to work at my job in the Boston YWCA, I passed the Hippocrates Health Institute on Exeter Street. I stopped one day to read a poster on the wall outside about the Institute's philosophy, liked what it said and walked in. That decision was to have huge implications for the future course of my life and Neil's.

Exercise instructing 1980, Boston Harbour 1983, gardening in Hippocrates 1984

At first I was wary, wondering had I stumbled on some kind of cult. Books were on sale in the lobby and I flicked through titles unfamiliar to me, such as *The Essene Gospel of Peace* translated by Edmund Bordeaux Szekley and *Survival into the 21st Century* by Viktoras Kulvinskas. The staff members looked alight from the inside out. They were gentle and friendly, their eyes were bright, their skin seemed to glow and they had a different energy about them. I learned they were not only vegetarians, but also raw food vegetarians.

Over the next few months, I often found myself calling by as I cycled home. I chatted to staff and guests and was invited onto their two-week programme. I met their founder Ann Wigmore and developed an awareness that change can be based in the chemical composition of our bodies, and that feeling good doesn't have to wait for outer change in society, or for the perfect personal situation to come along.

I had always been a happy, upbeat person. However, experiencing a 100% raw food vegetarian diet over that two-week stay at the Hippocrates Institute had a profoundly positive effect on me, psychologically and spiritually. I had boundless energy and felt happiness of a quality I had rarely experienced before.

Of course the Hippocrates diet was a lot more than vegetarian; it involved a radical cleansing of the physical system, introducing easily absorbable super-nutrition, which released a lot of extra energy into the system. As I was young and healthy, this extra energy was not just used for healing and boosting my immune system but had the effect of supercharging me psychologically.

While attending my two-week stint at the Institute, I cycled home every evening to see Neil. He was fascinated to see the change in me and said: 'Whatever you are on, I want some of it too.' Throughout the following year I continued to work at the Boston YWCA while volunteering at the Institute. I taught a gentle exercise class to the guests attending the two-week programme. Many of these were in poor health, and came to Hippocrates with diagnoses of life-threatening illnesses. It was thrilling to see the profoundly positive changes a raw food vegetarian diet had on them.

Becoming vegetarian and first recipes

Neil and I made the decision to become vegetarian that year. Neil rapidly developed a passion for vegetarian cooking, creating truly delicious food. Prior to this, we had enjoyed the full Irish diet, without a thought about its sources or consequences, and cooked meat, potatoes and two vegetables in the traditional way.

I had a very unsophisticated palate and was suspicious of anything unusual. Neil was more adventurous, and I remember him encouraging me to taste avocado. I thoroughly disliked the strange texture, but it is now one of my favourite foods!

Many of the early recipes for Cornucopia were created in our kitchen for our dinner table during this time. Our friends were thrilled to be invited around for dinner: vegetarian lasagnes, curries, soups, salads, and other experiments. It is amazing that such a talent had lain dormant in Neil for so long.

Sometimes we lived fully on a raw/living diet and other times we enjoyed cooked vegan and vegetarian foods. Our love of beautifully created cooked vegetarian foods eventually overrode the more radical and purist experience of a raw food vegetarian lifestyle, but my abiding memory of those in the raw food movement is that of happy, healthy people, full of energy and mirth!

During this period, the yearning to return home became a very strong voice within me. Ireland was going through tough times economically, socially and politically, but we, idealistic as ever, became very motivated by the dream of setting up a healing/vegetarian centre there.

Return to Ireland

In 1984 we made the difficult decision to return. At Shannon airport, when I excitedly told the customs official that I was back home after nine years, he asked me why and told me to turn back, that everybody else was leaving the country!

My excitement at being home was, however, unquashable. I was overjoyed to be back to the sights, smells and feel of Ireland – and of course to my family. We set up a sandwich business initially, supplying fresh sandwiches to staffrooms in local schools, and we made the decision to open a health food shop, as this seemed a practical way to begin.

Neil and I were idealists first and business people second. Had we realised that many restaurants didn't survive due to a 23% annual VAT bill and other huge economic challenges, we might not have ventured on. A seriously worked business plan would probably have projected huge losses and financial failure. Perhaps it's lucky we didn't have the business degrees or financial advisers to dampen our enthusiasm.

After a few false starts, we found a site on Dublin's Wicklow Street and became leaseholders in November 1985, converting the premises from a dry-cleaner's and shoe repair shop into a health food store. We did all this on a tiny budget of £11,000 – a £5000 overdraft from the bank and a £6000 loan from my parents, money that we paid back in incremental repayments of £100 per week. A simple and gentle record of these repayments was kept in a red notebook that was stored on the top shelf of their kitchen press. I found this notebook recently and was moved by memories of their loving support. And so, in January 1986, Cornucopia began.

The early days

The sheer hard work of those first years was exhausting but in many ways our youth, enthusiasm, innocence and lack of research protected us. The shop stocked fruit, vegetables and wholefoods – nuts, seeds, grains, herbs, spices, lentils and beans. Most of the wholefoods were sold loose from bins with plexiglass doors that Neil and I had artfully constructed in our backyard.

We also sold vitamins, minerals and food supplements and enjoyed dispensing health and healing information to the many customers that poured through the door from the first day. Our idea was that all the ingredients required to create a delicious vegetarian meal would be available in the one store. Crafts, cooking utensils for a wholefood lifestyle and books on health and healthful living, which we imported directly from America, were also available. At the back of the shop there was a small salad serve-over deli-area and a hot pie-dispensing unit, as well as about 25 high stools pulled up to benches constructed from louvre doors with glass coverings. There Neil, using inspiration initially from *The Moosewood Cookbook* by Mollie Katzen, along with his own imagination, cooked and served hummus, tabbouleh, Indonesian-style rice salad, vegetarian curries and lasagnes and delicious soups. My mother also helped in the beginning, baking fruit scones for us at home on a daily

1985   1986   1994

basis, which we collected from her house and brought in to sell from our counter. After a number of months she stopped this, feeling we were ready to produce our own baked goods. Some customers liked her baking so much that they were very disappointed. One gentleman from a local men's clothing shop put up a little joke petition on the wall with the heading 'Bring Back Mother's Scones'. We had a happy and jovial relationship from the very beginning with our daily regulars.

The shop was very busy and yet people squashed themselves together on the stools to partake of the delicious fare. As too few seats were available, customers creatively took the stock off the shelves and stood with their soups and salads perched on the space they had cleared. Vegetarianism was new and strange to many people, yet the delicious food kept people coming back. Cornucopia quickly won its way into the hearts of many customers who remain regulars to this day.

We ran Cornucopia as a health food shop and small café for the next seven years until December 1992. I worked in the health food shop and Neil ran the café. Those years were exciting and fulfilling; we were thrilled to be back in Ireland, the business was succeeding, we managed to buy a house and our two beloved daughters, Roisín and Dairíne, were born in 1986 and 1988. So many things were happening in the one small space that one customer told us we should rechristen the place 'Can you

cope with it?' Neil and I worked very hard and one of us was always present in the restaurant/shop, while one of us minded the children at home. The toddlers had Mammy minding them one day and Daddy the next and the eldest girl when she started to talk had the one name for us, which was Maddy. Life seemed perfect in many ways. We were grateful for all that we had achieved and were enjoying the changing Ireland of the early 1990s.

We were very close to both the staff and the regular customers and had a lot of fun together. Cornucopia has had a great Christmas party for the staff every year since we started, and it is a tradition we still stick to. Santa always comes, and often many former staff, still 'Cornucopians' at heart, join the festivities. I well recall the first time Neil and I left the premises with the staff running it by themselves, a big step for us, to go to a cousin's wedding. As we walked through the restaurant together, dressed in our finery, all the customers started clapping!

Within our first few weeks we became very busy, although money remained extremely tight. It was apparent to one customer, Mairéad De Faoite, that we might not make it if we didn't have help, as the service was not quick enough. We couldn't afford any more staff. Because she was vegetarian, she supported what we were doing and volunteered her services. Often she brought her young children with her, and they were kept busy packing bags of beans and herbs for the shop. She soon joined the staff and worked with us for many years and is a dear friend to this day.

We worked hard, and received our first accolade in 1988, Walker's Award for the Best Vegetarian Restaurant in Ireland. At this time an investor approached us, encouraging us to franchise, as he believed that fast-food health food was the new way forward. We declined, deciding not to go in that direction, as the dilution of product and the pressure to maximise profits for shareholders would probably remove the essential ingredient that makes Cornucopia what it is.

Eventually the demand for the café far outweighed the demand for the shop, so we passed the retail section on to one of our senior staff, Paula, and Cornucopia became fully a restaurant in January 1993.

Parting

Early in June that same year, Neil fell suddenly and dramatically ill. Over one very traumatic weekend, he became jaundiced and was diagnosed with pancreatic cancer. We were told that he had only a number of weeks to live. No medical treatment was offered, as it was considered that his liver and pancreas were too badly damaged. He was only 40

Family portrait 1990: Roisín, Neil, Deirdre and Dairíne

and I was 39. It is difficult to describe the utter shock and horror that we suffered.

When I could sleep at night, each morning was like waking up to a nightmare. Neil was very courageous. He instantly reverted to the lifestyle he had been taught at Hippocrates, eating a diet of raw vegetarian food, but our destinies, which had been so united and connected for twenty years, were now suddenly rent apart. Neil's destiny pointed towards early death and all the unknowingness that that entails. He would have to say goodbye, forever, to the beauty of human life, to his family and friends, to his young children, to his work, to the nature and music that he loved, to his future. And the destiny that now loomed before me was to live without him – as a widow, mother of two young children, running a business on my own.

Death was not something to which we had ever given much serious thought. Whatever spiritual muscles we had developed through our Irish Catholic upbringing and our dabbling in Buddhism were of tremendous help over this time, as were the many people who helped us ('human angels', as Ann Wigmore used to call them). Neil's wonderful sisters and family minded our children. The staff at Cornucopia, in particular our chef/manageress Pamela Windsor and our chefs Gina, Paula and Michelle, did a great job of running the business on their own while I nursed Neil.

We were grateful that we had some time together to take leave of one another, unlike the many that lose a loved one through sudden death. After a valiant battle against the cancer over the following three months, Neil died in my arms in September 1993.

Afterwards, I was in shock, as it had all happened so quickly. When the numbness wore off, the pangs of parting were intense. They reminded me of the pangs of childbirth, which is not unlike death in its intensity of experience.

I have certainly learned humility from my experience. We were Mr and Mrs Health food, and yet one of us met an early death through cancer. There are no certainties in life, no absolute answers. We fumble our way along, and the only certainty that we have as human beings is love for one another. I know that healthy, delicious food is a form of love and I have continued to work with, and love, the restaurant that Neil and I started together.

Recovery and taking the helm

With the assistance of loyal and talented staff members, I have succeeded in continuing to run Cornucopia. It is said that what does not break you makes you strong. One of my favourite books, *The Prophet* by Kahlil Gibran, states that 'pain is the breaking of the shell that encloses our understanding' and 'when we have reached the mountaintop that it is then that we begin to climb.' I have lived my life by such philosophy over the past years and have found it helpful.

I have gone on to rear two wonderful daughters and have recovered the joy of marriage with my loving husband, Osgur. I have enjoyed, or tried to enjoy, every moment of this tremendous experience we call life. I have become more knowledgeable about business and love being part of the vibrant, living community that is Cornucopia. There is not a day that my heart does not lift when I walk through its doors. It has a truly amazing atmosphere, emanating from the food and the people who are part of its daily routines and rhythms.

Philosophy

Cornucopia's food aims to achieve a happy union between health and taste. The philosophy I absorbed at the Hippocrates Health Institute has informed the health ethos and the overall ethics of Cornucopia since its inception. This philosophy is based on the axiom of Hippocrates, the philosopher and father of modern medicine, who said, 'Let food be your medicine'.

The quality of the food we eat on a daily basis and how it is prepared directly affect every aspect of our being. Food of the highest quality is fresh, natural, preferably organic, in season, vegan or vegetarian. It contains a high proportion of salads and uncooked or lightly cooked fresh vegetables and fruits and freshly made juices, all of which are vitamin and enzyme rich.

2008: Deirdre and Osgur, Corncupia counter staff, Deirdre and Eleanor

When our cells are properly nourished and the waste from our bodies, from a cellular level upwards, is efficiently removed, all aspects of our being, from mood and energy level to overall wellness, are greatly enhanced. Ensuring that all this is provided without compromising taste, flavour, texture or appearance is the true magic and alchemy that is worked in Cornucopia.

Each day, hour by hour, year by year, with the sense of urgency and deadline that is common to all restaurants, the fresh supplies arrive, and the fruit, vegetables and sacks of dried goods are transformed using a combination of skill, recipes, chopping, sprouting, blending, boiling, baking and sautéing into an array of salads, soups, breads, desserts, main dishes and fresh juices. Fresh herbs, fresh ingredients, skill, experience, creativity, imagination, research and consultation on the part of the chefs and management ensure a varied, lively menu that excites the palate of both staff and customers. Eighty per cent of our menu changes daily – and is planned a week in advance.

Many of our staff and customers are vegetarian and many are not. All enjoy the food and benefit from it. For those who make the decision to become vegetarian or vegan, the knowledge that they eat a cruelty-free, non-violent meal, where no animal has suffered, provides an additional positive dimension to the experience.

I truly believe that taking responsibility for the small things we do daily can have a far-reaching and cumulative ripple effect, both outwards to the larger world and inwards to our own beings. At a time in history when we can feel frustrated that there is little we can do to effect positive change in the world, why not start with our food, our most personal interface with nature? The right choice on a meal-to-meal basis can go on to affect all our interrelationships on this planet in a more profound manner than many of us can imagine.

The future

Cornucopia has had a presence on Dublin's Wicklow Street for over two decades now. Our third decade will see great changes for the restaurant. At the time of writing we are planning to expand from the current 50 to 100 seats, spread over three floors at both 19 and 20 Wicklow Street. Number 20 is a beautiful Georgian building that we intend to bring back to some of its former glory. This exciting development will provide scope for more customers, more creativity and more wonderful food.

Dublin and Ireland have obviously changed greatly in the years since we opened. Health awareness and culinary awareness have greatly improved, and Cornucopia has had, and will continue to have, an important role to play in this. I'm glad we didn't listen to that customs official and turn back in 1984!

The cookbook

Cornucopia is proud and delighted to present this cookbook, with a selection of tried and tested, life-enhancing and taste-thrilling recipes for you to try at home. A decision to walk away from processed food means that more time must be spent on shopping, chopping, preparing, cooking and cleaning up, but the rewards for this decision are numerous. Probably one of the most significant consequences is the personal taking back of power from a world that demands more and more speed and less personal satisfaction.

Processed foods are quick, convenient and sometimes tasty, but they steal from the body and the mind and even the spirit, taking away far more than they give back in time saved. Home producing more natural, healthy and energy-giving meals, as with any creative endeavour, yields pleasure and satisfaction on many levels.

Time, a most precious commodity, is well spent on our health, an equally precious commodity. Home cooking is indeed also a carrier, on an energetic level, of the positive emotions we fold in for our family and friends. Add to this the wonderful and welcoming aromas and visual beauty of homemade food and it truly becomes something we should decide not to live without.

A weekly shop at the organic farmers' market, the health food shop or the fruit and vegetable section of the local food market ensures that the ingredients required are there at your fingertips in your cupboards and fridge. Cooking/food-preparing two or three times a week, with proper storage, will ensure that fresh, delicious food becomes part of your daily fare. Your eyes will be brighter, your mind clearer, your mood lighter and your step springier!

Dedications

This cookbook is dedicated to many, but primarily to Neil, Cornucopia's original co-founder with me, without whose inspiration, talent, enthusiasm and hard work it would not have been possible to create Cornucopia. We worked side by side for seven years creating this amazing place and, for the fourteen years that he has been physically gone, Neil's spirit, love of life and love of great food have inspired me and those who work with me.

In 2004, Cornucopia endured a second loss, with the untimely death of one of our much-loved chefs, Eddie Bates. The loss of Eddie, and his passion for food, wry sense of humour, impeccable good manners and sense of fair play, has left a hole in all of our hearts. A number of Eddie's inspirational recipes are included here. We still love you and miss you, Eddie.

This book is further dedicated to all the people who make and have made Cornucopia happen on a daily, hourly basis — from its twenty-two years of staff, past and present, to its suppliers and its customers. Many staff, no longer working with us, have contributed to the living, breathing mini-community that is Cornucopia and are still proud to call themselves 'Cornucopians'. Thanks especially to Mairéad De Faoite, Gina, Paula, Pamela, Teresa, Maureen Nugent, Maureen O'Toole, Cathy, Paul, Peter, Inge, Michelle, Joan, Carol, Claire, John Swan, Josh, Sinead, Jean, Denise, Mo, Marie & Philip, Ann-Marie, Betty, Del, Ann & John Rahill (our accountant), who no longer work in our restaurant, but whose indelible recipes and systems have become part of who we are.

To all present staff, including my two daughters, Roisín and Dairíne, to my niece, Ciara, to Phil, Margaret, Tony, Eleanor, Josef, Eamonn, Chris, James, Marek, Eddie,

Podge, Lenka, Monika, Ruth and Jane and all kitchen porters and counter staff – too numerous to mention by name – much thanks and appreciation!

All this work and production is, of course, for the delight of our dear customers, who daily arrive for the food that we create to satisfy their appetites, tickle their taste-buds and enhance their health and life-force. This book is also dedicated to all these customers, past and present. Thanks for your custom, encouragement and appreciation and for the many requests for a Cornucopia cookery book over the years. Here it finally is.

Acknowledgements

Eleanor Heffernan, the main author of our book, has put her many creative talents to work to make the idea a reality – talents for writing, cooking, organisation, time management and for cajoling and forming me, the book team, the chefs, the managers, the customers and the suppliers into a team working for her and supplying her with the support, resources, recipes, pointers, creative space, equipment and feedback necessary to allow this book to emerge from her visionary pen and pan!

Eleanor worked within Cornucopia as waitress, manager, chef, translator and staff counsellor for seven years and knows and loves the restaurant and its feel and philosophy intimately. I will be forever grateful to her for her writing ability, charm and intelligence, for her unique ability to bring dreams and aspirations down to earth into practical charts, time-lines, check-lists and agendas, and most especially for the focus and dedication over the past year that it has taken to create the wonderful *Cornucopia at home*. We are all overjoyed that Eleanor and her partner John are expecting their first baby, whose tiny presence has imbued the book project with one further layer of excitement, delight and anticipation. Congratulations to Eleanor and John.

Orla Keeshan, our young and vibrant photographer, has lent her many talents to both the food design and the stunning collection of photographs in this book. Over the past year she has travelled to our suppliers' organic farms and gardens taking pictures of crops, flowers and markets. She worked with Eleanor as each recipe was tested, photographing the food in her own kitchen and garden as it was taken from her own oven, and styling the photographs with a collection of dish-ware and props, creatively sourced from builders' suppliers, art shops and homeware shops, with her talented eye. All the photographs are of the food in its natural state and only natural light is used. Orla, who until recently worked as a waitress in Cornucopia, is a Fine Arts student, specialising in photography, at Dún Laoghaire College of Art and Design. She now curates the art exhibitions that enliven the walls of Cornucopia.

Orlagh Murphy, also an ex-waitress from Cornucopia, and a recent graduate in Visual Communication (BDes) from the National College of Art and Design, is the young woman responsible for the design and layout of the book, the stunning hand-drawn illustrations and in particular the cover illustration and design. Orlagh has carefully designed a book with the texture and feel of Cornucopia coming from every page. When we were choosing a publisher, Orlagh in particular felt that it was important that we choose a company that would allow us complete creative control. The nature of this day-by-day creative process has allowed the choosing of the recipes, the testing and photographing of them and the design of the book to be intrinsically linked, and one has inspired the other.

A word of special thanks to Tony Keogh, our head chef, who has overseen all the recipes and checked them thoroughly before giving them his special stamp of approval, and to Claire McCormack, the talented pastry chef behind many of our cake and bread recipes, who approached this whole project with passion and dedication.

Thanks to Philip West, author of the first draft of the cookbook, who is now project managing Cornucopia's expansion into the building next door, and to manager Margaret Burke, who assisted so much in the choosing of the recipes and who, more than anyone else, has been responsible in recent years for the high standard of the food in Cornucopia. A special word of thanks also to Natalia and Willie, of the publishing company Stitchy Press, both also ex-staff members, who were involved in the initial planning and development of this book and with doing research.

Thanks also to Font Literary Agency in Clontarf, made up of a partnership of Aine McCarthy (novelist Orna Ross), a long-time customer of Cornucopia, and Ita O'Driscoll, coincidentally the aunt of our own author, Eleanor Heffernan. Thanks for their encouragement and assistance and for finding us the wonderful Cork University Press with Mike Collins and Maria O'Donovan, who have allowed us almost free rein with our creative process and have assisted us financially and practically. A special word of appreciation to my husband Osgur and to all my family for their love and support.

We hope you enjoy this book as much as we have enjoyed creating it!

Bon appétit, good health and sláinte!

Deirdre McCafferty
May 2008

A word from a customer

'You're a writer,' Deirdre said. 'We're doing a cookbook. Would you write a foreword?' A foreword to a cookbook from Cornucopia, my favourite restaurant, my home from home, in which I've been fed and nurtured for more than two decades?

'Of course,' I said. 'I'd be delighted.'

'Just a few paragraphs about your experience as a customer and your memories of Cornucopia and Dublin back in the 1980s and 90s.'

'Sure.' Then, putting on my professional hat – my day job is giving editorial and publishing advice – I asked, 'Who's publishing the book?'

'We're doing it ourselves. Three of the girls who work in the restaurant are cooking and writing and designing it. They're amazingly talented.'

As I returned to my meal – chickpea casserole with garlic potato, sprouted bean salad and fruit – I began to think of what I would write about and found myself thinking back to the time when there was no Cornucopia. When bombs went off, killing people North and South. When we weren't allowed to have a divorce or, in many parts of the country, a condom. When hard-pressed PAYE workers went on strikes and marches. When people emigrated in droves, with no intention of returning. When almost every month a building, or sometimes even a whole street, was demolished to clear the way for cars – our political masters' idea of progress.

In those days, few of us had ever tasted asparagus, avocado or artichoke. Bread came in two varieties: soda or sliced. Cooking oil was Mazola. Cheese was processed to a pulp, then cut into triangles and wrapped in silver paper (Why? Why?).

I was working in a city centre health club when I first heard about the young couple who had returned from the States to open a wholefood shop and vegetarian café on Wicklow Street. The food was said to be healthy, hearty, delicious and – big attraction in recession-hit Dublin – cheap.

To be vegetarian then was to take a road less travelled. I have never been vegan or even staunchly vegetarian. I would accept a meat meal if somebody offered it to me unknowingly or would eat fish if necessary. Even still, in those early days, it was challenging to be a vegetarian in Ireland. Trying to hold the line with people or restaurants that considered you a faddy inconvenience. Deflecting meatarians who interpreted your personal preference as an invitation to argument. For more strictly vegetarian friends, it was even harder: explaining that no, vegetarians don't eat fish, or trying to ensure that they weren't surreptitiously being fed meat stock by well-meaning relatives who were 'worried' about them.

The plus side was that, in renouncing meat you joined a community of like-minded souls, already predisposed to like and trust each other. The occasional fanatic aside, veggies tend to be a great bunch of people: tolerant, thoughtful, open-minded and progressive. Tolerance, thoughtfulness, open-mindedness and progressiveness were just what Dublin needed at that time. Which was why it was such a joy to see Cornucopia arrive. As I look back from here, it seems that the opening of Cornucopia heralded the coming of then unimaginable change. Other national institutions were born around the same time – TV3, Temple Bar, the National Lottery – but none that had more impact on my life. Impact doesn't come more fundamental than food.

'Cornucopia is doing a cookbook,' I said next day to my colleague, literary agent Ita O'Driscoll. 'I'm thrilled.'
'I know,' she said.
'You do?'
'My niece, Eleanor, is doing the writing.'
'Really? But that's amazing. It seems like a sign.'
'You and your signs. Is that your way of saying we should see if we can get them a publisher?'
'Do you think they'd want one?'
'Let's ask.'

We asked. Deirdre and the team were underwhelmed. A publisher might want to dilute their vision. Would they retain control over words, paper, design, cover and so on? We didn't know about that, but we could tell them that, as self-publishers, they were making their lives extra difficult, particularly when it came to distributing the book beyond the restaurant. If they wanted to see their book in the shops, they would find it costly and onerous to set it up and administer. Marketing and publicity to reach beyond their existing customers would be even more time- and money-consuming.

Deirdre listened. She still had qualms but we got the go-ahead to put out feelers. As we expected, the Cornucopia name ignited immediate interest and more than one publisher made a bid. In the end, Cork University Press (CUP) was felt to be closest to the spirit and aims of *Cornucopia at home* and had already produced some beautiful vegetarian cookbooks.

A round table meeting was set up with Deirdre, Orla the photographer, Orlagh the designer, Eleanor the writer, Ita, myself and the editors from CUP. Everyone was awed by the vision and the talent of the team. By the end of the meeting, we had an agreement.

'Isn't it great?' Deirdre said, beaming around at us. 'This is the Cornucopia way. Organic.' One of the things that delighted her most was not the size of the deal but that it had been brought together by a long-time customer and Eleanor's auntie. There are smarter restaurants, restaurants with more space and more style, where they will serve you at your table and pour your wine for you, but there is no restaurant in Dublin that takes my health more seriously, that works harder to make their food delicious, that has such considerate and interesting staff.

It is the people, as much as the food, that make Cornucopia special. Long before immigrants from other countries became commonplace in Dublin's restaurants, travellers, gap-year students and seekers of all kinds fetched up there — on both sides of the counter. Wherever they came from, the one thing they all had in common was that they were smiling. That level of satisfaction, in those who feed and those who are fed, arises only when a restaurant wants to do more than just serve food at a profit.

It is no small thing to set up your business, and your life, around deeply held principles. That is what Deirdre and Neil did when they came back from America and what Cornucopia continues to do. What goes on there day after day has always reminded me of that saying of Ghandi's: 'You must be the change you want to see in the world.' Cornucopia didn't try to change Dublin. Nobody ever preached or evangelised. It just calmly, steadily, persistently got on with *being* that change. Cornucopia is more than a restaurant; it is a vote for a way of being in the world. A signpost helping us to stay on the road less travelled. For me, its being here in Dublin has made all the difference. So I am proud to play my small part in its latest venture, this wonderful cookbook that captures the spirit of the restaurant. All its goodness is here — the food, the ambience, the ethos, the colour, the innovation, the creativity — beautifully presented for us to take home and take to heart.

Deepest thanks to all,
Orna Ross

www.ornaross.com

A word from the author

Welcome to *Cornucopia at home*, a collection of recipes from Cornucopia Vegetarian Wholefood Restaurant in Dublin. We present to the home cook an array of recipes from our extensive and enduring repertoire of soups, salads, main courses, breads and desserts. They are all, of course, vegetarian. Each section also contains a selection of suitable options for those adhering to the special diets catered for in our restaurant: vegan, gluten-free, wheat-free, yeast-free, egg-free, dairy-free, sugar-free and nut-free. Many recipes use entirely wholefood ingredients and we encourage use of local and seasonal vegetables, free-range organic eggs, 'good' fats and an awareness of nutritional balance. Our recipes are designed to create healthy, hearty, delicious, nourishing and heart-warming foods that are easy to make and delightful to eat.

What is this book and who is it for?

How many times over the years have we been asked, 'When are you going to publish a cookbook?' 'It's in the pipeline', we'd invariably reply. It was neither for want of recipes nor for want of an audience that the cookbook, until now, remained unwritten. We were just all too busy running the restaurant! Finally, persistence on the part of our customers via phone calls, emails, comment books and nabbing the restaurant owner, Deirdre, in her local food market demanding a cookbook, as well as a fortuitous freeing up of staff eager to embrace the project, has propelled the pipeline-dwelling promise into a hardback reality – a friendly and unique mish-mash of eastern and western vegetarian recipes, executed in a casual, home-cooked style with constant awareness of providing for those adhering to special or restricted diets. It is not a general reference book for vegetarian cookery, but rather a guide to recreating Cornucopia-style food at home.

   That is what this cookbook is all about – teaching people to cook in the

'Cornucopia way' — the organic amalgamation of cooking styles, methods, language and emphases that have evolved in our little space over the last two decades. It is for people who like vegetarian food, who like wholefood, who like comforting food, who like health food and who like to cook everything from scratch. It is for people who have eaten in Cornucopia for years and always wondered how to replicate that delicious dressing on their favourite sprouted bean salad, or what that herb in the Spanish chickpea casserole is or how exactly to go about making a flapjack without using butter and flour. It is for people who popped in once or twice and found a unique place where everything was just a little bit different from anything they'd ever experienced before, a refreshing change from the more generic food culture that has taken over our busy, convenience-oriented towns and cities, inspiring them to make an effort themselves to broaden their daily food experience.

This book is also for people who have never heard of Cornucopia but would enjoy an attractive, substantial cookbook with wonderful photographs and a narrative that not only describes the blow by blow of each recipe but also conveys a sense of the community that occupies 19 Wicklow Street — both staff and customers — its evolution over the years, its charm, its independence, its ethics and, above all, its commitment to real, honest food. At a very practical level, it is a book for vegetarians and non-vegetarians alike who like to cook, not hunt supermarket shelves checking labels, and for vegans, coeliacs and anyone else who would like to enjoy a varied and colourful menu whilst adhering to more specific dietary requirements. All recipes are marked with symbols to indicate their suitability for each special diet (see next section for details). We hope this book will provide you with some new-found favourite recipes that will become part of your repertoire for years to come.

Note: due to the extended timescale involved in bringing a book from conception to publication, recipes that have been added to the Cornucopia menu within the past eighteen months have not been included in this book. They will, of course, find their place in a subsequent publication.

A word of thanks

Cornucopia at home is truly a product of the Cornucopia community. From the creation of the original recipes to their recent adaptation for home use, from the photography, graphic design and artwork to the writing and editing, this book was put together entirely by members of the restaurant staff. The chefs, managers and

waiting staff had the know-how to visualise, plan, write, design and illustrate this
cookbook. It was wonderful to have a team of people who not only already knew
each other professionally, but who also all knew Cornucopia intimately — its food,
style, ambience, clientele and ethos — and as a result shared an overall vision of how
the book should turn out. That's not to say we cruised the steady waters of blissful
agreement from start to finish, not to say our tiny basement office wasn't witness
to the occasional stand-off between visionary chef, pragmatic writer and assuredly
gourmet manager, not to say that there wasn't wrangling over whether a photograph
of a half-licked teaspoon constituted appetising art or unpublishable sleaze. However,
as proprietor Deirdre exclaimed one debate-riddled day, 'Isn't it WONDERFUL that
we can all argue so animatedly about food, that that's all we have to disagree on?' She
was right — our differences were less about the fundamental aspirations of the book
and more about selfishly ensuring that our own personal favourites were represented
in it. And, in the end, we found a very simple formula for our uncertainties — when in
doubt, pose the question, 'What do the customers think? What have they eaten with
most gusto, what recipes have they asked most enthusiastically about, what catches
their eye, what ingredients do they get excited by?' Those questions have shaped the
content of our book, just as the profile of our customers has influenced the look and
feel of our book — which proved a really useful umbrella aesthetic for the unruly gang
of mad-hatters at the helm!

Thanks are owed to the many customers who have encouraged us over the years to
publish a recipe book. 'When is the book coming out?' has been almost as common a
question as 'Excuse me, where's the tap water?' ('There is a filter water machine just
by the front door') and 'What time does the queue die down?' ('Rarely, I'm afraid!').
Enormous thanks to all the counter staff, who patiently answered enquiries about the
cookbook with suitably non-committal vagueness for the many years that this book
was in the pipeline ('Oh soon, very soon, it's definitely on the way'). Thanks to every
chef past and present, whose ability to respect the tried and tested recipes at one
end of their bench, but be spontaneous and inventive at the other end, have kept our
repertoire both reliable and exciting over the years. Thanks to our managers Phil and
Margaret, who have somehow imbued our busy, dynamic and often chaotic 111m²
with sufficient calm, organisation and supportiveness for the book team to find a
creative space without disrupting the day-to-day running of the restaurant.

A special thanks to Freda Keeshan, who probably thought that she'd left the
catering world behind when the Wellfed Vegetarian Café Co-op (formerly of Crow
Street, Temple Bar), of which she was a founding member, closed in 1993. No
such escape! Freda, mother of our photographer, Orla, generously allowed us the

unlimited use of her kitchen and garden, which we invaded at least two days per week for the duration of the project, with her pets Paco, Sandy and Willow for company. Her terraced cottage provided the first home for the Cornucopia recipes, which, reduced from their original 'serves eighty' to 'serves four to eight', were cooked, tested and photographed, and fine-tuned for the domestic gods and goddesses who will use them to bring a slice of Cornucopia life into their homes. Enormous thanks also to my good friend Rose Brophy, whose generous provision of a mobile home in a secluded spot in Wexford regularly afforded me a perfect escape from the madding crowd to spend quality time alone with my laptop. Without that tin box by the sea, this project might never have come to fruition.

Thanks also to my proofreaders, Mary and Malachy Heffernan, James, Phil and Ed for all their astute last-minute help.

And a final word of gigantic appreciation to Deirdre McCafferty, our boss. Her trust in the good of humankind and her belief in the talents of every individual have fostered a liberal working environment where each member of staff can find their own special niche in which to work, create and contribute. Her faith in the abilities of three former waitresses to put together a book worthy of her restaurant's name has given us the confidence and freedom to find our own path towards the realisation of *Cornucopia at home*. She has been generous with resources, has remained constantly interested in, and impressed by, our efforts and has taken care of all the financial practicalities, leaving us to immerse ourselves in the fun parts of producing a cookbook.

Eleanor Heffernan
May 2008

Special diets

<table>
<tr><td>*v*</td><td>vegan</td><td>*df*</td><td>dairy-free</td></tr>
<tr><td>*gf*</td><td>gluten-free</td><td>*ef*</td><td>egg-free</td></tr>
<tr><td>*wf*</td><td>wheat-free</td><td>*cn*</td><td>contains nuts</td></tr>
<tr><td>*yf*</td><td>yeast-free</td><td>*cs*</td><td>contains sugar</td></tr>
<tr><td>♡</td><td>low fat</td><td></td><td></td></tr>
</table>

Cornucopia is known primarily as a vegetarian restaurant. However, we also specialise in catering for several more specific special diets. Our colourful menu boards are chalked up each morning, not only with the menu of the day, but also with a series of symbols to indicate what soups, hot dishes, salads, breads and desserts are suitable for particular dietary requirements. These same symbols appear next to each recipe throughout the book. An absence of symbols next to a recipe indicates that that particular dish is vegetarian, but not suitable for any of our other special diets.

Adhering to a special diet does not need to result in a sense of deprivation or craving. On the contrary, it can encourage a sense of adventure and appreciation of each meal. If you have been suffering from poor health or irritating symptoms due to food allergy, it can be exciting and liberating to have found a diet that will free you from these and bring your health and well-being to a new, improved level. Drawing on recipes and techniques from all around the world can increase your repertoire of dishes suitable for your special diet and lifestyle. And with a little imagination, many classic recipes, not originally suitable for certain diets, can be adapted into equally delicious versions that can be enjoyed by all. Cornucopia has spent twenty-two years compiling, inventing and adapting recipes to cater for the dietary needs of all our customers, so that everyone can eat their fill without compromising their health or ethos. This book presents delicious and satisfying recipes with consideration for the following dietary requirements.

Vegetarian

Naturally, all the recipes herein are vegetarian. Individuals may choose to be vegetarian for many different reasons, most commonly ethical, environmental, religious, health-based, political, cultural or economic beliefs.

Vegetarians do not eat anything that has been derived from a slaughtered animal, including all meat, poultry, fish and shellfish. Foods containing hidden products from slaughtered animals are also avoided, for example cheese made with rennet (most cheeses), wine filtered with isinglass or gelatine, confectionery, ice-cream and medicines made with gelatine and chocolate bars containing whey (which contains rennet). Lacto-ovo vegetarians do eat eggs (free-range), dairy and honey, though many individuals try to source such products from small, organic producers whose treatment of animals is more likely to be compassionate.

A well-balanced vegetarian diet, embracing as many different food types as possible, fulfils all the nutritional needs of the human body and does not require vitamin or mineral supplements.

Vegan *(v)*

Veganism is very often a philosophical lifestyle choice based on compassion, animal rights and environmental responsibility, rather than a special diet based on food intolerance. However, there are also those who choose veganism for its many nutritional advantages, particularly when facing a personal health challenge. Some extensive and prominent scientific studies (e.g. *The China Study*, by Colin Campbell) propose that an exclusively plant-based diet has the capacity to optimise health and can help to heal and prevent certain illnesses.

Vegans try, as far as is possible and practical, not to eat or use any products derived wholly or partly from animals. From a dietary point of view, this means avoiding dairy products, eggs and honey. Like vegetarians, vegans do not eat confectionery or medicine capsules that are made from gelatine. Strict vegans do not wear leather, fur, wool or silk and do not use any cosmetics or cleaning products that have been tested on animals.

Vegans are well catered for in this book. All but two of both the soups and salads are vegan, half of the main courses are vegan, all but one of the breads are vegan and the dessert chapter contains eight vegan options.

Gluten-free *(gf)*

An allergy to gluten is usually associated with coeliac disease, though some people are intolerant to gluten without necessarily carrying the disease. Coeliac disease is a condition of the small intestine, which, when exposed to gluten, becomes inflamed and incapable of absorbing nutrients properly. Thus, the symptoms of coeliac disease are often fatigue, digestive problems, anaemia or weight loss. The only effective treatment for those suffering from coeliac disease is to adhere to a lifelong gluten-free diet. Items that must be avoided are: wheat (flour, bran, couscous, bulghar wheat), all wheat-based products (pasta, bread, pastry, semolina, soy sauce, sauces thickened with flour such as béchamel), barley, spelt, rye and oats.

Cereals that are safe for consumption by those adhering to a gluten-free diet are corn (cornmeal, polenta, cornflour), quinoa, millet and rice. Non-wheat-based flours that can be used in gluten-free cooking are soy flour, rice flour, potato flour, maize flour (cornmeal) and gram flour (made from chickpeas). As many baking powders contain a small quantity of flour, health food shops stock gluten-free baking powder alternatives. One common brand of supermarket baking powder, Royal Baking Powder, uses maize rather than wheat and is therefore suitable for gluten-free baking.

Potatoes and rice are the main unprocessed sources of carbohydrates available to coeliacs. In Cornucopia we also have a selection of polenta-based dishes, which serve as popular alternatives to lasagnes and gratins for those on gluten-free diets. In this book, all the soups are gluten-free, all but one of the salads are gluten-free and half of the main courses are gluten-free. A recipe for gluten-free bread is included in the bread chapter and the desserts chapter offers five gluten-free options.

Wheat-free *(wf)*

Eating a wheat-free diet may be due to wheat hypersensitivity (allergy), wheat intolerance (a milder allergy) or a conscious decision to reduce the amount of wheat-based products in one's diet to encourage a more varied nutritional spectrum. Common symptoms of wheat allergy/intolerance include eczema, asthma, rashes, a bloated or swollen stomach, abdominal cramps and digestive problems. Untended wheat allergy can cause severe stomach discomfort, headaches, breathing difficulties, nausea, tiredness, itchiness and irritable bowel syndrome (IBS).

Wheat allergy is distinct from coeliac disease, as those allergic to wheat are not necessarily reactive to the gluten protein in wheat and other wheat-like grains, but rather to other allergens specific to wheat. Unlike coeliac sufferers, some people with wheat allergy, especially those with a mild intolerance, can tolerate spelt flour, rye flour and oats. Those adhering to a wheat-free diet should avoid flour, couscous, bulghar wheat, semolina and wheat-based products such as bread, pastry, pasta, soy sauce (but not tamari), sauces thickened by flour (rather than cornflour), wheat crackers and biscuits. All the cereals and non-wheat flours listed as safe for a gluten-free diet, as well as potatoes and rice, are also suitable for those adhering to a wheat-free regime.

People on a wheat-free diet can enjoy all the soups in this book, all but one of the salads, half of the main courses, gluten-free bread (and, in some cases, spelt bread) and seven of the desserts.

Yeast-free *(yf)*

There are two main reasons to avoid yeast in one's diet: a dietary yeast allergy and the presence of a yeast infection in one's body. A common question posed to those with suspected yeast allergy is, 'Do you feel tired or swollen after eating a slice of bread, but not after eating pasta?' This would suggest that the person is not allergic to wheat, but rather to the yeast used to leaven the bread.

Common foods containing yeast are: yeast bread (but not soda bread), some cakes and buns (such as hot-cross buns and Danish pastries), alcohol (beer, cider, wine and most spirits), vinegar (and condiments containing vinegar, such as mayonnaise and many pre-packaged salad dressings), olives and capers that are stored in vinegar, Marmite, fermented soy products (miso paste, shoyu, tamari), some fruit skins (especially grapes and plums), some dried fruits, mushrooms, cheese, sour cream and buttermilk. Some people allergic to yeast must also avoid all forms of sugar (see below).

The other common reason to cut out yeast is the presence of a yeast infection, candidiasis, in the body. Those who have been diagnosed with candidiasis must avoid worsening their condition by eating foods that contain yeast. Additionally, they are advised to starve the yeast infection by avoiding sugar, which is the most direct food source for yeast. This includes refined and unrefined sugar, honey, molasses and concentrated fruit syrups.

Although sugar does not actually contain yeast, it is a yeast-encouraging foodstuff. As a result, none of the desserts that contain sugar in this book have been marked as yeast-free (*yf*). If you are adhering to a yeast-free diet but can tolerate small amounts of sugar on occasion, check the dessert recipe for the presence of any other yeast-containing ingredients (vinegar or alcohol). If these are not contained in the recipe, it may be suitable for you. In the case of soups, salads, main courses and breads that use sweeteners (sugar, honey, apple concentrate, molasses), the sugar level is so low that we have not considered it high enough to render the recipes unsuitable for those on a yeast-free diet.

All of the soups in this book are yeast-free. As we use lemon juice rather than vinegar in many of our salad dressings, seven of our salads are suitable for those on a yeast-free diet. The chapter on main courses has six yeast-free options and the bread chapter offers soda bread and gluten-free bread as well as savoury scones. As elaborated above, due to the presence of sugar, apple concentrate or a high quantity of natural fruit sugars in all the dessert recipes, we have not marked any of them as suitable for a yeast-free diet.

Note: candidiasis is not usually treated by diet alone, but by a combination of special diet and medical or alternative medical treatment, including the use of probiotics.

Dairy-free *(df)*

Dairy allergy is a reaction to proteins in cow's milk. The symptoms, similar to many food allergies, can range from skin rashes and irritation to respiratory problems such as asthma and from mild stomach discomfort to pronounced digestive problems.

Those who have been diagnosed with dairy allergy must avoid all items generated from cow's milk, including cheese, butter, yoghurt and cream. Some people enjoy alternatives such as rice milk and soymilk. Non-dairy milks and butters can be made from nuts such as cashews and almonds. Many people with dairy allergy can tolerate sheep's milk and goat's milk and cheeses made from them.

As we have long been catering for the vegan diet, many of Cornucopia's recipes are suitable for those adhering to a dairy-free food plan. Everything marked as vegan (V) is, by default, dairy-free. Some recipes also contain egg but not milk, and are therefore marked *df* but not *v*; for example, the garlic potato salad with toasted hazelnuts, which contains egg in the mayonnaise (check the label) but no dairy.

Egg-free *(ef)*

There are two common reasons for avoiding eggs in one's diet. One is egg allergy and the other is an ideological desire not to consume the potential life contained in a chicken's egg – for example, the Hare Krishna religion does not permit its followers to eat eggs, nor do some forms of Hinduism. Egg allergy occurs most commonly in young children, many of whom outgrow their allergy between the ages of five and seventeen. Some people, however, maintain a lifelong allergy. As with the dairy-free diet described above, those adhering to an egg-free diet are well catered for in Cornucopia by our many vegan options, with the addition of several recipes that contain dairy but not eggs (for example, the Mediterranean chickpea salad is not vegan, but it is egg-free).

Cooking without eggs is relatively easy (with the exception, of course, of omelette and quiches). All the soups in this book are egg-free, as are all but one of the salads, most of the main courses and all of the breads (as long as you don't glaze your scones with eggwash). The toughest culinary area to tackle without eggs is desserts, in particular cakes and pastries. The binding and aerating qualities of eggs in certain kinds of cakes brings a lightness and moistness that is difficult to replicate with commercial egg replacements, such as banana purée or apple sauce, so we haven't tried. Instead we stick to recipes that work well without eggs. The repertoire of egg-free (generally vegan) desserts presented herein includes oat bars, apple crumble, vegan cheesecakes, fig and banana tarts, date squares and coconut petit fours.

Nut allergy *(cn — contains nuts)*

Allergy to nuts, like eggs, is most common in children, who often outgrow the condition by their early or late teens. Nut allergy can have quite severe effects on the sufferer, who must adhere to a total exclusion diet. Those with very severe hypersensitivity may not be able to eat in any restaurant where nuts are used, as even dishes without nuts may have been contaminated sufficiently to cause a reaction.

When cooking at home, where you can be vigilant about the cooking environment and utensils, many of the recipes in this book are nut-free: all but one of the soups, eleven of the salads, sixteen of the main courses, all of the breads and nine of the desserts.

Sugar-free *(cs — contains sugar)*

There are several common reasons for avoiding or limiting sugar intake: diabetes (difficulty regulating blood sugar), hypoglycaemia (overproduction of insulin), yeast infection (candidiasis: see yeast-free section, page 29) or simply a health-conscious decision to avoid processed foods with high calories and very little nutrition such as sugar. Each of these conditions represents different levels of sugar intolerance. Many people on a sugar-free diet will not be adversely affected by the addition of two teaspoons of brown sugar to a two-litre pot of soup, but cannot eat a sugar-free dessert that has very high levels of fruit sugar. As a result, labelling of sugar and non-sugar foods in this book has been quite cautious.

Rather than mark sugar-free (*sf*) on the vast majority of soups, salads, main courses and breads, we have, instead, marked contains sugar (*cs*) on the occasional savoury recipe that requires a teaspoon or two of brown sugar. Such incidences are usually accompanied by an alternative sweetener for those who want to avoid sugar. On the other hand, in the baking chapter, assume that each recipe contains sugar, unless clearly marked no added sugar.

Notes

The Cornucopia cupboard

Every kitchen, be it professional or domestic, contains its own unique combination of ingredients, utensils, aspirations and constraints. Every chef and home cook strikes their own personal balance between factors such as taste, health, ethics, time and budget, hence the infinite variety of restaurants, the invariable novelty of dining at friends' and the absolute comfort of food dished up from your own kitchen.

Enjoying this cookbook by no means requires replicating the Cornucopia kitchen, nor assuming the Cornucopia attitude to food and cooking. However, there are a number of basic shopping-list items that really define our cooking, which we consider essential for delicious, healthy and conscientious cooking, reminiscent of the Cornucopia experience. In addition, there are a few hardware items that, though not indispensable, are used often enough to merit investing in, which we have described below. At the end of this section, we have included a description of the Cornucopia cupboard: a definitive guide to the ingredients used in Cornucopia, for those who enjoy lists and minutiae!

Organic brown rice

Cornucopia uses organic brown rice to accompany our stews and curries and to make our rice salads. It has a lovely, nutty texture with a satisfying chewiness. Good-quality organic brown rice is available from health food shops. Many supermarket brown rice varieties are of comparably poor quality.

Of all forms of rice available, organic brown rice is by far the healthiest choice. All rice starts off as brown rice – it just gets whiter the more it is processed. First, the outer layer, the hull, is removed, producing the grain that we recognise as brown rice and causing almost no nutritional loss to the rice. At this point, the rice is rich in fibre, protein, vitamin B, manganese, iron and magnesium, as well as cholesterol-reducing bran oil. To make rice white, it is then milled and polished, a process that removes the bran, leaving a pearly white grain that has lost much of its good stuff, including vitamins, minerals, bran oil, essential fatty acids and fibre. As a result, nutritionally, white rice is to brown rice what white sliced pan is to wholemeal brown bread – a filling, but low-grade alternative.

Brown rice is available in both short-grain and long-grain forms. When cooked, short-grain brown rice tends to be a little softer and stickier, while long-grain is chewier, as well as fluffy and separate. Long-grain rice also has a slightly higher protein content. Nutritionists recommend that vegetarians combine brown rice (or, indeed, any wholegrain) with beans/lentils (or tofu) at one sitting, to create a whole protein – i.e. a meal that fulfils all the body's protein requirements for maintaining and repairing tissue.

For guidelines about cooking brown rice, see page 184.

Vegetarian cheese

Cheese is made by coagulating (curdling) milk, which separates into curds (solids) and whey (liquid). The curds are then matured into various types of cheese. The active ingredient used to coagulate milk is rennet, which is most commonly sourced from the abomasum (fourth stomach) tissue of a newly born slaughtered calf. Vegetarian cheese is made using rennet from non-animal sources, usually fungal or bacterial. In the past, fig leaves, wild thistle and safflower were all sources of plant rennet for cheese-making. Nowadays, most vegetarian cheeses are produced using the fungus *Mucor miehei* or the bacterias *Bacillus subtilis* or *Bacillus prodigiosum*.

The difficulty in buying vegetarian cheeses lies not in their general availability, but rather in distinguishing them from non-vegetarian cheeses. No one particular type of cheese is exclusively vegetarian; each manufacturer has their own method of production. To add to the confusion, cheese producers are not obliged to list their active ingredient, therefore making it impossible to know from the packing if it was made with vegetarian or non-vegetarian rennet.

Some cheeses (especially supermarket own-brand cheeses) are now marked 'suitable for vegetarians'. If you are buying cheese at a farmers' market, simply ask the producer directly what kind of coagulant they use. Other than that, you can look up individual companies' websites for information. The Vegetarian Society of Ireland has a (not exhaustive) list at www.vegetarian.ie that names some of the vegetarian cheeses available on the Irish market. The Vegetarian Society UK has a more comprehensive list of approved cheese products at www.seedlingshowcase.org.uk. You can also turn to the end of this chapter for information on the Cornucopia cupboard, where you will find a list of the vegetarian cheeses we purchase weekly.

The great Italian cheese-makers that hold the production rights to Parmigiano-Reggiano have not come up with a vegetarian version of their popular cheese, as it goes against their laws of purity. Some vegetarian Parmesan-style cheeses are available. In Cornucopia, we use an Irish-made Parmesan-style cheese called Regato.

As Ireland is a great cheese-producing nation, it is very easy to source all your cheeses in Ireland, between the popular brands stocked in supermarkets and small producers selling their farmhouse cheeses at markets and in specialist food stores.

Vegetarian wine

Many wines are unsuitable for a vegetarian diet; even more are unsuitable for a vegan diet. After harvesting, grapes are pressed and then placed in vats to ferment, converting the sugars in the juice into alcohol. As the initial pressing of the grapes is quite coarse, the juices are filtered several times during fermentation to remove residual sediment from the wine, making for a clear, unclouded consistency. This clarification process often involves using animal-derived products such as isinglass (from fish bladders) and gelatine (boiled bones). For those concerned with animal welfare, another common filtration substance is egg white, from eggs that are not necessarily free-range.

However, there are many vegan and vegetarian options for wine filtration. Bentonite and kaolin are two minerals that are used for fining by some winemakers. Natural clay-based filters also exist. Some very patient vintners simply allow the sediment to settle naturally at the bottom of the casks and then decant off the wine several times. As this is considered a very traditional and specialist method, unfiltered wine is sought out by certain connoisseurs and therefore the wine label may boast unfiltered wine, which is more likely to be vegetarian.

As with cheeses, the main difficulty with sourcing vegetarian wines is that the bottles do not supply information as to what method of clarification was used, nor do they list the additives used in production. Many supermarket own-brand wines are now labelled suitable for vegetarians when appropriate. Other than that, it is a matter of doing your research. The Vegetarian Society UK has quite a comprehensive list of acceptable wines at www.seedlingshowcase.org.uk. Another option is to buy your wine from a small, specialist wine shop, where the proprietor is likely to have detailed information to hand about the wines in stock.

Wine for cooking should not be cheap, nasty 'plonk' — which is rather like pouring a generous glug of vinegar into your dish. Of course, you don't need to buy enormously expensive wine either, just make sure it is palatable. Ideally, the wine that goes into the dish can subsequently be enjoyed by the glass with the meal itself.

Note: organic wine is sometimes presumed to be vegetarian, as it is considered natural. Although many organic wines are vegetarian, this is not always the case. Organic simply means that the grapes were grown in organic soil without artificial fertilisers or insecticides. Even organic winemakers are not required to put on their label which clarifier is used, since it is removed from the final product.

Vinegar

Vinegar comes from the French *vin aigre* (literally sour wine). The vinegars used in Cornucopia are red and white wine vinegar, balsamic vinegar, apple cider vinegar and rice vinegar. With the exception of rice vinegar (which is charcoal or machine filtered), all these products are made by the oxidisation of ethanol in alcohols that are commonly purified by non-vegetarian means. As described in the case of wine (see above for details), alcohol filtration methods often involve isinglass (fish bladder), gelatine (boiled animal carcass) or the whites of non-free-range eggs. Manufacturers are not obliged to list products used in filtration, as they do not form part of the finished goods. To identify suitable vinegars, buy in health food shops, where products are more commonly marked as suitable for vegetarians. You can also look for specialist vinegars that are unfiltered.

Beans and pulses

Beans are, of course, an essential part of the Cornucopia kitchen. We use borlotti beans, butter beans, cannellini beans, chickpeas and kidney beans to bulk up casseroles, stews, bakes and salads with a low-fat, high-fibre, nutrient-rich source of protein. We use red lentils and split peas to thicken soups and sauces. Puy lentils, considered the Mercedes of lentils, are added to moussakas and casseroles. Haricot beans are used for our homemade baked beans on the breakfast menu.

We purchase enormous 25kg sacks of dried beans and pulses every week. Every night, the evening chef soaks whatever beans are necessary for the next day's menu. On a domestic scale, dried beans are available from most supermarkets. Health food shops tend to have a greater selection.

If you are short of time, good quality tinned beans are an alternative. Choose brands that do not add sugar or preservatives. Unlike many vegetables, beans do not lose many nutrients in the canning process and, if you are cooking a small quantity, sometimes the whole process of soaking overnight and cooking for one and a half hours can seem a bit arduous. Always drain and rinse tinned beans before using them.

However, from both a cost-effective and environmental point of view, dried beans are preferable to tinned ones. They can be stored in an airtight container for up to a year. All dried beans need to be soaked overnight or for twelve hours. This is because they contain a digestive inhibitor which is rinsed away with soaking. Lentils and split peas do not require soaking, as they can be cooked quite quickly from dry.

Cooking beans

1. Check the dry beans for pebbles or grit by spreading them out on a tray and sifting through them.
2. Rinse them well by placing them in a sieve or colander and running cold water on them.
3. In a suitable container, cover the beans with about triple their volume of cold water.
4. Leave to soak overnight, or for approximately 12 hours.
5. Discard the soaking water and rinse the beans thoroughly under cold water again.
6. Now transfer to a suitable pot and cover with plenty of unsalted cold water.
7. Bring to the boil, reduce the temperature and then simmer until tender but not mushy. For cooking times, see below.

Borlotti beans	—	1-1½ hours
Butter beans	—	1-1½ hours
Cannellini beans	—	1-1½ hours
Chickpeas	—	2-3 hours
Kidney beans	—	1-1½ hours
Pinto beans	—	1-1½ hours

Free-range eggs

There is an EU directive in place requiring that the raising of battery hens be eliminated by the year 2012 as it is considered a practice too cruel to be continued. After that date, all hens servicing the egg industry are to be housed in open barns and provided with free access to outdoor scratching areas at all times.

Why wait until 2012? Free-range eggs should be the undisputed choice of anyone who cares about animal welfare. An added bonus is that hens that scratch and enjoy fresh air also produce tastier eggs. If possible, choose organic eggs, which are sure to be free of chemicals from antibiotics, hormone-enhanced foodstuffs and pesticides, which may have been consumed by non-organically raised hens. Organic free-range eggs are lower in fat, higher in vitamin A and higher in essential omega-3 fatty acids. They taste richer, sweeter and come with the feel-good factor of doing good for yourself, the environment and the well-being of the hens.

Unrefined natural sea salt

In Cornucopia we use only natural sea salt, and never refined table salt. Natural sea salt is a rich source of a huge variety of minerals necessary for the human body to function properly, whereas refined table salt contains only sodium and chloride. When harvesting sea salt, an area is flooded with seawater, which is left to evaporate. The heaviest salt sediment sinks to the bottom and the lighter salt particles settle on the top. Table salt comes from this top layer, as it is finer and whiter. It is then treated with preservatives, additives and bleaches to ensure an attractively smooth, dry, free-flowing, pearly-white consumer product.

By contrast, unrefined natural sea salt comes from the lower layers of salt sediment, where many more minerals have settled. It is not treated with any chemicals and is simply packaged in its natural form. Compared to table salt, it is darker in colour, rougher in texture and slightly damp, so it is considered less marketable. However, as salt is absolutely necessary for life, then why not choose the best-quality, highest-nutrition product available? Serve it in a small bowl, rather than a shaker as it is more suited to pinching than shaking. Unrefined natural sea salt is available from health food stores and specialist food shops.

Oils

As anyone who pays any attention to health matters well knows, not all oils are made equal. In Cornucopia, we select unrefined oils that have been exposed to minimum processing and therefore retain maximum natural goodness.

Some things to look out for when purchasing oils

· Try to choose unrefined oil. This means that the oil has simply been extracted from the vegetable/fruit/nut/seed source, mechanically filtered and bottled. It has not been bleached or stabilised and it retains its full natural flavour, colour and aroma. Refined oils, by contrast, may have been exposed to numerous chemical processes to extend their shelf life and remove their pigments and odour, processes that render the oil attractive, especially to the food manufacturing industry, but far removed from its natural state.

· Try to choose expeller-pressed rather than solvent-extracted oils. This means that the oil has been removed from source by mechanical rather than chemical methods. If possible, choose cold-pressed oil which refers to oil that has been extracted without exposure to heat, which can compromise the nutrients in and digestibilty of the oil.

· Select oils in light-resistant plastic containers or tinted glass containers. Store your oils in a cool, dark press.

In Cornucopia we predominantly use the following oils

· **Good-quality unrefined sunflower oil**. This can be found in health shops. Sunflower oil is high in vitamin E and low in saturated fat (as are most plant-origin oils, with the exception of coconut oil and palm oil). Sunflower oil is made of polyunsaturated fat, a healthy source of essential fatty acids required by the body for controlling inflammation and blood clotting and facilitating brain development and healthy skin and hair, as well as allowing the body to absorb and transport vitamins A, D, E and K through the bloodstream. Used in moderation, unrefined sunflower oil produces good cholesterol, reducing risk of heart disease. Although unrefined sunflower oil is more expensive than lower-quality, refined vegetable oils, it is chemical-free and retains both its natural colour and flavour and its natural goodness. Its mild flavour makes it suitable for all kinds of cooking, as well as for use in certain salads in which the more pungent flavour of olive oil is not desired.

· **Extra-virgin olive oil.** Virgin in terms of olive oil means that the oil is extracted from the olives by mechanical rather than chemical means. Virgin olive oils are never refined (chemically treated to remove strong odours, tastes or acidity). Extra-virgin is the result of the first cold pressing of the olives and is the highest quality olive oil available. It has a delicate, fruity flavour, a rich colour and very low acidity. Later pressings of the olives use both heat and chemical methods, both of which affect the nutrients (vitamins E and K, chlorophyll, polyphenols, etc) and taste. Cold-pressed olive oil, by contrast, retains all its natural goodness. Olive oil is composed of monounsaturated fats (good fats) and has long been associated, in small quantities, with fighting heart disease and lowering cholesterol. It is a delicious oil for salads, dips and roasting vegetables and enhances all types of Mediterranean cooking. You can find good-quality extra-virgin olive oils in both supermarkets and specialist food stores. Olive oils that are not marked 'virgin' are usually a blend of unrefined and refined oils and should be avoided.

The olive oil that we use in Cornucopia is, at time of writing, sourced from small, organic producers in Italy who use a granite-stone crushing method for extracting the oil – a system that, we are told by our trusty Italian supplier, Franco, has not changed much since the time of the Romans. This tried and tested system ensures an ambient temperature throughout the processing, retaining a deep and wonderful flavour.

Note 1: for deep fat frying use a refined oil as unrefined oil will be too unstable and change the flavour of the dish unfavourably.

Note 2: raised heat levels cause a chemical change in all oils, rendering them more challenging for the human digestive system. Butter and coconut oil are the two oils that have been observed to be most stable when heated. For the home cook adhering to a very strict health regime, these two fats are the safest to use when cooking.

Herbs

Fresh herbs are the most wonderful visual, olfactory and gustatory addition to savoury cooking, both hot and cold. The simple addition of a small handful of fresh basil can transform a plain vegetable soup into a tasty and aromatic sensation. A handful of chopped parsley adds lightness and freshness to a garlic potato salad. A few sprigs of rosemary added to a tray of roasting vegetables enhances them with an earthy depth of flavour and an aroma that you can drift away on.

Although fresh herbs can seem pricey, they are infinitely preferable to dry herbs. Not only do they have a much better flavour, colour and texture, but they also retain their nutritional benefits in the form of antioxidants and chlorophyll. Listing the benefits of herbs as natural medicine (and the original source of most modern medicine) would require a whole other book, but be confident that by adding lots of fresh herbs to your food as often as possible, they are working their natural magic for you as you enjoy their tasty tones. Supermarkets and farmers' markets both stock a good array of fresh herbs, where you will find some or all of the common cooking herbs: basil, chervil, chives, coriander, dill, mint, oregano, parsley, sage, tarragon and thyme. It is also a wonderful (and economical) pleasure to grow herbs in your own back garden. Herbs can thrive either in beds or in pots so can be adapted to any size

Organic items used daily in Cornucopia:

★ <u>brown rice</u>
★ <u>Pastas</u>: penne, fusilli + spaghetti
★ <u>flours</u>: white, brown, granary, spelt, rye, potato flour, rice flour, soy flour
★ <u>beans</u>: chickpea, cannellini, butterbean
★ <u>Soy products</u>: soy sauce, tofu, tamari, soy milk, cream, yoghurt
★ <u>drinks</u>: cola, lemonade, red + white wine
★ <u>hot drinks</u>: green + blacks hot chocolate, selection of herbal teas
★ <u>condiments</u>: jam, marmalade, red sauce, cider vinegar, red wine vinegar
★ <u>Other</u>: wheatgrass, gluten-free wraps, brown sugar
★ <u>oil</u>: all olive oil

GMO FREE ZONE
WWW.GMFREEIRELAND.ORG

WELCOME TO ORGANIC LIFE, please wait to be seated!

of garden, or even just a side passage or window-ledge.

If planting in beds, you can either devote a separate section to your herb garden or you can disperse the herbs amongst your other plants, as they are an attractive addition to any flower and shrub bed. If you are using pots, you might like to divide your herbs into two planters. Herbs that enjoy full sun are chives, rosemary, thyme, sage and oregano, so you can plant them together in one pot. Herbs that don't mind a bit of shade at midday (although, in the Irish climate, this is not as crucial as in hotter countries) include parsley, rocket, basil, chervil, mint, lemon balm and sorrel, so any combination of them can be grown together in a second planter that receives part-sun, part-shade. It is recommended, particularly for pot planting, that you use a soil-based compost rather than peat moss. Water regularly, especially from March to September, to prevent the pots drying out. Herb plants and seeds can be purchased from gardening centres. You may also find a selection of seeds in some supermarkets and DIY shops.

Local, seasonal & organic fresh produce

Insofar as is practical and affordable, buying locally grown, seasonal organic fruit and vegetables is best practice where shopping for fresh produce is concerned. Unless you have your own vegetable patch, farmers' markets are the most reliable suppliers of locally grown, seasonal fruit and vegetables. Unlike imported produce, their wares have not spent several days in transit. As they are harvested a few days before selling (sometimes that very morning), they do not require any treatment with chemicals to improve their shelf life. They have spent a minimum of time out of the earth and have therefore lost as few of their nutrients and as little of their natural moisture, colour, taste and life as possible. Imported fruit and vegetables not only have lost some of their natural goodness and flavour, but they are also often treated with chemical sprays to keep them looking fresh. In addition, international exporting of fresh produce is responsible for an enormous annual carbon print as the world market demands that tropical fruits be available all year round in Northern Europe and Irish potatoes be constantly on sale to homesick ex-pats in Tokyo. As buying from a local farmers' market is not always a practical possibility, look out for products labelled Irish-grown in your local supermarket or greengrocer.

There is something very wholesome about eating locally. I remember sitting in a caravan park in France as a young teenager eating *pain de campagne* (artisan bread) covered with a local soft cheese and picking at cherries from a nearby outdoor fruit market as my parents sipped a local table wine. There was nothing remotely costly on the table, but altogether it made for a superb lunch. I was struck by the notion that these items were made to be consumed together, having all come from the same soil under the same climate in the same region. They had all been produced by people who spoke the same language with the same accent and a similar history. No wonder the flavours and textures complimented each other perfectly. It took being abroad to drive this point home to me, but the same phenomenon applies to Ireland. By buying locally produced fresh produce and fruit and vegetables that are in season, you are bringing an effortless coherence to your cooking, as well as optimising freshness and flavour and minimising environmental damage.

Selecting organically grown goods is also an ideal worth aiming for. Chemical-free farming provides you and your family with a healthier, safer diet, whilst reducing the detrimental effects that fertilisers and pesticides have on our environment. Organic farmers are more often small, independent (or co-op) operators than big businesses. They have chosen a method of farming that is environmentally responsible over one whose principal aim is to optimise profits. Rather than using chemicals, organic farmers use natural crop rotation to ensure that their soil remains rich and replete with minerals. Instead of resorting to weed killers and pesticides, they rely on farm husbandry (manual labour) to maintain the health of their crops. Those who raise chickens for eggs or livestock for milk and cheese are more likely to treat their animals as creatures worthy of a good life rather than as non-sentient industrial products. Supporting organic farming is both a positive contribution to the environment and a strong defence of small, local industry in the face of the often crippling competition from exclusively profit-driven international businesses. And at a culinary level, it ensures that your foods do not contain potentially harmful chemicals, nor are their natural quirks, variations and unique flavours masked or manipulated into glossy, monotonous standards.

Buying organic, local vegetables also inspires a greater awareness of and connection to one's environment. At the time of writing, Cornucopia's organic vegetable supplier is Marc Michel (Wicklow), who is occasionally unreachable because he doesn't hear his phone 'over the noise of the tractor', in case we ever wondered how close he remains to hands-on farming now that his business has expanded and experienced far-reaching success. Ordering from Marc Michel has made us pay avid attention, not only to the seasons, but also to the weather. On a sunny Friday, it might be remarked 'Oh good, a spot of sunshine! The lettuces will have a good day of growth and we'll get a fine delivery on Monday'. Or after a prolonged spell of heavy rain, 'I hope the sky clears soon to give the poor vegetables a spot of sunshine'. Vegetables in the supermarkets arouse no such sentiments, as often their origins are too remote and their presentation too clinical to suggest that they were ever rooted in the earth at all!

GM-free

In so far as possible, Cornucopia tries to ensure that none of our food contains genetically modified (GM) ingredients and we ask our suppliers to verify this. As a consumer interested in GM-free living, there are a number of things you can do:

- Buy organic certified produce. As organic farming outlaws all GM crops and contamination by GM crops, certified organic goods are suitable for GM-free living.
- Look for GM-free labelling. More and more Irish producers are applying for GM-free certification and displaying the GM-free logo on their packaging.
- Use the internet to research particular items. The GM-free Ireland organisation offers information and guidelines at www.gmfreeireland.org

Kitchen equipment

To tackle the recipes in this book, you will benefit from having some or all of the following items. We recommend basic kitchen essentials such as good sharp knives, various small and medium pots, a heavy-based frying pan, baking trays, a grater, a pepper grinder, a large mixing bowl (and several small ones), a citrus juicer and a selection of ladles, spoons and lifters.

Handheld stick blender
This is an inexpensive and safe blender suitable for blending soups, sauces and salad dressings. It is a wonderfully useful item and very easy to clean. A must.

Food processor
This is useful for breadcrumbs, grinding nuts, mixing thick purées, mixtures and dips, rubbing butter into flour, and lots of other time- and muscle-saving applications.

Mixer with balloon, paddle and hook attachment
This is not an absolute necessity, as much of what a mixer does can be achieved by hand, but it does save time and effort for whipping cream, combining cake mixes and kneading bread.

Large heavy-based stainless steel pot with lid

This is a perfect pot for the soup and casserole recipes in this book. We used a four litre pot for all the recipe testing. Any similar-sized pot will do.

Rectangular baking dish

Many standard household baking dishes are oval. An oval dish is fine for most of the bakes in this book, such as the nut roast, moussaka or gratin. However, for the lasagne and polenta bakes, which involve layering rectangular sheets of pasta and polenta, a rectangular dish is preferable.

Roasting trays

At least two heavy roasting trays are beneficial, as many of the recipes involve roasting large quantities of vegetables at the same time.

Good chopping board

Considering the amount of chopping you will do, particularly for many of the salad recipes and main course recipes, it is worth investing in a good-quality, large chopping board rather than fiddling with a small, lightweight one. A good tip if you find that your chopping board tends to slip on your work surface while you are chopping is to spread a slightly damp tea towel underneath it.

Your cupboard

The Cornucopia store cupboard

For those who enjoy lists, this is (probably!) an exhaustive list of the ingredients that we use each week in Cornucopia

Rice, grains & flours
Long-grain brown rice, wild rice, bulghar wheat, couscous, polenta, barley, jumbo oats, unbleached strong white flour, unbleached plain white flour, wholemeal flour, granary flour, wheat bran, semolina, spelt flour, rice flour, potato flour, soy flour, maize flour, cornflour

Oils & fats
Organic extra-virgin olive oil, unrefined and refinedsunflower oil, toasted sesame oil, 100% butter, vegan sunflower margarine

Beans & pulses
Borlotti beans, butter beans, cannellini beans, chickpeas, kidney beans, haricot beans, lentils (red, puy), pinto beans, split peas (green, yellow), fresh sprouted beans from David Ashe in Kildare

Sea salt & pepper
Unrefined natural sea salt, freshly ground black peppercorns

Spices
Bay leaves, caraway seeds, cardamom seeds, cayenne pepper, chilli pepper (fresh and ground), cinnamon (quills and ground), cloves, coriander (seeds and ground), cumin (seeds and ground), fennel seeds, fenugreek (seeds and leaves), galangal, garam masala, ginger (fresh rhizomes and ground), lemongrass, lime leaves, mustard seeds (brown), nutmeg (freshly ground), paprika, sumac, star anise, tamarind, turmeric

Soy products
Tofu, silken tofu, tamari/shoyu, soymilk, soy yoghurt, soy cream

Wines & vinegars
Organic vegetarian red and white wine, mirin, aged balsamic vinegar, brown rice vinegar, organic cider vinegar

Ready-mades
Mustard (Dijon, English, wholegrain), organic pasta (spaghetti, fusilli, penne), cannelloni, fresh lasagne sheets, creamed coconut, buckwheat noodles, rice noodles, glass noodles,

wheaten noodles, vegan yeast-free low-sodium bouillon, tomato purée, peanut butter, tamari, pita bread, vegan sosmix (for breakfast sausages), sugar-free organic jams, marmalade and tomato sauce

Pre-packaged
Olives, capers, peeled plum tomatoes, dried arame seaweed

Baking ingredients
Psyllium husks, 70% dark, 53% dark and white chocolate, frozen raspberries, frozen blueberries, cocoa powder, Royal Baking Powder, dried yeast, natural vanilla extract, vanilla pods, natural almond essence, bread soda, apricot jam

Dried fruit
Prunes, dates, unsulphured apricots, sultanas, raisins, currants, figs

Nuts and seeds
Almonds (flaked, ground), cashew nuts, hazelnuts, peanuts, walnuts, desiccated coconut, sunflower seeds, pumpkin seeds, sesame seeds, poppy seeds, linseeds

Sweeteners
Organic apple concentrate, organic runny honey, maple syrup, raw cane sugar, caster sugar, cane molasses, golden syrup, icing sugar (confectioner's sugar)

Dairy, cheese & eggs
Whole-fat milk, Greek-style natural yoghurt, dairy cream, crème fraîche, cream cheese, buttermilk, cheddar, Gubbeen or Applewood smoked cheddar, Seriously Strong Cheddar, Cashel Blue cheese, Chèvre log goat's cheese, Salakis feta cheese, Haloumi cheese, Regato cheese, free-range eggs

Fresh herbs
Basil, chervil, chives, coriander, dill, mint, oregano, parsley (flat-leaf and curly), rosemary, sage, tarragon and thyme

Fresh fruit
Apples, Bramley apples, bananas, grapes, oranges, grapefruits, lemons, limes, pineapple, honeydew melon, Galia melon, watermelon, pears, peaches/nectarines, rhubarb, strawberries

Vegetables & leaves
Aubergines, baby corn, beansprouts, beetroot, broccoli, butternut squash, cabbage (white, savoy), carrots, cauliflower, celeriac, celery, courgettes, cucumbers, fennel, garlic, green beans, kale, leeks, lettuce (baby gem, frisée, oakleaf, butterhead, lollo rosso), mangetout beans, mushrooms (button, field, portobello), onions (Spanish, red), peppers (green, red, yellow), parsnips, potatoes (baby, baker), pumpkin, radicchio, radishes (baby, daikon), red chard, rocket, spinach (regular, baby), spring onions, sugarsnap peas, sweet potatoes, vine tomatoes (cherry, beef, plum), turnip, watercress, wheatgrass

Soups

Introduction to soups

Steaming bowls of soup were available in Cornucopia from the very first day of opening as a health food shop combined with a small café in 1986. Customers perched at the back of the shop on high stools pulled up to handmade benches imaginatively fashioned from wooden louvre doors with glass panels on top. It was not quite luxury dining, but that never stemmed the flow of enthusiastic punters, who found in Cornucopia something comforting and nourishing. The word 'restaurant' comes from the French verb *restaurer*, which means 'to restore'. In the 16th century, Parisian street vendors began to sell a thick, inexpensive soup called *restaurer* to passers-by, advertised as an antidote to physical exhaustion. In 1765 an entrepreneur opened a shop specialising in restaurer soups and thus was born the word restaurant – a place to seek restoration. Deirdre and Neil McCafferty were continuing in this tradition when they opened Cornucopia. In the front, they sold ingredients and products to encourage a life of health and wellness and, in the rear, they fed people wholesome vegetarian food to restore their energy in the middle of a busy city day. Just like on the streets of Paris, thick, inexpensive restaurer soups were one of the main sellers.

The soups were cooked and served on the premises by Neil, the original chef, while Deirdre, his wife, our current proprietor, looked after the shop end of things. Amongst the first flavours, as far as Deirdre can recall, were vegetable with green split pea and cream of mushroom. They were sipped from brown, hand-thrown earthenware bowls, made in Dún Laoghaire by the husband and wife ceramics team, Helena and Peter Brennan. The bread for dunking was supplied by Crusty Kitchen Bakery on Grafton Street (imagine, a bakery could afford Grafton Street rent back then!).

Since those days, our culinary repertoire has increased, as has our seating capacity, and we've progressed to orange (or terracotta, as the catalogue so grandiosely refers to them) bowls as well as an extensive selection of our own homemade breads and scones. But one thing has certainly not changed and that is the central role that good, hearty soups play in the Cornucopia menu. Hailed for their flavour, wholesomeness and student-budget friendliness, our two daily varieties (and, more often than not, a third and fourth when the first ones run out) vary between simple classics and more adventurous flavours, between blended and chunky textures and between wintry root vegetables and lighter, more refreshing summery ingredients.

Some of our most regular customers have been requesting 'a bowl of soup and a slice of soda bread' day in day out since long before Dublin became a wealthy and fashionable capital of fashion, food and frolics. One much-cherished gentleman customer has been known to consume three large bowls of soup consecutively of an evening – but only when tomato, lentil and basil is on the menu. Other nights he limits himself to one big bowl and a pot of tea! Colette, our longest-standing and highly respected member of staff, has been a familiar face behind the Cornucopia counter since 1990. Heaven knows how many bowls of soup she has served to customers in her time, but I do know how many bowls she has served for herself – one for every working day. Colette loves her soup. And one of the first things that one learns as a supervisor is that Colette must be warned of her impending ten-minute break well in advance so that she can dish up her soup and set it aside to cool. Our soups are so thick and hearty that their heat retention is quite astonishing. Colette knows from experience that unless she pours her soup a little in advance, she might spend her entire break blowing on her soupspoon. This same phenomenon has worked to our advantage in terms of selling takeaway soups. People have time to purchase their soup to go, walk back to their office, perhaps pick up a message or two along the way, and their soup will still be hot when they sit down at their desk to enjoy it. For those who have the time to sit and enjoy their lunch in the restaurant, one of the great pleasures of a nice thick, substantial Cornucopia soup is that it demands to be eaten at a leisurely pace and simply cannot be rushed: starting from around the rim of the bowl, where it is a little cooler, and working one's way across the surface, before dipping into the hotter depths and allowing each spoonful to get a little air before sipping it down, no slurping or guzzling possible.

Customers have often requested recipes for their favourite soups. Until now, it has been difficult to give them a satisfactory answer. Whilst we could list off the ingredients that go into a particular soup, it was just about impossible to specify the quantities suitable for making a pot of soup at home. We measure things in Cornucopia using 12-litre containers rather than cups, ladles rather than teaspoons and handfuls rather than pinches. Soups have never been an exact science, but rather the craft of a skilled chef who senses quantities rather than measures, so writing down recipes for a home cook took a bit of time and experimentation. Now, finally, customers who want to try Cornucopia soups on their own turf have a handbook to get them started.

The selection of soups that follow are all easy to make. Most require little more than a stick blender, a large pot with lid and the ingredients listed, though some also involve a bit of extra blanching, sautéing or oven roasting. The results will not be wispy broths that leave room for four more courses to come, but thick, hearty soups that, with a hunk of bread on the side, will provide a filling and healthy lunch or tea. Depending on the size and hunger of the parties in question, the recipes will serve between four and eight: eight small bowls served as a starter before a main course; six medium bowls to satisfy average soup appetites; and four large bowls, with top-ups, for people who are returning from a hard day's graft. The blended soups in particular will keep well in the fridge for reheating the following day. (Soups left overnight may thicken somewhat, as the vegetables and pulses absorb the liquid, so you may need to add a little extra water upon reheating.) You can also freeze portions of soup for defrosting as required. When reheating soups, make sure to bring them gently to a high heat and then simmer for several minutes.

One great thing about making soup is that there is great potential for flying by the seat of your pants. You can substitute an ingredient you would need to shop for with something you already have in the fridge, or reject a listed herb that the kids really hate in favour of a sprig of something you have growing in the garden. None of these recipes rely on an exact scientific balance between the different elements, so you can be quite relaxed in 'interpreting' them to suit yourself. There are also plenty of hints and suggestions along the way for how to use the basic techniques and ideas in this chapter to make many more soups than we have actually provided recipes for; for example, by varying the vegetables seasonally, by experimenting with presentation, by adding an extra spice here or a drop of cream there. Soon you will be writing your own book of soups!

This chapter is by no means a general education in soup-making. Instead it contains several varieties of classic Cornucopia daily soups as well as a selection of our more occasional flavours, be they season-dependent, ethnic or just a bit more labour-intensive. If you are just embarking on your soup-making career, try any of the soups listed in 'The basics' or 'Cream soups', as they are the most straightforward and they will give you the fundamental skills to eventually invent your own flavours.

Soups: some basic information

Soup starter: mirepoix

Mirepoix is the French name for the classic combination of onion, carrot and celery (traditionally in the ratio of 2:1:1), which forms the basis of many types of soup, stews and sauces. The vegetables are usually sautéed or roasted in butter or oil before liquid is added. This liquid will be a flavourful base for cooking. Over the centuries, further aromatics, such as leeks, tomatoes, garlic, mushrooms and chilli peppers, have been added to vary the mirepoix.

The common Cornucopia soup mirepoix consists of onion, carrot, celery and leek. This medley is used extensively throughout this chapter and is also referred to as the soup starter. For the purpose of most soups, the vegetables are chopped roughly, softened in a little oil, then cooked in liquid until soft and, eventually, blended into the soup. As a result, unless otherwise noted, you need not be terribly fussy about how you chop the starter vegetables; similarly-sized medium chunks that will cook evenly are fine.

Stock

If you do happen to have some vegetable stock in the fridge or freezer, it is a welcome flavour-enhancing addition to any soup. Replace some or all of the water in the recipe with stock (see page 184 for a stock recipe), but be careful in subsequent seasoning – if the stock is already seasoned, the soup may require no further salt and pepper.

One of the recipes listed (Eddie's kale and barley broth, page 112) absolutely requires that you use stock rather than water. As it is a thin base broth and none of the vegetables are blended into the liquid, that liquid must be independently flavourful. A recipe for the required amount of stock is integrated into the recipe for Eddie's broth.

Thickeners

The mirepoix vegetables provide an aromatic, tasty liquid base for your soup. Another factor, particularly in Cornucopia-style soups, which aim to be both filling and highly nutritious, is an ingredient to thicken the soup. Thickeners are not always necessary; sometimes the main vegetable ingredients will make for a hearty consistency when blended. However, for the purpose of texture and nutritional variety, some of the following are often included in Cornucopia soups. They do not dominate the flavour of the soup, but rather act as good wholesome carriers for other flavours.

Lentils and split peas

Lentils and split peas can be cooked in the soup, which means they do not require advance preparation. They go well with almost any vegetable, making them the most versatile and convenient healthy soup thickener. They should be added to the soup at the same time as the liquid, after the mirepoix has been sweated. Red lentils are the fastest cooking, requiring only 15 minutes to soften. Green and yellow split peas require at least 30 minutes. They are then blended into the final soup, bringing a wholesome, slightly grainy texture as well as plenty of protein, fibre and iron. Puy lentils, as they hold their shape quite firmly after cooking (other lentils and split peas turn mushy), are not so suitable for blending into soups. They can, however, be cooked separately and stirred in whole.

Beans

Unlike lentils and split peas, beans must be cooked before being added to a soup. For information on soaking and cooking different types of dry beans, see page 38. You can also use tinned beans, making sure to drain and rinse them before use. Beans commonly used in Cornucopia soups are chickpeas, butter beans, cannellini beans and kidney beans. You can blend them all into the final soup, or reserve a few and stir them in whole to add some chunky bits to the soup. Just like lentils and split peas, beans will broaden the nutritional profile of your soup, as well as making it a satisfyingly substantial lunch or tea.

Potatoes

Potatoes are another ingredient with which to thicken soup without taking over the flavour. Potatoes make for a smoother, creamier thickener than beans and pulses. They work particularly well with other root vegetables and with alliums (onions, garlic, chives, leeks, shallots, scallions, etc). Potatoes should be added to the soup at the same time as the liquid and blended in at the end. Potatoes can also form the main vegetable of a soup – for example potato, lentil and rosemary or cream of potato and spinach.

Blending

For blending all soups and sauces, we recommend using a hand-held stick blender. This piece of equipment is inexpensive to buy, easy to clean and safe to use, as it does not require you to transfer hot ingredients from one container to another. A standard food processor will also work, but you may have to liquidise the soup in several batches and it will be dangerously hot, so take care.

Note: when using a stick blender, always remember to unplug it before washing it under the tap.

Herbs

Many of our soup recipes include fresh herbs, which fall into two categories for the purpose of soup-making: those which should be added early and cooked in the soup to soften them and release their flavour and those which should be added as late as possible to retain their freshness and prevent them from losing their flavour.

Herbs that require a bit of cooking tend to have woody stems or have thick leaves (thyme, rosemary, oregano, sage); they should be added at the end of the soup starter and simmered with the liquid. In the case of thyme and rosemary, you either put whole sprigs into the soup and make sure to remove them before blending, or you pick the leaves off the stalk, in which case they can be blended into the final soup. In the case of oregano and sage, simply remove the thickest part of the stalks; the rest will soften sufficiently during cooking.

Herbs that should be reserved until the soup is cooked are the light, leafy ones (basil, coriander, flat-leaf parsley, dill, chervil, mint, tarragon, etc). They should be added at the final blending stage or, if finely chopped, stirred in just before serving. This will allow them to retain optimum colour, flavour and nutrition.

Chunky soups

Smooth soups are fully blended. Chunky soups can be either partly blended, with some ingredients kept whole, or light, aromatic broths filled with unblended ingredients. If you enjoy chunky soups, cook some of the ingredients separately and stir them in after the main soup has been blended. A good example of this is the roast leek and split pea soup on page 72. The mirepoix and cooked split peas are blended smooth. The leeks are roasted separately and stirred in at the end, making for a beautifully rich and chunky soup.

Other ingredients that make delicious chunks:

Beans — cook them separately (or use tinned beans) and stir them in at the end

Puy lentils — cook them separately and stir them in at the end

Barley — boil it separately (about 1 hour) and stir it in at the end

Savoy cabbage/kale — slice thinly, blanch until just softening and stir it in at the end

Roasted vegetables — such as little chunks of parsnip, butternut squash, leeks and red peppers – roast them separately and stir them in at the end

Cooked vegetables — diced pepper, courgettes, fennel, potatoes – chop them into attractive small pieces and add them to the soup after blending (or the unblended broth), return to the heat and cook until soft

Sweet corn, green peas — simply stir them in at the end

Dressing up your soup

When serving soup, warm the bowls slightly beforehand if possible, so the soup stays nice and steaming hot until your guests tuck in. In recognition of the fact that many people like to dip a hunk of bread into their soup, choose a nice chewy, crusty bread – try any of the yeast bread recipes in this book, or any fresh artisan bread. All sorts of fancy additions can make a bowl of soup both look great and add an extra dimension of flavour or texture.

Cream
A little swirl of cream or soy cream in the centre of a flavourful soup looks fantastic. Cream compliments tomato soups particularly well. Bear in mind that cream softens the original flavour somewhat, so a tiny amount is sufficient to enrich the soup without clouding its tastiness.

Herb oils
As with cream, swirling a little herb oil into the centre of each bowl of soup adds a dramatic bit of flair to the presentation. A nice zingy herb oil will also lend a pleasant contrast of flavours. Depending on the base flavour of your soup, try basil oil, coriander oil, mint oil or mixed garden herbs (chervil, parsley, dill, chive, etc). Blend 100ml of olive oil with about 1 tablespoon of lemon juice, a good handful of herbs and a pinch of salt and pepper. The oil should be thin enough to drizzle.

Croutons
Croutons are simply toasted chunks of bread, which can be spooned onto a bowl of soup and immersed in its flavour. Preheat your oven to 200°C. Using day-old bread, remove the crusts and then cut the rest into small squares (about 1cm). In a mixing bowl, toss the bread in a little extra-virgin olive oil and sprinkle on some salt and pepper. Transfer to a baking tray (or two if necessary – the bread should be only one layer deep) and toast until golden brown (10-15 minutes), shaking the croutons around once or twice to ensure even cooking. Cool in the tray and then either sprinkle some on top of each bowl of soup just before serving or place in a bowl in the centre of the table for guests to help themselves. Croutons can be stored for two days in an airtight container.

Note: if using shop bread, check packaging to ensure it does not contain E920, which is a non-vegetarian food additive.

Fresh herbs

Apart from herbs blended into the soup for flavour, or herb oils drizzled onto the surface of the soup, you can also garnish your soup with a fine fresh sprig of basil, coriander, mint or parsley, whichever is most compatible with the base flavour. To keep your sprigs alive and looking healthy, place them in a glass of water until just before serving. You can also chop some herbs finely and sprinkle them on top of the soup, or stir them in at the last moment. A scattering of chopped chives can look really attractive and their oniony pungency enhances the flavour, especially of cream soups.

Toasted nuts

Toasted nuts, when appropriate, bring a pleasant crunch to blended soups. You need to choose lightweight nuts that will float on the surface of the soup. Toasted flaked almonds and toasted pine nuts both work really well. Place them on a baking tray in a medium oven until turning golden, tossing once or twice. Flaked almonds take about 5 minutes, pine nuts about 7 or 8 minutes. Scatter a small amount onto each bowl of soup and serve immediately.

Cook's notes

The basics

These first three recipes are all variations on a basic vegetable, pulse and herb formula. All require a soup starter (see page 56) as well as the main vegetable, pulse of choice, water and herb. When everything is cooked, the ingredients are blended to smooth and seasoned to taste. The nutritional profile of these three vegetable and lentil/split pea soups is extremely balanced. They are a low-fat, zero-cholesterol source of slow-release energy, protein, fibre, vitamins and minerals. They are quick, easy and inexpensive to make and can be refrigerated for up to three days, as long as they are gently reheated to a high temperature. They are a great food for children, especially those who are more hesitant about eating whole vegetables, or even for adults who you are hoping to encourage towards healthier habits.

This vegetable, pulse and herb formula is the basis of many Cornucopia soups and can be used with any number of combinations. There are only small differences to be found between these first three soups. The main vegetable in the first one (carrot) is cooked in the soup itself, whereas the main vegetables in the second two (butternut squash and leek) are both roasted in the oven first. Secondly, the carrot and butternut squash are both blended into the soup, whereas the roast leek is stirred in whole at the end. Lastly, the herbs in the first and third soups (basil and dill) are added at the end of cooking to retain freshness and pungency, whereas the sage in the second soup is added during cooking, to soften its thick leaves and draw out the flavour. These variations simply demonstrate the versatility of this basic vegetable, pulse and herb soup and, hopefully, will inspire you to try all sorts of experimentation.

Some guidelines to creating your own basic soups

Vegetables
Most vegetables that you can think of can be used in soup. Some can be cooked in the soup itself, added at the same time as the liquid and cooked until soft (carrot, fennel, tomato, celeriac, potato, sweet potato, turnip). Other vegetables are infinitely more flavourful if roasted first in a little olive oil until soft and added to the soup before blending (butternut squash, parsnip, red peppers, leeks, courgettes, aubergines, red onions).

Pulses & beans
You can use red lentils and yellow or green split peas. The cooking times will vary slightly (see page 57). Green and yellow split peas tend to form a crust on the surface

of the soup when it goes cold. This is nothing to be concerned about; it will dissolve back into the soup as soon as it is reheated.

You can also use tinned or dried beans rather than lentils/split peas. Dried beans are rather less convenient, as they have to be soaked overnight and then cooked for between one and two hours. If using tinned beans, one tin per 2 litres of soup is sufficient. If using dried beans, for the same amount of soup soak 100g beans overnight and then cook them as per page 38. As they are cooked already, beans should be added to the soup just before blending.

Herbs
As with vegetables, most herbs are suitable for trying out in soup. Think about the flavour combinations with the keynote vegetable. For example, carrot goes well with most herbs, in particular basil, chervil, coriander, parsley and tarragon. Roasted root vegetables marry well with earthy herbs such as thyme, rosemary and sage. Tomatoes are delicious with basil, oregano or bay. Potatoes team up with chives, rosemary, thyme and dill. Mushrooms and tarragon compliment each other, as do green peas and mint, onions and sage. These are only examples, and your own taste buds will come up with their own combinations. As described on page 58, delicate, leafy herbs should be added to the soup at the last minute, whereas thicker, woodier herbs need to be cooked in the soup to soften them and allow their flavours to emerge.

Sample soups

Below are some of the popular variations of the vegetable, pulse and herb soup that are not included in this book. Using the basic recipes that follow as a guide to quantities and cooking methods, you can try any of these soups:

Potato, lentil & rosemary
Sweat mirepoix, add 4 large potatoes, 125g red lentils, 2 litres of water and 4 sprigs of rosemary. Cook for 30 minutes and blend.

Tomato, split pea & oregano
Sweat mirepoix, add 2 tins (or 1kg peeled, quartered fresh) tomatoes, 1 litre of water, 150g split peas and a small handful of fresh oregano leaves. Cook for 30 minutes and blend.

Turnip, split pea & cumin
Sweat mirepoix, add 700-800g chopped turnip, 150g yellow split peas and 2 litres of water, cook for 30 minutes then blend with 1 tablespoon of toasted cumin seeds (5 mins, medium oven).

Fennel, butter bean & dill
Roast 6 bulbs of fennel. Sweat mirepoix, add 2 litres of water and cook for 20 minutes. Add roast fennel, medium bunch of dill and 1 tin of butter beans (or 100g dry beans, soaked overnight and cooked as per page 38) and blend.

Roast celeriac, split pea & thyme
Roast 700-800g celeriac. Sweat some mirepoix. Add leaves from a small bunch of thyme, 150g split peas and 2 litres of water. Cook for 30 minutes. Add roasted celeriac and blend.

Cook's notes

Carrot, red lentil & basil soup
v gf wf yf ♡

This is possibly the easiest but also one of the most satisfying soups that we make in Cornucopia. The carrots are added at the same time as the soup starter (mirepoix) and sweated for 15 minutes to soften them and draw out the flavours. Then the water and lentils are added and the soup is cooked until the vegetables and lentils are all soft. Finally the basil is added and everything is blended until smooth. All you need then is a ladle and some hungry mouths.

Lentils are considered one of the world's healthiest foods. With 26% protein content, they are a staple of the many vegetarian communities of India as a source of vegetable protein. They are often combined with brown rice or other grains to produce a complete protein (i.e. all eight essential amino acids required by the human body to build and repair tissue). In the case of the lentil soups described in this book, a slice of brown bread on the side will create a complete protein. Lentils are also an excellent source of folic acid, a very good source of dietary fibre and iron and a good source of vitamin B1. Identified as a healthy heart food, lentils are completely fat-free and cholesterol-free and their high soluble fibre content helps to lower cholesterol. They rate as low on the recently popularised Glycaemic Index, meaning they are digested slowly and steadily and released gradually into the bloodstream, rather than causing sugar spikes which force the body to produce an unhealthy amount of insulin.

Lentils have formed part of the human diet for many millennia. There is evidence of primitive lentil cultivation right back to the Neolithic era (about 10,000 years ago) in the Near East. They are now grown all over Europe, throughout Northern Africa, in the Middle and Far East and in North America. They grow in small pods (see diagram), each of which contains one or two lentil seeds, which are either split and then dried or dried whole. They can be stored in a sealed package or an airtight container in the kitchen cupboard for up to a year.

This carrot soup is an excellent place to start or continue cooking with lentils. If you can source organic carrots, all the better. Other herbs that you could try instead of basil are: coriander, chervil, dill, chive and tarragon.

1 onion
5 carrots
2 sticks celery *(including leaves)*
½ leek
150g red lentils
75-100g *(big bunch)* fresh basil
Unrefined sunflower oil
Salt and pepper
2 litres of water

Start by roughly chopping the onion, carrot, celery and leek. If using organic carrots, there is no need to peel them, just rinse them. Wash the chopped leek under cold water to remove any soil or grit and drain thoroughly.

Now generously coat the base of a large pot with sunflower oil and place over a medium heat. Add the chopped vegetables. Stir briefly to coat them with oil, cover with a lid, turn down to a low heat and sweat for 15 minutes, stirring occasionally.

Next, add 2 litres of water and the red lentils. Stir carefully to ensure that the lentils do not stick to the base of the pot. Bring to the boil and then turn the heat down, cover with a lid and simmer for 30 minutes or until the lentils have turned yellow and the carrots are soft.

Remove the pot from the heat. Add the fresh basil, reserving some sprigs for garnish. Blend until smooth using a stick blender. If the soup seems a little thick, add a drop of water to reach the desired consistency. Season with salt and pepper. Bring back to a simmer and serve. Garnish each bowl with a sprig of basil.

Lentil plant

Roasted butternut squash, lentil & sage soup

v gf wf yf ♡

Recently my 96-year-old grandmother was at dinner in my parents' house. Having cleaned her plate, she requested 'more of those orange things', by which, it emerged, she was referring to chunks of roasted butternut squash. I'm sure she would have no idea what a whole butternut squash looks like, nor would she recognise the name, for it came onto the Irish market long after her culinary patterns were definitively established, but she was, nevertheless, much impressed by the soft, sweet, slightly charred 'orange things'. I have no doubt that she declared them 'grand', the absolute highest compliment in her food critique lexicon. Roast squash is, indeed, a taste that almost everyone seems to particularly enjoy.

Roast squash is a great favourite in Cornucopia and it makes several appearances in this book – here as a soup, in two salads (borlotti bean and bulghar wheat), in several main courses (thai curry, pumpkin and courgette pie, cannelloni, lasagne and polenta) and it even pops its head up once more in a savoury scone. It has a sweet and smoky depth of flavour as well as a lovely soft, but not mushy, texture. Tossed in olive oil, seasoned and roasted with perhaps a sprig or two of rosemary, it makes a delicious side vegetable. It is almost impossible to resist popping one or two chunks into your mouth the minute it emerges, glowing from the oven.

This soup is another delicious use of squash. It is a bright, happy-looking soup, full of lentil goodness, sweet with squash and earthy with sage, with across-the-board appeal. If sage is not a favourite herb of yours, try rosemary, thyme or oregano, all of which marry beautifully with squash. Should Irish winter pumpkins be in season, you could replace the squash with 900g of good-quality pumpkin.

Peeling a butternut squash can sometimes prove challenging. One relatively easy method is to top and tail it. Then, using a regular peeler, widen the circle at the fat end of the squash, so that most of the skin at that end is gone. Now, starting at that bald circle, drag the peeler over the big bump, right down to the bottom of the thin end of the squash. Repeat until all the skin has been removed. Then, cut the vegetable in half lengthways and use a soupspoon to scoop out the seeds from the two hollow parts. Your squash is now ready for chopping.

1 butternut squash *(about 900g)*
  — *or pumpkin if in season*
1 onion
1 carrot
2 sticks celery *(including leaves)*
½ leek
150g lentils
3-5 sprigs sage *(about 15 leaves)*
Extra-virgin olive oil
Unrefined sunflower oil
Salt and pepper
2 litres of water

Preheat your oven to 180°C.

Peel the butternut squash and chop it into medium cubes. In a bowl, toss the squash in a little olive oil, salt and pepper. Transfer to the baking tray and roast in the oven until soft (30-40 minutes), agitating once or twice.

Meanwhile, roughly chop the onion, carrot, celery and leek. Wash the chopped leek under cold water to remove any soil or grit and drain thoroughly. Now generously coat the base of a large pot with sunflower oil and place over a medium heat. Add the chopped vegetables. Stir briefly to coat them with oil, cover with a lid, turn down to a low heat and sweat for 15 minutes, stirring occasionally.

When the vegetables have sweated, add lentils, sage leaves (remove the stalks) and water to the soup pot. Stir carefully to ensure lentils do not stick to the base. Bring to the boil, then cover, reduce to a low heat and simmer for 20 minutes, or until the lentils have turned yellow and all the vegetables are soft. Now add in the chunks of roast squash.

Remove the pot from the heat and blend until smooth using a stick blender. If the soup seems a little thick, add a little water to achieve the desired consistency. Season with salt and pepper. Return to the heat, bring back to a simmer and serve.

Cook's notes

Leek, green split pea & dill soup

v gf wf yf ♡

This is a blended split pea and vegetable soup into which whole pieces of roasted leek are stirred, making for a pleasantly thick and chunky texture. If you are feeding children who would rather their soup be smooth, then some or all of the leeks can be blended in. Do not be alarmed if, when it cools, the soup forms a thick, moonscape-like skin – this is a common feature of split peas. As soon as it is reheated, a quick stir and the skin will disappear back into the soup.

Dill is a sweet herb with a mild anise flavour and long, feathery leaves. It looks for all the world like the punkish hairstyle that grows out of the top of a fennel bulb. In fact the two are closely enough related within the plant kingdom that it is recommended that they not be sown beside each other as they can cross-pollinate. Dill comes from the ancient Norse word *dilla*, which means to soothe or to lull. The name is derived from the relaxing effects that dill, especially dill seeds, can have on the muscles of the digestive tract. Teas made from dill seeds have been used throughout the ages in both Eastern and Western medicines to ease the stomach. Dill is an ingredient in the original Woodward's Gripe Water and many subsequent versions of the natural remedy for easing colic in babies. The oil in dill seeds is known to have a mildly antiseptic quality, which Hippocrates, the ancient Greek father of medicine (460-370BC), must have known something about when he prescribed the following method for cleaning one's teeth: 'Clean teeth with a ball of wool dipped in honey. Rinse with one spoon of dill seeds boiled in one cup of white wine.'

Now that we have more convenient tooth-cleaning products on the market, dill is more commonly used as a versatile and delightful herb in cooking. Chopped finely, it makes for a wonderful herb butter, delicious served on baked potatoes. It can also be stirred into yoghurt or crème fraîche with a little seasoning, olive oil and lemon juice as a dip or a salad dressing. Stir some finely chopped dill into a cream or béchamel sauce just before serving. Or mix it with breadcrumbs, pumpkin seeds and grated cheese for a wonderful gratin topping. Dill also marries successfully with egg dishes – add it to quiches, omelettes or even sprinkle a little over some mid-morning scrambled eggs.

4 large leeks
1 onion
1 carrot
2 sticks celery *(including leaves)*
2 cloves garlic
150g green split peas
50g *(medium bunch)* fresh dill
Extra-virgin olive oil
Unrefined sunflower oil
Salt and pepper
2 litres of water

Preheat your oven to 180°C. Chop the leeks lengthways into halves and then widthways into small squares (bearing in mind that they will not be blended into the soup but will be stirred in whole at the end). Rinse thoroughly under cold water and drain well. In a bowl, toss the leeks in a little olive oil, salt and pepper. Spread over the two baking trays and roast in the oven until completely soft, turning occasionally. They will take about 20 minutes. Set aside.

Meanwhile, roughly chop the onion, carrot, celery and garlic. Generously coat the base of a large pot with sunflower oil and place over a medium heat. Add the chopped vegetables. Stir briefly to coat them with oil, cover with a lid, turn down to a low heat and sweat for 15 minutes, stirring occasionally.

Now add the split peas and water and stir carefully to ensure the split peas don't stick to the base of the pot. Turn up the heat and bring to the boil. Cover, reduce to a low heat and simmer for at least 30 minutes, or until the split peas and vegetables are soft.

Remove the pot from the heat, add the fresh dill and blend until smooth using a stick blender. If the soup seems a little thick, add enough water to achieve the desired consistency. Stir in the roast leeks and season with salt and pepper. Bring back to a simmer before serving.

Cook's notes

Tomato soups

There are so many different kinds of tomato soup – from chilled gazpacho to spicy Mexican bean soup to rich cream of tomato soup. When I was a younger, the only tomato soup I ever tasted was the tin of condensed product immortalised by Andy Warhol. Due to its excessive sweetness and general lack of resemblance to real tomatoes, it was not a soup I had any love for. I remember how astonished I was, when I cooked real tomato soup from scratch when at university, at how remarkably simple and delicious it was. It was a recipe I resorted to many times, with a swirl of cream in each bowl and a sprig of basil if I was trying to impress.

For a really quick and nutritious tomato soup, cook a soup starter (see page 56) then add two tins of tomatoes, 150g lentils and 1½ litres of water and simmer for 30 minutes. Blend with a fresh herb of your choice and season. If you would like to use fresh tomatoes, choose 1kg of really ripe plum tomatoes. Cut an 'X' into the skin of each and plunge them into boiling water for about a minute. Drain them and remove the skins, which should slip away easily. Now quarter the tomatoes and add them to the soup, after the mirepoix has been sweated, along with the lentils and water. Simmer for half an hour and then blend with a herb of your choice.

For a really special, intensely flavoured tomato soup, use 1kg of vine-ripened cherry tomatoes. Halve them and toss them in a little extra-virgin olive oil, salt and pepper. Roast them in a medium oven for about 25 minutes, agitating once or twice. These caramelised, almost jammy gems can be used instead of freshly skinned or tinned tomatoes in the basic tomato soup recipe described above or either of the two recipes that follow.

Tomatoes combine beautifully with many different herbs – try basil, oregano, rosemary, sage and mint, to name but a few. Chilli can also be a welcome addition to tomato soups; one very popular winter-warmer soup in Cornucopia is tomato, chilli and mint, which has a pleasant kick on a cold, wet evening.

Some people find that the natural acidity of tomatoes needs to be balanced by a small amount of sweetener. This is not generally something we do in Cornucopia. However, if you do find that your tomato soups taste a little bitter for your liking, add a scant teaspoon of unrefined brown sugar or apple concentrate to rebalance the flavour.

Tomato, roast red pepper & roast garlic soup
v   gf   wf   yf   ♡

This recipe was introduced to Cornucopia by our ever-inventive chef, Eddie Bates. When working to a strict noon deadline, as Cornucopia chefs do on a daily basis, one might be tempted to choose a straightforward, all-in-one-pot soup that does not involve fiddling with hot, oily bulbs of garlic as the lunchtime queue fast approaches. However, Eddie was never a man to shrink from the excitement of a culinary challenge. And though it sometimes entered him into a high-pressure race against time, he often went the extra mile with his soups. This utterly mouth-watering tomato, roast red pepper and roast garlic soup is a fine example of how a little extra preparation brings depth and sumptuousness to a simple combination of basic ingredients.

This tomato soup has long been a staff favourite. Upon arrival at work, if they spot it on the lunchtime menu, several members of staff will immediately stash a bowl of it in a safe corner, in the knowledge that it will be long since sold out by the time their lunch break rolls around. And more often than not, they're absolutely right. Many customers can't resist a nice tomato soup. And if it's a tomato soup enriched by roasted red peppers and roasted garlic, the second soup option of the day stands little chance of competing!

Roasting garlic, as is the case with many vegetables, dramatically changes the original flavour. Whereas raw or lightly cooked garlic is sharp and pungent, roasted garlic has a mellow, sweet, almost buttery taste and a soft, creamy texture. If you feel like experimenting with roast garlic, roast a second (or third) bulb along with the one required for this recipe. Orla, our photographer, likes nothing more than a few cloves of roasted garlic eaten, still warm, from the bulb. You can also pick or squeeze out the cloves and mash them with a fork. This roast garlic purée is delicious mixed through mashed potato or spread on fresh or toasted crusty bread as instant, fresh garlic bread. Roasted garlic is also a tasty addition to gravies, cream sauces and dips.

Although roasting the garlic breaks down many of the compounds responsible for causing the infamous garlic breath, should you be concerned about possible social disasters after eating this soup, or any other garlic-heavy foods, chew on (and swallow) a healthy sprig of parsley or drink a full cup of hot mint tea.

Preheat the oven to 180°C.

Chop the peppers in half and remove the seeds. Cut the top off the bulb of garlic. Toss both the peppers and the garlic in a little olive oil, salt and pepper and transfer to two separate baking trays.

4 red peppers
1 bulb garlic
1 onion
1 carrot
2 sticks celery *(including leaves)*
½ leek
2x400g tins of plum tomatoes
    (organic if possible) or 1kg
    ripe plum tomatoes
1½ litres water
Extra-virgin olive oil
Unrefined sunflower oil
Salt and pepper

Cook's notes

Pour a little extra olive oil into the top of the bulb of garlic (see page 143), coating the cloves on the inside. Roast until soft and set aside. The pepper will take about 20 minutes, the garlic about 30 minutes. When cool enough to handle, hold the uncut end of the bulb of garlic and squeeze all the flesh out through the cut end. Discard the skins.

If you are using fresh tomatoes, they must first be deskinned. Cut an X into the skin of each, place them in a suitable bowl and pour boiling water over them. After one minute, drain the tomatoes and the skins can now be removed with ease. Chop the tomatoes in quarters and set aside.

Cover the base of a large pot generously with sunflower oil and place over a medium heat. Add the carrot, onion, celery and leek. Stir briefly to coat them with oil, cover with a lid, turn down to a low heat and sweat for 15 minutes, stirring occasionally. Next, add the freshly skinned or tinned tomatoes and water. Turn up the heat and bring to the boil. Cover, reduce to a low heat and simmer for 20 minutes, or until all the vegetables are soft.

Remove the pot from the heat and add the roasted peppers and garlic flesh. Using a stick blender, blend until smooth. If the soup seems a little thick, add enough water to achieve the desired consistency. Season to taste and return to a gentle simmer before serving, perhaps with a slice of basil bread, as described on page 346.

Tomato, white bean & savoy cabbage soup with basil oil   *v gf wf yf* ♡

This is a chunky, farmhouse-style combination of tomatoes, beans and cabbage, lifted by a lovely tangy basil oil drizzled on top. This soup is like dinner in a bowl — it is both filling and wholesome and it contains such an array of flavours and textures that you will feel you've experienced more than a common-or-garden bowl of soup, but rather a delicately balanced meal. With a hearty hunk of crusty bread to mop up the inside of the bowl, this rustic broth will keep you satisfied for hours to come.

Savoy cabbage is now commonly available in Ireland all year round. Having used a quarter of the cabbage for this soup, you may wonder what to do with the rest. Savoy cabbage is delicious pan-fried in a dash of olive oil with some finely chopped garlic, salt and a good twist of black pepper. It is also used as a leaf wrap in the dolmades (page 278). Blanched, it is a great ingredient for creamy gratins (page 218), or try it in traditional Irish mashed potato and cabbage colcannon (page 115). When curly kale comes into season in late autumn, you can use it instead of savoy cabbage — it has a slightly darker colour and deeper flavour, and it works wonderfully well in this recipe.

A word of warning: it is recommended that the consumption of this soup be accompanied by a large cloth napkin (it's not that I'm posh, it's just that paper napkins are yet another disposable burden on the environment), tucked in firmly at the collar. This will serve to limit the damage that stray lengths of tomato-drenched cabbage can do to one's clothing. Apart from that residual danger, this is an absolute pleasure to dip your spoon into.

The small quantity of basil oil cited below is enough to drizzle an artistic swirl into six bowls of soup, with perhaps a little over for whoever likes it best to have a second swirl. You might consider doubling or trebling the quantities, making it actually easier to blend and leaving you with extra basil oil for drizzling over stews, salads, toasted cheese sandwiches, bakes and quiches. You could also cook some baby potatoes and toss them, still hot, in a little basil oil and serve them as a side dish with, amongst other things, roast vegetable ragout, quiche, omelette, leafy green salad or with some grilled (or roasted) asparagus topped with a cheesy béchamel sauce. Basil oil will store in the fridge for five days. For convenience, store it in a custom-made drizzler bottle, or alternatively an empty mineral bottle.

For the soup:
1 onion
1 carrot
2 sticks celery *(including leaves)*
½ leek
2 cloves garlic
2 sprigs oregano
2 sprigs thyme
2 sprigs rosemary
2x400g tins of plum tomatoes
    (organic if possible) or 1kg
    ripe plum tomatoes
¼ of a large *(⅓ of a medium)*
    savoy cabbage
1x400g tin of cannellini beans
    or butter beans or 100g
    cannellini beans or butter
    beans soaked overnight and
    cooked as per page 38
Unrefined sunflower oil
Salt and pepper
1½ litres of water

For the basil oil:
100ml extra-virgin olive oil
Juice of ½ lemon *(or 1 tbsp*
    lemon juice)
25g *(small bunch)* fresh basil
Pinch each of salt and pepper

If you are using fresh tomatoes, they must first be deskinned. Cut an X into the skin of each, place them in a suitable bowl and pour boiling water over them. After one minute, drain the tomatoes and the skins can now be removed with ease. Chop in quarters and set aside.

Roughly chop the onion, carrot, celery, leek and garlic. Rinse the chopped leek under cold water to remove any soil and drain thoroughly. Now coat the base of a large pot with sunflower oil and place it over a medium heat. Add the chopped vegetables. Stir briefly to coat them with oil, cover with a lid, turn down to a low heat and sweat for 15 minutes, stirring occasionally.

Next, remove the stalks from all the herbs. When the vegetables have sweated, add the freshly skinned or tinned tomatoes as well as the herbs and water to the soup pot. Turn up the heat and bring to the boil. Cover, reduce to a low heat and simmer for 20 minutes, or until all the vegetables are soft.

Meanwhile chop the savoy cabbage into thin, bite-size strips (bear in mind it has to fit into a soupspoon). Bring a pot of water to the boil and plunge in the cabbage for 2-3 minutes. It should retain a pleasant bite. Refresh immediately in cold water, drain and set aside.

Next, place all the ingredients for the basil oil into a suitable container and use a stick blender to blend until smooth. When the soup is cooked, remove the pot from the heat, blend thoroughly with a stick blender and season with salt and pepper. If it seems a little thick, add enough water

to achieve the desired consistency. Just before serving, drain and rinse the cannellini beans (or butter beans) and stir them in, along with the blanched cabbage. Return the pot to a medium heat and bring to a simmer.

To serve, dip the ladle deep into the pot to make sure each bowl of soup gets plenty of beans and cabbage. Finish with a generous swirl of basil oil on top of each portion.

Cream soups

Adding cream to soup certainly enriches it, thickens it and makes for a wonderfully velvety consistency. However, as cream also softens the intensity of other flavours, a 'cream of' soup must be made with great attention to seasoning and keynote flavours. Below are some tips to avoid blandness and ensure that your creamy soups remain titillating to the tastebuds as well as being rich and luxurious.

Tips for flavouring cream soups

Butter
An important start to your 'cream of' soup is to use a good knob of butter (with a dash of oil to raise the flashpoint slightly) as the fat in which you sweat the mirepoix (onion, carrot, celery, leek). Butter develops specific flavour compounds when it is used in frying, quite different to the effects of oil. Using butter with your mirepoix brings a nutty, smoky taste to the vegetables, deep flavour tones that won't be lost in the later addition of cream.

Vegetable stock
Another hint when making creamy soups is to use vegetable stock instead of water, if you have some lying around. For a recipe for vegetable stock, see page 184. As with the use of butter described above, this will intensify the flavour of the soup.

Flavourful vegetables
Cream of tomato soup works really well, because tomatoes are naturally sharp and tangy enough to cut through the cream. Other vegetables that work well are alliums (leeks, shallots, onions, garlic), as they are quite pungent, and also mushrooms, as they are strong and earthy in taste. Roasting vegetables also makes them more suitable for 'cream of' soups, as their flavours become sweeter and more intense in the oven – for example roasted butternut squash, beetroot, parsnip or red onion.

Garlic and nutmeg
Almost regardless of what other ingredients are used, a few cloves of garlic and a generous pinch of freshly grated nutmeg are welcome additions to a 'cream of' soup. Add the garlic (about 4 cloves for 2 litres of soup) to the mirepoix at the beginning of the cooking and grate in the nutmeg at the same time as adding the cream. The garlic brings a little pungency to the underlying vegetables and the nutmeg, a classic partner of all things creamy, adds warmth and depth to the final flavour.

Herbs and spices

Using plenty of fresh herbs or carefully chosen spices will also inject punch into a 'cream of' soup, so that as well as the richness of the cream there remains an interesting vibrancy of flavour. Herbs that work particularly well are parsley, chives, basil, dill and tarragon. Spices that you might like to try are paprika, cumin, coriander, chilli and cayenne.

Spicy croutons

If you would like to serve croutons with your 'cream of' soup, the standard croutons described on page 60 cannot be faulted. However, for a variation, you might try these spicy croutons, as their added kick will contrast pleasantly with the smooth creaminess of the soup. Having removed the crusts from day-old bread and cut it into 1cm pieces, place them in a mixing bowl and toss with a little olive oil, salt, pepper, 1 teaspoon of minced garlic, a scattering of finely chopped mixed herbs (thyme, oregano, rosemary, etc), 1 teaspoon of paprika and a good pinch of cayenne pepper. Toast in the oven for 15 minutes, or until crispy and golden.

Note: if using shop bread, check packaging to ensure it does not contain E920.

Reheating

If you have any creamy soup left over, take great care when reheating it that you just bring it to a gentle simmer. If you boil it the cream may split into oils and milk solids, thus ruining the nice creamy texture.

Soups to try

Using the two 'cream of' soups that follow as guidelines to quantities and methods, here are some other delicious combinations to try:

Cream of turnip, yellow split pea & parsley
Cook a mirepoix with garlic. Add 800g (approx) turnip, 100g yellow split peas and 2 litres of water/stock. Cook for 30 minutes, then blend in 200ml cream, nutmeg and a good handful of fresh flat-leaf parsley.

Cream of roast beetroot & dill
Roast 6 beetroots as per page 171. Cook a mirepoix with garlic. Add 2 litres of

water/stock and cook for 20 minutes. Blend in the chunks of roast beetroot, 200ml cream and 50g fresh dill.

Curried cream of sweet potato
Cook a mirepoix with garlic. At the end of sweating, add in 1 heaped tsp ground cumin, 1 heaped tsp ground coriander, 1 tsp ground cinnamon, 1 tsp ground ginger, 1 tsp turmeric and ½ tsp chilli powder. Cook for 3 minutes, then add water and 5 sweet potatoes and cook until soft. Blend with 200ml cream. You can also try curried cream of cauliflower, carrot or potato.

Cream of roast leek, garlic & chives
Roast 4 leeks and 1 bulb of garlic. Cook a mirepoix. Add 2 litres of water/stock and cook for 20 minutes. Blend in the leeks, garlic flesh, 200ml cream, nutmeg and a good handful of fresh garden chives.

Other vegetables to try in 'cream of' soups
Fennel (include the anise-flavoured leafy tops), celeriac, asparagus, broccoli, roasted pumpkin, roasted red pepper, spinach, onion.

Cook's notes

Cream of mushroom & ginger soup
gf   wf   ef

This is a spectacularly flavourful soup, a cream of mushroom soup, possibly unlike any you have tasted before. The earthy flavour of the mushrooms, as well as the spiciness of the fresh ginger and the deep tones of the tamari (or shoyu) and sesame oil, contrast wonderfully well with the velvety smoothness of the cream. It is not necessary to roast the mushrooms to enhance their flavour, as the other ingredients are aromatic enough to create a strong symphony of flavours that cuts through the cream.

Ginger is an ingredient quite extensively used in Cornucopia, both in its ground form and its fresh form. As it is native to India and China, ginger occurs quite often in the traditional cuisines of both of those countries. Ground ginger is an essential ingredient in many Indian curry pastes, as well as popular drinks such as chai (spiced tea) and lassi (chilled spiced yoghurt drink). Chinese cooking tends to favour using fresh ginger – which is a common ingredient in dressings and marinades and sauces. Finely sliced pickled ginger is a much-loved Japanese palate cleanser and grated ginger is often added to shoyu, mirin and garlic as a dip for tofu. In Korea, fresh ginger is an important ingredient in kimchi, the traditional spicy pickled cabbage.

When ginger was imported from the colonies to Europe, it became a much sought-after ingredient, particularly for baking, with the creation of ginger biscuits, gingerbread and stem-ginger cakes. The children's fairy story about the runaway gingerbread man was first published in 1875 but was a firm favourite bedside tale long before. Deeply flavoured ginger beer was developed in England in the mid-eighteenth century and became established as a non-alcoholic (or very low alcohol) drink of choice.

Ginger, as well as being a pleasantly spicy and warm flavouring for food, has healing properties, in particular for the stomach. It stimulates increased production of saliva and digestive fluids, helping with nausea, indigestion and upset stomachs. It is recommended as a remedy for travel sickness and morning sickness, by either nibbling on gingernut biscuits or drinking ginger tea. To brew yourself a nice pot of ginger tea, be it to soothe your stomach, to combat cold symptoms, or just for pleasure, choose the youngest, juiciest-looking rhizome of fresh ginger that you can find. Peel 2 or 3 thumb-size pieces into a pot as well as some slices of lemon. Add 1 litre of water, bring to the boil and simmer for half an hour. Sweeten with honey or unrefined brown sugar and add some more lemon to taste. Strain the tea into a pot and enjoy it hot and steaming.

1 onion
1 carrot
2 sticks celery *(including leaves)*
½ leek
4 cloves of garlic
2 thumb-size pieces of
    fresh ginger
8 large field mushrooms *(or
    500g any kind of mushroom)*
200ml cream *(and a little extra
    to swirl)*
A good dash of freshly grated
    nutmeg *(about 1 tsp)*
Unrefined sunflower oil
1 tbsp butter
1 scant tbsp sesame oil
1 scant tbsp tamari *(or shoyu/
    soy sauce if not required to
    be gluten-free)*
Salt and pepper
2 litres of water *(or vegetable
    stock, see page 184)*

Roughly chop the onion, carrot, celery, leek and garlic. Rinse the chopped leek under cold water to remove any soil and drain thoroughly. Peel the ginger and chop it into little pieces. Place the knob of butter and a little sunflower oil into a large pot and heat over a medium ring. When the butter has melted, add the chopped vegetables and ginger. Stir briefly to coat them with fat, then cover with a lid, turn down to a low heat and sweat for 15 minutes, stirring occasionally.

When the vegetables have sweated, add the water (or stock), bring to a boil and, still lidded, simmer for 15 minutes. Next, chop the mushrooms roughly and add them to the soup. Simmer for a further 10 minutes, at which point all the vegetables will be soft.

Remove from the heat, add the cream and nutmeg and, using a stick blender, blend until smooth. If the soup seems a little thick, add enough water to achieve the desired consistency. Now stir in the sesame oil and tamari. Season with salt and pepper, bearing in mind that the tamari is quite salty, so very little extra salt, if any, will be required. Return to the heat and bring to a gentle simmer. Serve with a swirl of cream in the centre of each bowl.

Cook's notes

Cream of potato & spinach soup
gf   wf   ef

This is a lovely, filling soup that is very easy on the stomach and perfect for a cold winter's day. It is good soup for feeding to children, as the flavours are quite mild and the texture wonderfully smooth. They will love the fancy swirl of cream in the centre of the bowl. You can add a final flourish with some finely chopped chives or flat-leaf parsley, just to give the soup some extra freshness.

Some variations on this cream of potato soup that are well worth trying out are: cream of potato and leek (use 3 potatoes and 3 leeks) or cream of potato and roasted red onion (use 3 potatoes and 4 roasted red onions).

When choosing potatoes for potato soup, use floury potatoes for soups into which the potatoes will be blended (such as this one) and waxy potatoes for soups (usually broths) in which diced potatoes will be left whole. The floury potatoes will soften and release their starch, which helps to thicken the blended soup. In the case of a broth, you don't want the potatoes to release starch, which would cloud the clarity of the broth, but rather to stay firm and intact, pleasant for chewing rather than falling apart into a mushy mess. For a list of the different kinds of floury and waxy potatoes on the Irish market, and their appropriate uses in cooking, see page 229.

Vegan option
If you would like to make a vegan version of this rich potato soup, replace the 150ml of cream with 150ml of tinned coconut milk. Use sunflower oil rather than use butter to sauté the starter vegetables in. You can create the creamy swirl effect in the centre of each bowl with a little extra coconut milk.

Roughly chop the onion, carrot, celery, leek and garlic. Rinse the chopped leek under cold water to remove any soil and drain thoroughly. Place the knob of butter and a little sunflower oil into a large pot and heat over a medium ring. When the butter has melted, add the chopped vegetables. Stir to coat them with butter, cover with a lid, turn down to a low heat and sweat for 15 minutes, stirring occasionally.

Meanwhile, peel the potatoes and chop them into medium chunks. When the vegetables have sweated, add the water (or stock) and potatoes to

1 onion
1 carrot
2 sticks celery *(including leaves)*
½ leek
4 cloves of garlic
4 large floury potatoes *(such as roosters) — about 1kg*
400g spinach
150ml cream *(& a little extra to swirl)*
A good dash of freshly grated nutmeg *(about 1 tsp)*
Unrefined sunflower oil
1 tbsp butter
Salt and pepper
2 litres water *(or vegetable stock, see page 184)*

the soup pot. Bring to the boil, again cover with a lid, turn down to a low heat and simmer for 20 minutes, or until all the vegetables are soft.

Next, remove the stalks from the spinach and wash and drain it thoroughly. When the soup is cooked, stir the spinach into the pot. It will cook in 1 minute.

Remove the pot from the heat, add the cream and nutmeg and use a stick blender to blend until smooth. If the soup seems a little thick, add enough water to bring to the desired consistency. Season with salt and pepper. Bring back to a simmer and serve with a little swirl of cream in the centre of each bowl.

Soup adventures

When I was a schoolgirl in the 1980s, my mother or father made a big pot of chunky vegetable soup every Sunday night. A portion of it was heated in a little pot every weekday morning (in pre-microwave days) and I brought a yellow *Muppet Show* thermos flask of it to school with me. At lunchtime, I'd pour my thick, hearty soup into the little plastic cup that screwed on to the top of the flask. It never came out very smoothly, more a 'plop, plop' effect that used to elicit squeals of disgust all around me. No one seemed to like the smell of my soup, nor the texture of my soup, never mind the fact that I dared bring it into a sliced pan sandwich and tetra-pack juice dominated lunchroom. My whole soup custom was considered downright weird. It was really just a plain old rustic vegetable soup, but a lot of the kids around me only knew tinned or packet commercial soups, which were not 'lumpy' and 'smelly' like mine, but rather thin, smooth and predominantly free of anything resembling a real vegetable.

Things are a lot different now. Fresh soup has received great press of late as a healthy food for everyone and a good way to get children to eat some of their five-a-day vegetable portions. Supermarket fridges are replete with all sorts of farmhouse soups, homemade soups, gourmet soups and several lines of 100% organic soups. A vast array of flavours is available, no longer restricted to the few traditional standards, introducing new and innovative ingredients, tastes and textures. The vast majority of fresh soups are free of artificial flavours and colours and still contain much of the goodness of the vegetables that have gone into them. Alongside this surge of interest in good-quality, wholesome soups, we have an ever-developing availability of delicious, artisan breads to dip into them — further encouragement to embrace the soup revolution.

The only possible downside of the much-improved selection of soups on offer to the Irish market is that it discourages the tradition of making soup at home. Why go to all that bother when you can buy a pretty passable fresh soup in a carton in the local convenience store? There is a great reason to bother: why settle for passable? I challenge you to find a soup as interesting and, indeed, as delicious as any of the six soups that follow (or, indeed, any that have gone before) packaged and sold in any fridge in any retail outfit, north, south, east or west. Homemade soup, just like homemade most things, sings a melody all of its own. Choose the best-quality ingredients you can afford to buy, organic where possible. You will never tire of homemade soup, as each and every pot will be unique, for, as you are not bound by strict industrial standards, the vegetables, your mood, the weather, the seasoning will all vary from soup to soup, with a slightly different effect each time.

So far this chapter has presented some of our standard Cornucopia soups, along with tips and ideas about varying those soups and making them your own. The next six soups are some of our more unusual and occasional soups, soups for customers who like a bit of a change, who like to take a gamble on something they may never have tasted before. The recipes use nuts, spices, herbs and techniques that, we hope, will cause you to raise an eyebrow in an 'I simply have to try that one' response. Here begin our adventures in soup.

Honey-roasted parsnip, toasted almond & cumin seed soup
v   gf   wf   yf   cn

This soup was created one Sunday morning in 2005. It being a Sunday, there was an air of calm and (relative) relaxation in the kitchen, Sunday being a day when (A) we do not serve breakfast, so the chefs have some extra cooking space, and (B) a slightly shorter and quieter day of service lies ahead, so the chefs are under a little less pressure. Crucially to this soup, there was also, for whatever reason, a rare and unsettling excess of empty oven space. Usually the opposite is the case — chefs regularly have a queue of trays of vegetables waiting to go into the packed ovens and the salad chef and main food chef enter into daily negotiations about who gets to use what oven, and when. However, on this particular Sunday, there must have been less roasting on the menu. So the chef du jour, Josh Whitney, not one to let an empty oven go to waste, filled lots of trays with flaked almonds and chopped parsnips and set them a-roasting. A delicious sweet aroma of toasting nuts emerged from the kitchen, the first sign that an unexpected treat was on the way. There followed the earthy, caramelised tones of roasting parsnip.

Several hours later, delighted waiting staff gave the seal of approval to the brand new taste sensation — roast parsnip, toasted almond and cumin seed soup. We had all eaten soups made with ground almonds in the past. Not a patch on using toasted flakes, which are sweet and buttery and a little mysterious. Needless to say, the soup proved a popular choice amongst customers that Sunday and it has lived on in staff memory and in our menu ever since.

The only amendments that have been made for domestic use is that we've added a little honey to the roasting parsnip to balance out the slight bitterness of the cumin seeds. As we try to keep most of our soups vegan in Cornucopia (with the obvious exception of cream soups), we don't use honey in the restaurant version of this soup, but it does work wonderfully well. For vegans who would like to mimic the effects of honey, sprinkle a little unrefined brown sugar on the roasting parsnip. Should you prefer to avoid sugar, use a dash of apple concentrate. Allow plenty of time for roasting the parsnips — they are quite woody and take a famously long time to soften. And make sure to taste one before they are blended into the soup — they are astonishingly delicious.

Preheat your oven to 180°C.

Peel the parsnips and chop them into medium pieces. Toss them in a little olive oil, salt and pepper, as well as the runny honey, making sure each piece is coated. You might like to warm the honey slightly to help it spread. Transfer to

5 medium parsnips
1-2 tbsp runny honey
150g flaked almonds
1 onion
1 carrot
2 sticks celery
½ leek
2 tsp ground cumin
½ tsp ground cinnamon
Extra-virgin olive oil
Unrefined sunflower oil
Salt and pepper
2 litres water

two baking trays and roast until completely soft, agitating occasionally. This will take about 45 minutes.

Meanwhile, roughly chop the onion, carrot, celery and leek. Rinse the chopped leek under cold water to remove any soil and drain thoroughly. Coat the base of a large pot generously with sunflower oil and place over a medium heat. Add chopped vegetables and stir briefly to coat them with oil. Cover with a lid, turn down to a low heat and sweat for 15 minutes, stirring occasionally. Next add the ground cinnamon and cumin and, stirring constantly, cook for a further 3 minutes.

While the oven is hot, spread the flaked almonds on a dry baking tray and toast for about 5 minutes, until golden brown. Set aside. Turn the oven off.

When the spices have been cooked, add the water, turn up the heat and bring to the boil. Cover again, reduce to a low heat and simmer for 20 minutes, or until all the vegetables are soft.

Remove the pot from the heat. Add in the roast parsnips and most of the toasted almonds (reserve a few) and, using a stick blender, blend until smooth. If the soup seems a little thick, add enough water to achieve the desired consistency. Season with salt and pepper and return to a simmer. To serve, sprinkle a few of the remaining toasted almonds onto each bowl.

Cook's notes

Sweet potato, coconut & coriander soup
v gf wf yf cn

This soup truly is a one-pot wonder — it has no sticking lentils to worry about, no roasting, no blanching, and no drizzling. Its defining twist is the simple addition of a block of creamed coconut — a cheap and cheerful hint of the exotic in your vegetable soup.

Creamed coconut is basically coconut milk that has had all the water extracted from it, leaving a concentrated cream that is solid at room temperature. It is commonly used to enrich curries and broths in both Indian and Thai cuisine. Blocks of creamed coconut are very inexpensive and are available from Asian food stores, health food shops and many supermarkets. As with many rich and sumptuous ingredients, creamed coconut is fairly high in calories, most of which come from fat. However, coconut fat is now considered a good fat by many health practitioners, made up as it is of health promoting, immune boosting medium-chained saturated fats (similar to those in breast milk), which the body requires for building cell membranes, for absorbing calcium into the bones, for transporting fat-soluble vitamins (the anti-oxidant ones) into the bloodstream and for building good cholesterol, which enables the body to break down fats. Short- and medium-chain saturated fats, consumed in moderate amounts, are converted into quick energy by the body, not stored as fat. So although the calorific value of this soup is a little higher than a vegetable and lentil soup, for example, it is a nutritious source of some of the fats required by the body to function properly.

This soup is the first recipe from this book ever to have been tested by the public. Back in September 2007, when *Cornucopia at home* was in its embryonic stages, a very preliminary soup chapter was written as a sampler with which we hoped to attract a publishing deal. We laid it out and illustrated it and sent it to Font Literary Agency, which had expressed an interest in representing us. We couriered our tentative proposal to them on a Friday afternoon, along with the fledgling soup chapter. We expected to hear nothing until the following week, but, on Saturday evening, I received a text from Ita and Aine, the team at Font, saying that, not only had they read and enjoyed our proposal, not only did they really like the soup chapter, but they were tucking into a bowl of this very soup, which they had not been able to resist making. That text message sealed my enthusiasm for writing this book. I was delighted, not at the positive reaction to our work, but at the fact that real people in a real household had used our manuscript to make, eat and enjoy a delicious soup. That thrill has fuelled me through the highs and lows of long days spent writing, much as this soup will fuel you and your army through the ups and downs of an average afternoon.

Note: this recipe uses coriander. An alternative herb to use is basil, which compliments coconut equally well.

1 onion
1 carrot
2 sticks celery *(including leaves)*
½ leek
5 medium sweet potatoes
    (about 1kg)
1x200g block creamed coconut
50g *(medium bunch)* fresh
    coriander
Unrefined sunflower oil
Salt and pepper
2 litres water

Roughly chop the onion, carrot, celery and leek. Rinse the chopped leek under cold water to remove any soil and drain thoroughly. Coat the base of a large pot with sunflower oil and place over a medium heat. Add the chopped vegetables and stir briefly to coat them with oil. Cover the pot with a lid, turn down to a low heat and sweat for 15 minutes, stirring occasionally.

Meanwhile, peel the sweet potatoes and chop them into medium pieces. When the vegetables have sweated, add the sweet potatoes, as well as the block of coconut (break it up a bit) and the water. Turn up the heat and bring to the boil. Cover, reduce to a low heat and simmer for 30 minutes, or until the sweet potato is soft.

Remove the pot from the heat, add the fresh coriander (reserve a few sprigs for garnish) and use a stick blender to blend until smooth. If the soup seems a little thick, add a little water to reach the desired consistency. Season with salt and pepper and return to a simmer. To serve, garnish with a fine, healthy sprig of coriander in each bowl.

Spicy corn & kidney bean soup
v gf wf cs ♡

This is an unusual Mexican-style soup with a deep barbecue flavour. It is pleasantly chunky, each spoonful a unique combination of kidney bean, corn and green pepper in a smoky, slightly spicy, corn broth. The smoky tones are achieved by frying half of the sweetcorn with a little brown sugar in a dry pan until it starts to caramelise and turn brown. This corn will be blended into the main soup, while the unfried kernels will be stirred in whole. Use frozen corn rather than tinned corn if possible. Tinned corn is stored in water with sugar and salt and exposed to a high temperature to kill bacteria. It loses nutrients and goes a little limp during that process. Frozen corn, however, is flash-frozen at the point of harvesting, loses few nutrients and, once defrosted, has far more natural taste and texture.

As for the kidney beans, in a perfect world you would plan this soup the day before, reach into your well-stocked dry store for 100g of kidney beans, soak them overnight, rinse them the next morning and cook them for an hour and a half, ready for stirring into the soup just before lunchtime. However, in the real world, this is not always possible and the good news about tinned beans is that, unlike the sweetcorn mentioned above, they do not lose a significant amount of nutrients in the canning process. They are preserved in salted water, but most of this is washed away when you rinse them. So as a practical solution to time limitations, precooked tinned beans are a nutritious alternative to dried ones, although you might like to offset the carbon print of the tin can by using locally grown, organic vegetables in the soup!

Kidney beans (native to Peru) are ideal for using in soup, as they hold their shape well in cooking and their robust, chunky texture makes for a lovely bit of chewing. Their deep, burgundy colour stands out dramatically in this golden yellow corn broth. As with all legumes, kidney beans are high in cholesterol-lowering soluble fibre, as well protein, iron and folic acid and their slow-release energy helps prevent blood sugars rising too rapidly after a meal. Combine this soup with a grain to provide the body with a whole protein; for example, serve it with thin slices of brown bread or some fresh, crusty wholegrain baguette. Or, to remain true to the Central American origins of this recipe, why not try making a version of Native American cornbread (see the recipe overleaf for details). It makes a delicious, crumbly round, which is cut into warm wedges, a perfect companion for this healthy, spicy soup.

400g frozen sweetcorn
  (not tinned)
1 tbsp unrefined brown sugar
1 onion
1 carrot
2 sticks celery *(including leaves)*
½ leek
4 cloves of garlic
1 tsp ground cumin
1 tsp ground coriander
½ tsp chilli
½ tsp ground cinnamon
2 green peppers
1x400g tin of kidney beans
  (standard tin) or 100g dried
  kidney beans soaked
  overnight and cooked as per
  page 38
25g *(small bunch)* fresh coriander
Unrefined sunflower oil
Salt and pepper
A dollop of crème fraîche for
  garnish *(optional)*
2 litres of water

First, roughly chop the onion, carrot, celery, leek and garlic. Rinse the chopped leek under cold water to remove any soil. Coat the base of a large pot with sunflower oil and place over a medium heat. Add the chopped vegetables and stir briefly to coat them with oil. Cover with a lid, turn down to a low heat and sweat for 15 minutes, stirring occasionally. Next add the four dried spices and, stirring constantly, cook for a further 3 minutes. When the spices have cooked, add the water to the soup pot and bring to the boil. Cover again and simmer for 20 minutes or until all the vegetables are soft.

While the soup is cooking, deseed the green peppers and dice them into small, neat squares. Set aside. In a dry pan, fry half of the sweetcorn (direct from frozen) with the brown sugar, stirring regularly, until it turns a light brown barbecued kind of colour. Set aside.

Remove the soup pot from the heat and add in the fried corn (not the unfried corn). Blend until smooth using a stick blender and season with salt and pepper. If the soup seems a little thick, add a little water to achieve the desired consistency. Now, return to the heat and add the diced green peppers. Cook for about 10 minutes, until the peppers have softened. Finally, drain and rinse the kidney beans and stir them in, as well as the remaining (unfried) sweetcorn. Heat thoroughly. Just before serving, chop the fresh coriander and stir it into the soup.

As an option, you can place a small dollop of crème fraîche in the centre of each bowl, a cool contrast to the steaming, spicy soup.

Cook's notes

Hot-baked skillet cornbread

This was unlike any bread I had ever tasted. It is short and crumbly and served in warm, wholesome wedges with chilli or soup or topped with spicy tomato and melted cheese. It's a fabulous and filling treat for enjoying with the spicy corn and kidney bean soup.

Extra-virgin olive oil
425g cornmeal *(polenta)*
100g unbleached plain
    white flour
2 tsp salt
2 tsp baking powder
1 scant tsp baking soda
250ml buttermilk*
225ml regular milk*
2 free-range eggs
3 tbsp (45ml) melted butter

* Alternatively, use 475ml
buttermilk & no regular milk

9in or 10in (22cm or 25cm) skillet pan (cast-iron frying pan) or round baking tray

Preheat your oven to 200°C. Put 1 tablespoon of olive oil into the skillet pan (baking tray) and place it in the oven to heat.

Next, place the cornmeal (polenta) and salt into a mixing bowl. Sift in the flour, baking powder and baking soda and mix thoroughly. In a separate bowl, whisk together the milks and the eggs and then add the melted butter. Make a well in the centre of the dry ingredients and pour in the wet ingredients. Fold them together to make a sloppy batter.

Carefully remove the hot skillet/baking tray from the oven. Gently swirl around the hot oil (or use a pastry brush) so that it coats the sides. Pour in the batter and smooth it over so it is evenly spread. Bake it in the centre of the oven for 30-40 minutes, until set in the centre and golden brown. A skewer or toothpick inserted into the centre should come out clean.

Cool in the skillet/tray and then slice into generous wedges. Serve while still a little warm with spicy soups or stews. Cornbread should be eaten on the day of baking. It can be rejuvenated by giving it 5 minutes in a warm oven the next day, or toasted with cheese on top.

Moorish spiced carrot & lentil soup with gremolata
v gf wf ♡

The Moors were originally a people of mixed Arab and Berber descent who inhabited Spain, Portugal and Northern Africa in the Middles Ages. The term now generally refers to a predominantly Muslim ethnic group that is spread across Morocco, Western Sahara, Algeria and Niger. Calling this soup Moorish is really an allusion to the herb and spice combination typical of the hot lands of Northern Africa: fresh mint coupled with a spice medley of chilli, cumin, coriander, turmeric, cinnamon and cardamom.

This recipe, whilst ethnically Moorish, is also exceedingly moreish. Onto each bowl of warm, richly spiced carrot soup is placed a generous portion of gremolata – a light and zingy leafy garnish – bringing two culinary cultures face-to-face: the Moorish combination of spices and mint in the soup brought to life by the punchy gremolata, an expression of the Italian partiality to garlic, lemon zest and fresh herbs. This makes for a truly refreshing combination. A word of warning: don't make the gremolata too long in advance, as it is essential that it be really fresh for optimum flavour and crunchiness. The soup, however, keeps particularly well overnight, as the spices release even more flavour over the course of time.

This is a great dinner party soup. The bright colours and contrasting textures are so striking your guests are sure to be impressed. The soup, although spiced, is not too spicy; it is more warm and cosy – so children, or adults sensitive to spices are unlikely to find it contrary to their taste. As it is quite a filling recipe, serve small portions if there is a main meal to follow. Or serve big bowls with crusty bread and follow it up with a selection of light and leafy salads instead.

Roughly chop the onion, carrots, celery, leek and red chilli. If you are using organic carrots, there is no need to peel them, just wash under cold water. Run the chopped leek under cold water and drain thoroughly. Measure the five dry spices into a bowl, so they are ready when you need them.

Coat the base of a large pot with sunflower oil and place over a medium heat. Add the carrots, onion, celery, leek and chilli. Stir briefly to coat them with oil, cover with a lid, turn down to a low heat and sweat for 15 minutes, stirring occasionally. Next add the mix of dried spices and, stirring constantly, cook for a further 3 minutes.

For the soup
1 onion
5 large carrots
2 sticks celery *(including leaves)*
½ leek
1 red chilli
1 tbsp cumin seeds
1 tbsp coriander seeds
1 tsp turmeric
½ tsp ground cinnamon
4 cardamom pods
150g red lentils
25g *(small bunch)* fresh mint
Unrefined sunflower oil
Salt and pepper
2 litres of water

For the gremolata
4 cloves of garlic
Zest of one lemon
50g *(medium bunch)* fresh
    flat-leaf parsley

Now add the water and lentils, stirring carefully to ensure the lentils don't stick to the base of the pot. Turn up the heat and bring to the boil. Cover, reduce to a low heat and simmer for 20 minutes, or until the vegetables are soft and the lentils have turned yellow.

While the soup is cooking, make the gremolata. Chop the parsley and garlic extremely finely and stir in the lemon zest. Alternatively, grind the ingredients together with a pestle and mortar, being careful not to overdo it and turn it into a paste — it should retain a light, leafy consistency.

When cooked, remove the soup from the heat. Add the fresh mint and use a stick blender to blend until smooth. If it seems a little thick, add enough water to achieve the desired consistency. Season with salt and pepper and return to a simmer. To serve, place a generous spoonful of gremolata onto each bowl of soup. Leave any extra gremolata in the centre of the table for guests to help themselves.

Minted fennel, courgette & green pea soup
v gf wf yf ♡

In an ideal world this soup is consumed al fresco in mid-June. The sun is beating down on a garden filled with scented sweet-pea blossoms swaying gently in a mere hint of a breeze. At the bottom of the garden, there is a little vegetable and herb patch which has, just an hour earlier, surrendered a small crop of mouth-wateringly fresh garden peas (perhaps shelled while listening to Vivaldi's Concerto No 2 in G minor) and a healthy handful of mint, both of which arrive onto the parasol-shaded table in the guise of this light, yet filling, summery soup. If you live in Ireland, or anywhere of equally unreliable clime, it tastes good indoors too. And if your green fingers have not yet found expression in the form of a flourishing vegetable patch, then frozen garden peas and supermarket or farmers' market mint both rise to the occasion very successfully.

There are three stages to this soup. First, make a blended vegetable and lentil broth. Next add the chunks of fennel and courgette to cook in that broth. Finally add the mint and peas just before serving. Encourage diners to add a twist of lemon to their soup from the wedge on the side of their bowl for an extra-refreshing bit of zing. This is one of those soups that should definitely be consumed immediately upon completion rather than made in advance — reheating will make the nice chunky vegetables sag a little and the mint lose lustre.

To complete the summery lunch spread, make a big plate of crudités and a bowl of hummus (see page 193) and serve it all with a basket of fresh bread. All you need then is a nice pot of Earl Grey tea and some strawberries and cream. For a supremely special strawberry treat called Eton Mess, chop some strawberries and sprinkle with a little caster sugar (or honey). Whip up some cream and, if you have a real vanilla pod at your disposal, cut it open and scrape in the seeds. Add the strawberries (reserving a few for garnish), along with some crushed-up meringue. Fold it all together gently and serve in small bowls topped with some extra strawberries and (if you have some left over from the soup) a sprig of mint. Then loll about chatting and possibly sipping chilled Chardonnay for the rest of the afternoon. In an ideal world …

Roughly chop the onion, carrot, celery and leek. Run the chopped leek under cold water to remove any soil and drain thoroughly. Coat the base of a large pot with sunflower oil and place over a medium heat. Add the chopped vegetables and stir briefly to coat them with oil. Cover with a lid, turn down to a low heat and sweat for 15 minutes, stirring occasionally.

1 onion
1 carrot
2 sticks celery *(including leaves)*
½ leek
2 large *(3 small)* fennel bulbs
2 medium *(3 small)* courgettes
200g frozen peas *(or fresh
    garden peas)*
1 lemon — *cut into wedges*
50g *(medium bunch)* fresh mint
75g red lentils
Unrefined sunflower oil
Salt and pepper
2 litres water

Cook's notes

Next, add the water and lentils, stirring carefully to ensure the lentils don't stick to the base of the pot. Turn up the heat and bring to the boil. Cover again, reduce to a low heat and simmer for 20 minutes, or until the vegetables are soft and the lentils have turned yellow. While the soup is simmering, chop the fennel and courgette into spoonable-size pieces and, keeping them separate, set aside.

When the vegetable and lentils are soft, remove the pot from the heat and, using a stick blender, blend until smooth. Season with salt and pepper. Remove one ladle of soup and set it aside in a small container to cool slightly. This will be used as a base for blending the herbs. Return the soup pot to a medium heat and add the chopped fennel. Five minutes later, add the chopped courgettes and simmer for a further 5 minutes until both vegetables are soft.

Meanwhile, add the fresh mint to the reserved ladle of soup (keep a few sprigs for garnish) and, using the stick blender, blend until smooth. Blending the mint separately means it can be combined as late as possible with the hot soup for optimum freshness, colour and intensity of flavour.

Just before serving, stir the minty mix and the green peas into the soup, check the seasoning and bring back to a gentle simmer. Chop the lemon into wedges. Garnish each bowl of soup with a sprig of mint and a wedge of lemon for guests to drizzle over their soup if they'd like some extra zing.

Eddie's kale & barley broth

v wf yf ♡

Full credit for the creation of this soup goes to our dear chef Eddie Bates (1955-2004). Eddie was a shining star of the make-it-up-as-you-go school of cooking – and his love of seasonal ingredients and talent for subtle seasoning brought about many tasty and surprising sensations over the years. When we came to compile a list of soups for this book, memories of eating Eddie's infamous autumn broth abounded. But no one had ever paid close attention to precisely how he made it. Weeks of trials ensued, during which kale obligingly remained in season. Eddie, if you've watched our efforts in amusement, we hope that the resultant recipe comes close to the magic you worked with these ingredients. Thanks for the inspiration!

This soup requires more time and attention than many of the other recipes in this chapter. It is an unblended soup – little chunks of vegetables, delicate strips of curly kale and chewy pearls of barley submerged in a delicious, herby broth. Unlike most other soups described in this chapter, it is absolutely essential to make a vegetable stock in advance to enrich this broth. As the barley takes a good hour to soften, it too should be put on to cook well before the soup itself starts coming together. Although it is a little more labour intensive than a blended vegetable soup, this broth is well worth all the effort. It is delightfully light and delicate, flavourful and textured – a perfect starter or, with some hunks of brown bread, a perfect lunch.

Although kale is preferable, it is only in season in Ireland around late autumn. Should it be unavailable, savoy cabbage, which is on sale all year round, is a good substitute. We selected chervil to partner flat-leaf parsley in our broth but noticed that, although readily available wholesale, fresh chervil is something of a rarity in the shops. If you can't find it, replace with extra parsley.

While the vegetables for the stock can be chopped as erratically as you like, it is worth investing some effort into carefully dicing the vegetables for the actual soup, so that each spoonful will contain a dainty selection of all the finely chopped ingredients rather than one ungainly chunk of carrot.

Each element of this soup has been described separately below, for purposes of clarity. However, it may also make the whole process seem dauntingly complicated and time-consuming. Perhaps a two-sentence summary will make the recipe a little more accessible: While the barley and stock are both simmering, blanch the kale and sweat the vegetables for the broth. Then add the stock water to the broth vegetables, blend the herbs, bring everything together in one pot, simmer and tuck in. Should you be making this lovely broth as an autumn treat, and therefore have curly kale at your disposal, why not use the remainder of the head to make yummy mashed potato colcannon (see page 115 for details).

For the barley
100g barley (*dry weight*)
2 bay leaves

For the stock
1 onion
2 carrots
2 sticks celery (*including leaves*)
1 leek
5 bay leaves
10 whole black peppercorns
A few sprigs of thyme
Unrefined sunflower oil
2½ litres of water

For the soup
1 onion
2 carrots
1 stick of celery
1 leek
2 cloves garlic
200g kale (*if unavailable, savoy
cabbage or regular cabbage*)
50g (*medium bunch*) fresh
flat-leaf parsley
25g (*small bunch*) fresh chervil
(*if unavailable, use extra
parsley*)
Extra-virgin olive oil
Salt and pepper
2 litres of vegetable stock
(*see above*)

Start by cooking the barley

Rinse the dry barley in a sieve under cold water. Place it in a medium pot, cover with plenty of cold, salted water, pop in two bay leaves and bring to the boil. Cover and simmer for one hour (until soft with a little bite), then rinse under cold water, drain thoroughly and set aside. Discard the bay leaves.

Meanwhile, make the stock

Roughly chop the onion, carrots, celery and leek. Rinse the chopped leek under cold water to remove any soil. Coat the base of a large pot with sunflower oil and place over a medium heat. Add the chopped vegetables and stir to coat them with oil. Cover with a lid, turn down to a low heat and sweat for 15 minutes, stirring occasionally. Now add the bay leaves, peppercorns and thyme and water. Bring to the boil and simmer for 1 hour.

Remove from the heat and strain the stock using a sieve or colander. Use the back of a ladle to press through as much liquid as possible. Reserve the stock water and discard the vegetables and herbs. You should retrieve about 2 litres of stock.

Blanch the kale

Destalk the kale leaves and chop them finely into thin 3cm-long strips. Bring a pot of salted water to the boil and blanch the kale for 3-5 minutes, until beginning to soften but still a little *al dente*. Rinse immediately in cold water, drain and set aside.

Next, make the soup

As the soup vegetables will not be blended, they should be chopped neatly and very small. Dice the onion and carrot and celery into very small pieces. Slice the leek lengthways into quarters and widthways into medium squares. Rinse the chopped leek under cold water to remove any soil. Slice the garlic finely.

Coat the base of a large pot with extra-virgin olive oil and place over a medium heat. Add the neatly chopped vegetables and stir to coat them with oil. Cover with a lid, turn down to a low heat and sweat for 10 minutes, stirring occasionally. Next, add the stock and bring to the boil. Still covered, simmer for 10-15 minutes, or until the vegetables are soft. Check them regularly as, if they have been chopped nice and small, they will cook quickly.

Remove one ladleful of soup and, using a stick blender, blend it with the fresh parsley and chervil and set aside.

And finally ...
All the elements for the kale broth are now ready. They should be brought together into a steaming hot autumnal treat just before serving, so, before advancing to the final stage, make sure the table is laid and all interested parties have been summoned.

Bring the soup back to a simmer. Add the cooked kale and barley. Stir in the ladleful of herbed broth and season with salt and pepper.

When serving, plunge the ladle to the base of the pot to make sure everyone gets a full medley of barley, chopped vegetables and kale.

Colcannon *gf wf ef*

Colcannon is traditionally eaten in Ireland at Hallowe'en, when curly kale is in season. (It can be made with savoy cabbage or white cabbage when kale is out of season.) On 31 October, there was a custom of hiding coins and rings in the colcannon, much like the British tradition of hiding a ring in the barmbrack. Finding a ring meant marriage within the year. Finding a coin meant wealth would come your way. A thimble sealed your fate as a spinster and a button condemned you to a life of bachelorhood. Although health and safety concerns have probably all but eliminated such frivolities, colcannon remains a popular comfort food, especially on the cusp of winter.

6 floury potatoes
    (such as roosters)
    — about 1.5kg
500g curly kale
1 bunch spring onions
    (or a good handful
    of chives)
150-200ml milk
50g butter
Salt and pepper

Peel and quarter the potatoes and place them in a pot with plenty of lightly salted water. Bring to the boil and simmer until soft. Drain the potatoes and return them to the empty pot. Place over a low heat for a couple of minutes to evaporate off any excess water and then mash and set aside, covered to stay hot.

Meanwhile, remove the thick stalks from the kale leaves, slice them into thin strips and plunge into a pot of salted water. Boil vigorously until soft. Depending on the thickness of the leaves, this may take between 5 and 10 minutes. Drain and set aside. Chop the spring onions finely and place them in a small pot with the milk. Simmer gently for 5 minutes and then add the milk and scallions and a good knob of butter to the pot of potatoes. Whisk together until smooth and then fold in the kale. Season with salt and plenty of black pepper and then serve.

If you have any leftover colcannon, the following day form it into burger-shaped patties. Place a knob of butter and a splash of oil in a pan over a medium heat. When the pan is hot, add the patties and fry them on both sides until browned and a little crispy. Delish!

Salads

Introduction to salads

Since its inception, Cornucopia has prided itself on serving a broad, adventurous and constantly evolving range of salads. Though some old reliables have remained on the menu for many years, so too has there been the constant addition of new and unique recipes as we strive to resemble as little as possible the standard salad bar formula that has established itself in every corner of the Western world since its emergence in the 1960s. 'A medium salad plate please' is probably the most common customer request in Cornucopia — it must be one of the most popular lunches this side of the River Liffey and, if the choice of four salads is made with balance, one of the healthiest and most satisfying. We have taken ideas, recipes and ingredients from all around the world, sourced the freshest and most delicious products and stayed abreast of all the latest healthy-eating trends. Every day the salad chef chops, rinses, blanches, dresses, tosses, seasons and boxes up about 200 litres of salad — vegetables and fruit, grains and beans, salads of every colour and texture imaginable, spicy, zingy, herby, light, crunchy, filling, flavourful, nutty, seedy — a veritable cornucopia of chilled delights, which elicits no shortage of 'oohs' and 'aahs' from animated customers as they peer into the salad display fridge to choose from the day's offerings.

That very display fridge caused us an unexpected hiccup back in 2005 when we ordered a new one to replace the old, rather senior one that had housed our daily selection of ten salads for more years than we cared to remember. After a spot of late-night lugging and tugging and plugging, the spanking new specimen stood proudly in place and the now defunct golden oldie was loaded into a van and driven off to enjoy some well-deserved years of retirement. All appeared well until disaster struck the following day. Over the course of the morning, as the chef turned out one salad after another, it became apparent that the new fridge was ever so slightly smaller than the old one. As a result, our long-serving stainless steel salad bowls, ten of which had fitted neatly and snugly into the old fridge, could now only be squashed in eight at a time and at ungainly angles at that. A few unsettling days of mild pandemonium followed as we wrestled with this new pared-down salad situation, when a matter of two or three millimetres of fridge had changed the face of Cornucopia salads from a reliable assortment of ten to a comparatively meagre eight. The customers knew something was amiss, though not many could put their finger on what exactly. As we manoeuvred the bowls awkwardly in an out of the new fridge every time they needed to be refilled, we began to wish to have our bockety old fridge back.

Finally someone applied some lateral thinking and made a call to our catering supplier. Quicker than you could say 'SOS salad fridge emergency', he was in with his measuring tape jotting down dimensions and the very next morning we had a set of ten shiny new stainless steel bowls lined up smartly in the salad fridge, as if they had been tailor-made to fit. The old set of bowls was redeployed into the areas of homemade baked beans and proving yeast breads. A communal sigh of relief was breathed as the ten-salads-a-day system was restored, a system around which our plastic containers, cold storage units, menu boards, vegetable delivery and chef's shifts had evolved over the years – isn't it amazing how the size and shape of a fridge can dictate the natural balance of a whole living, breathing restaurant.

Of the aforementioned ten salads available each day, generally there are two potato salads, two bean salads (one sprouted, one cooked), two grain salads (pasta, bulghar, noodle, rice) and four raw vegetable salads. Sound nutritional advice would be to combine two parts raw with one part bean and one part potato or grain. Or, if you lead an active life that requires plenty of high-energy foods, especially at lunchtime, choose one part raw, one part bean and one part each grain and potato.

The importance of integrating plenty of raw fruit and vegetables into one's daily life has been well publicised in recent years, having been almost forgotten by a progress- and profit-hungry food industry. The advent and proliferation of highly processed convenience foods in the 1960s had, towards the end of the last century, all but eliminated raw food from many Western diets, which were increasingly calorie-rich, yet lacking in basic nutrition, due to the loss of vitamins, minerals and enzymes in processing. Convenience meals do not generally contain raw food, as it cannot be preserved, transported or stored with the same success as cooked, packaged or frozen foods. As the selection of bland snack foods and microwave-able instant dinners increased, so too did the once excitingly dappled range of fruit and vegetables on offer become industrialised – cultivated into standard sizes, colours and shapes. You'd be hard-pressed to believe that there are over 140 identified varieties of native Irish apple, considering the standard supermarket offering of Granny Smith, Golden Delicious and Royal Gala. The mainstream food economy often directs the consumer away from fresh and raw fruit and vegetables, towards the aisles full of tins and packets and frozen this and preserved that.

Fortunately, despite the exponential rise of the international supermarket chain as the main supplier of food and drink to the Western world, fresh, wholesome and raw food continues to be valued by groups as diverse as dieticians, the slow food movement, organic farmers, radical restaurateurs and fans of real food, warts and all. Many people testify to the life-enhancing benefits of eating a good proportion of food in its natural state (uncooked, unprocessed and organic) – from enhanced immune system to smoother digestion, from increased energy levels to weight loss, from improved moods and alertness to an overall sense of well-being. Raw plants represent food in the form that nature provides it, cells still vibrating with life-force, packed with vitamins, minerals, enzymes, protein, fibre and energy. In a busy life, it is always tempting to reach for cooked food to provide instant gratification, rather than spend time preparing, chewing and digesting raw food. However, omitting raw food means missing out on a natural, health-giving and purifying way to counterbalance some of the stresses and strains that modern life places on our mental and physical selves. Moreover, overlooking raw food also means missing out on a lot of very delicious, crunchy, flavourful food, as the six raw food recipes in this chapter will testify. Each of the salad recipes that follow makes one big bowl of salad – suitable for four to eight servings, depending on what else is on offer. Vegetables for salads are, ideally, locally grown and, whenever possible, organic. Delicate leaves such as lettuce, baby spinach, watercress, red chard and chopped herbs should be folded in gently just before serving to keep them from wilting and bruising.

Salads: some basic information

Dressings

The fifteen salads presented in this chapter employ fifteen different dressings, from light herb oils to nutty pestos, all of which can be whipped up in a matter of seconds with a stick blender. The dressing ingredients are listed separately from the salad ingredients in the text, as, if you particularly like a certain dressing, it is entirely possible to apply it to your own unique medley of vegetables, pulses or grains. Orla, our photographer, rescued all remnants of herb oils from our many afternoon salad-photographing sessions to drizzle onto her dinner that night. Her mother was rewarded with a jar of the following vinaigrette in part payment for lending us her home for the same photography sessions.

Cornucopia wholegrain mustard vinaigrette   *v   gf   wf*

100ml extra-virgin olive oil
100ml unrefined sunflower oil
75ml vegetarian cider vinegar
25ml apple concentrate
   (*available from health
   food shops*)
1 tbsp wholegrain mustard
Pinch of salt and pepper

For regular customers, this is the vinaigrette that is to be found in a self-service drizzler bottle right next to the cash desk. This dressing keeps very well, so you can treble or quadruple the quantities and store in a dressing bottle or an empty mineral bottle with two holes punched in the cap. Drizzle over mixed leaves or chopped raw vegetables for instant green salad. Whizz all the ingredients together with a stick blender.

Oils for salads

Three oils are necessary to negotiate this salad chapter: high-grade extra-virgin olive oil, unrefined sunflower oil and organic toasted sesame oil, which is available from health food shops. Extra-virgin olive oil comes from the first pressing of the olives as soon as they are harvested from the olive groves. It is extracted using a cold press, which avoids the loss of taste, freshness and nutrition that the subsequent heat-based processing (for lower-grade oils) causes. It should be stored in a cool, dark environment to maintain its quality, but not refrigerated, as it will solidify. The aromatic flavour of olive oil is integral to the European-style salads included herein.

Toasted sesame oil is to oriental salad dressings what olive oil is to Mediterranean salad dressings – both are highly flavoured good oils, which, consumed in moderate quantities, lower cholesterol, benefit skin, hair and joints and contain anti-oxidants, which help fight cardiovascular disease. Sesame oil is often combined with ginger, rice vinegar, garlic and shoyu (or tamari, the gluten-free version) to dress oriental-style salads or to marinate ingredients before cooking.

The health-giving qualities of both olive oil and sesame oil make them preferred choices in salads, as long as the flavour that they impart enhances the recipe. This is not always the case, so sometimes we use unrefined sunflower oil to allow the flavour of other components of a salad to come through; for example, in the Gujarati carrot salad the flavour of the toasted mustard seeds is central and would be overpowered by olive oil, so the recipe uses comparatively flavourless sunflower oil instead.

Vinegar & lemon juice

In Cornucopia, we regularly favour lemon juice (or lime juice) over vinegar as the acid ingredient in our salad dressings. This is partly because of the natural freshness of a squeeze of lemon compared to bottled vinegar, but also to accommodate people who have been diagnosed with yeast allergy and need to avoid fermented products, amongst other things, to maintain a healthy digestive system.

However, some recipes do require the specific flavour of a particular vinegar; in this chapter we use rice vinegar in some of the Asian-style salads and balsamic vinegar in the Italian tomato and rocket salad. As with choosing oils for salads, it is really worth investing in high-quality vinegars. In the case of balsamic vinegar, the older the vinegar, the more deep and intense the flavour.

Bear in mind that both red and white vinegar, as well as cider vinegar, are made from alcohols that are commonly filtered using non-vegetarian methods, such as isinglass or gelatine. Look for vinegars specifically marked as vegetarian, which can be found, in particular, in health food shops.

Mayonnaise *gf wf df*

Mayonnaise is made by mixing egg yolk and lemon or vinegar, then very slowly adding oil while whisking vigorously. The oil and the lemon form a thick, smooth emulsion, while the lecithin in the yolks acts as a stabiliser, preventing them from separating. It is usually flavoured with a little mustard, salt and pepper.

Homemade mayonnaise is infinitely superior to even the best of shop-bought ones, as it uses fresh, free-range egg yolks instead of powdered (and often not free-range) pasteurised eggs. It is more vibrant in colour and flavour and is free from the preservatives and additives required in commercial mayonnaise. Below is a recipe for simple mayonnaise that will keep for four to five days in the fridge. Make sure to use the freshest of free-range eggs, both for the purposes of food safety and also because lecithin, the agent in the yolks which binds the mayonnaise, is stronger in fresher eggs.

Note: because homemade mayonnaise is made with unpasteurised eggs, it is not recommended for pregnant women or the very young or very old. This is because raw eggs have a small risk of containing salmonella.

2 free-range egg yolks, very fresh
300ml unrefined sunflower oil
50ml extra-virgin olive oil
2 tbsp lemon juice *(or vegetarian white wine vinegar)*
1 or 2 tsp Dijon mustard
Pinch of salt
Generous twist of black pepper

Place everything except the oil in a mixer/blender and combine until smooth. Add the oil, literally drop by drop, combining thoroughly between each drop. When the mix has become smooth and thick, the oil can be added slightly more quickly, still beating thoroughly between each addition. Add extra salt and pepper if necessary.

Delicious as a dip for crudités (sticks of raw carrot, celery, red pepper, cherry tomatoes, broccoli, etc) or spread onto pretty much anything, from baked potatoes to steamed broccoli to sandwiches or used as a salad ingredient for the Cornucopia garlic potato salad with toasted hazelnuts (see page 128). Warning: once you've made your first batch of homemade mayonnaise, you may find it difficult to pick up a convenient jar of shop-bought stuff ever again.

Vegan mayonnaise   *v gf wf cn*

Although mayonnaise is a classic egg-based condiment, it is possible to make a very tasty vegan alternative. This recipe for a mayonnaise-like cashew nut cream comes from Veronica O'Reilly, a friend of Cornucopia and member of the Servants of Love community in Wicklow. She develops vegan living food products as part of her contribution to promoting healthful and wholesome food in Ireland.

175g cashew nuts *(or blanched, peeled almonds)*
125ml extra-virgin olive oil
125ml water
1 level tsp Dijon mustard
2-3 tbsp lemon juice

Soak the cashew nuts (or almonds) in water overnight. The following day, drain and rinse them. Then place all the listed ingredients into a blender and blend until a very smooth texture is achieved. Season to taste with salt and pepper. Refrigerate for at least two hours before using, during which time the mayonnaise will thicken.

This mayonnaise will keep for 3 days in the fridge. Use it just like regular mayonnaise: as a dip, as a spread or as a dressing.

Garlic mayonnaise potato salad with toasted hazelnuts
gf wf df cn (vegan if desired, see below)

This salad is a bit of a phenomenon. Those who like it, rarely just like it. They love it. Dream about it. Order it every day, without fail, as one of the two salad choices with their main course. They tell their friends about it. Who in turn come to try it … When Cornucopia's first chef (and co-owner) Neil McCafferty created the Cornucopia garlic potato salad back in 1986, he could not have anticipated that his simple, tasty combination of baby potatoes, toasted hazelnuts, mayonnaise and garlic would be on the menu every single day for the next twenty-two years (so far) and would, to this day, bring a smile to the face of fans and first-timers alike.

The garlic potato salad is a welcome option for people who cannot eat dairy products, but would like to eat something quite creamy. Potato salads in general are great for filling you up and providing you with immediate energy. Potatoes are an excellent source of vitamin C and a good source of iron and potassium. The advantage of salad potatoes (baby potatoes) is that they are eaten skin and all, ensuring a rich supply of dietary fibre. One word of warning, however. Mayonnaise, though delicious and creamy, is also extremely high in fat, so this salad should be served in moderation and combined with an equal amount of raw salad: perhaps some light, crispy lettuce leaves, barely drizzled with zingy vinaigrette to counterbalance the richness of the mayonnaise and the sweetness of the hazelnuts.

Note: to make this salad vegan, use homemade cashew nut (or almond) mayonnaise, as described on the previous page.

Preheat the oven to 180°C. Spread the hazelnuts on a baking tray and roast them for 8 minutes. Set them aside to cool and then rub them between your hands to remove the loose skins.

Chop the baby potatoes into bite-size pieces – either halves, quarters or slices, depending on how big they are. Place them in a large pot, cover with lightly salted cold water, bring to the boil, cover and simmer for about 15 minutes or until tender. Drain and set aside.

Meanwhile, make the dressing by blending the mayonnaise, lemon juice and garlic with a stick

150g hazelnuts
1kg baby potatoes
50g *(medium bunch)* parsley

Garlic mayonnaise dressing
100g good-quality mayonnaise*
    *(see page 126 for homemade
    mayonnaise)*
Juice of ½ lemon
2-3 cloves of garlic — *peeled &
    chopped roughly*
Salt and pepper

** If using commercial
mayonnaise, ensure it is made
with free-range eggs. Some
commercial mayonnaises may
contain milk powder, so if you
require this salad to be dairy-
free, be sure to choose a suitable
mayonnaise.*

blender or in a food processor. Season with salt and pepper.

When the potatoes and hazelnuts are cool, place them in a large bowl. Chop the parsley and add it to the bowl, reserving a little for garnish. Fold in the dressing evenly, taking care not to break up the potatoes. Serve sprinkled with parsley with a crisp green salad.

Sicilian-style potato with olives and capers
v gf wf

'Sicilian-style', in the case of this potato salad, means a generous proportion of olives and capers, as well as an intensely herby dressing. There are so many tastes to enjoy in this *insalate siciliane di patata*: the sweet and juicy cherry tomatoes, the salty tartness of the capers, the smoky depth of the olives, the crunchy bite of the red onions and the earthy marriage of extra-virgin olive oil and oregano. Sicilian potato can also be served as a warm salad. Prepare as below, but, instead of cooking the potatoes first and setting them aside to cool, cook them at the last minute. Get everything else ready and, when the potatoes are tender, drain them, toss the salad and serve straight away.

For a balanced lunch, this salad could be served with a simple omelette, with just some seasoning and fresh herbs and a little grated cheese if you like. Whisk two free-range eggs per person, add a pinch of salt and pepper and some finely chopped flat-leaf parsley or chives. Heat a little butter or olive oil in the base of a non-stick pan. When hot, pour in the egg mix. As the omelette cooks, tilt the pan and use a spatula to push the cooked egg towards the centre so that any runny egg flows towards the edges to cook. When almost all of the egg has set, add the grated cheese if using, and then fold one half of the omelette onto the other half. Turn the heat off and allow the omelette to sit for a minute so the ambient heat will complete the cooking. Transfer to a plate, add Sicilian potato and enjoy.

1 kg baby potatoes
400g vine cherry tomatoes
1 red onion
150g good-quality black olives
100g capers

Oregano oil dressing
200ml extra-virgin olive oil
1-2 cloves of garlic
50g *(medium bunch)* fresh
    oregano
Salt and pepper

Chop the baby potatoes into bite-size pieces, either halves or quarters. Place them in a large pot, cover with lightly salted cold water, bring to the boil, cover and simmer for about 15 minutes or until tender. Drain and set aside. Chop the cherry tomatoes in half and the red onion into thin moon-shaped slices. Drain the olives and capers. Meanwhile, make the dressing by blending the oil, garlic (peeled) and oregano (stalks removed) with a stick blender or food processor. Season with salt and pepper, using only a very small pinch of salt, as the capers and olives are quite salty already. When the potatoes are cool, combine all the ingredients in a large bowl, folding gently so as not to break up the potatoes. Check the seasoning and serve. If you have used unpitted olives, warn everyone eating the salad to watch their teeth.

Potato, red chard & sugarsnap peas in lemon & mint
v gf wf yf cn

This is a perfect salad for the early summer, when the two key ingredients, sugarsnap peas and red chard, are in season in Ireland. Of course, with the grand selection of fresh goods available in almost every corner of Ireland in supermarket chains, it could quite easily be made at any time of the year. But imported sugarsnaps and chard can be a little lacklustre compared to the locally grown, vivacious specimens available from June — youthful, sweet sugarsnaps and proud, crisp red chard; well worth waiting for.

The dressing, too, caters to a summer palate. When the weather is warm, lemon and mint are deliciously refreshing and invigorating. This particular dressing has an interesting twist — it is halfway between herb oil and pesto. Although most of the toasted flaked almonds in the ingredients remain whole and form part of the body of the salad, a small handful are blended into the dressing, thickening it slightly, so that its nutty texture can really coat the vegetables with minty, lemony flavours.

Red chard is a fantastic salad leaf, not only for its delicate peppery flavour, but also for the dramatic visual effect of its vibrant red stems and veins — it lightens and brightens wherever it goes. It should be folded into the dressed salad just before serving to prevent it from wilting. If red chard is unavailable, replace with baby spinach, rocket or mizuna.

150g flaked almonds
1kg baby potatoes
200g sugarsnap peas *(or mangetout if unavailable)*
100g red chard — *washed & drained*

Lemon & mint dressing
200ml extra-virgin olive oil
Juice of 2 lemons
25g *(small bunch)* fresh mint, plus a few sprigs to garnish
25g *(small bunch)* fresh basil
Salt and pepper

Preheat the oven to 180°C.

Chop the baby potatoes into bite-size pieces, either halves or quarters depending on how big they are. Place them in a large pot, cover with lightly salted cold water, bring to the boil, cover and simmer for about 15 minutes or until tender. Drain and set aside.

Meanwhile, spread the flaked almonds on a baking tray and roast them until golden, tossing once or twice. As they are very thin, they will toast quite quickly (about 5 minutes). Set aside to cool.

Bring a small pot of salted water to the boil and blanch the sugarsnap peas for 2 minutes. Drain and rinse in cold water immediately.

Meanwhile, make the dressing by blending together the olive oil, lemon juice and herbs with a stick blender or in a food processor. Add one handful (30g) of the flaked almonds that have been toasted for the salad and blend again. Season with salt and pepper.

In a large bowl, combine the potatoes, sugarsnap peas and remaining toasted almonds. Add the dressing and fold together, taking care not to break up the potatoes. Just before serving, gently mix in the red chard (don't add it earlier as it will go limp). Garnish with a sprig of mint.

Mediterranean chickpea in a sun-dried tomato dressing
gf wf ef

Mediterranean chickpea. The name of this salad really makes me smile. Firstly, because it reminds me of the many misspelt versions of the word Mediterranean that have graced our menu boards over the years, despite the active participation of qualified chefs, avid international travellers and first-class honours Trinity College scholars. It joins broccoli (broccolli? brocolli?), parsley (parsely? parsly?) and coriander (corriander?) as the most commonly rubbed out and rewritten words in Cornucopia. For a couple of months, Makhanwala curry was contender for the crown, but, fortunately for the board-writers, it only enjoyed a brief sojourn on the menu. The other reason Mediterranean chickpea amuses me is that, as a name for a salad, it really is rather vague. I mean, considering the vastness of the Mediterranean, touching three continents and bordered by eighteen countries, each of which has its own distinct cooking traditions and local ingredients, what on earth could the term 'Mediterranean chickpea' actually mean?

In 2008 Celtic Tiger Ireland, we're used to more sophisticated culinary terminology. But twenty years ago on Irish shores, there was still Irish food and foreign food. Within the foreign food category, two adjectives stood head and shoulders above the rest — 'Mediterranean', which generally meant 'something tomatoey with maybe a roast vegetable thrown in', and 'exotic' which inevitably involved pineapple. Common features of pizza menus, these two broad-sweeping adjectives paid scant respect to the subtleties and traditions of other culinary cultures, they were just two different ways of boasting the inclusion of imported ingredients. Nowadays, we are far more food-savvy. Cosmopolitan Ireland has developed the taste buds and language to appreciate the nuances and variety of cooking from all over the world. There are ethnic restaurants serving authentic food from every country imaginable, cooked by chefs from those very regions. Supermarkets have speciality sections stocking everything from Polish pickles to Japanese sea vegetables, from Provençal courgette flowers to fresh Neapolitan biscotti. Children can, not only name their favourite Indonesian dish, but eat it with chopsticks and have seen how to cook it on one of the many glamorous cookery programmes that fill the channels. Mediterranean chickpea seems innocently generic in the context of all our new-found foodie knowledge, but changing the name to the unwieldy 'chickpea salad with fusion influences from Greece, North African and Italy' would take up a lot of room on the menu board. So we stick with the original name, a hark-back to the not-so-distant days when this salad was a truly exotic offering in a much more monocultural Ireland.

This recipe suggests 2-3 teaspoons of toasted cumin seeds. Three will give a strong flavour with spicy warmth. If you are unsure as to your appreciation of cumin, when you blend the dressing start with one teaspoon and add more according to taste.

2 medium aubergines
3x400g tins of chickpeas
    (standard-size tins) or 300g
    dry chickpeas soaked
    overnight, and cooked as per
    page 38
250g vegetarian feta cheese
    (or haloumi)
200g baby spinach — *rinsed &*
    drained if not pre-washed
Extra-virgin olive oil
Salt and pepper

Sun-dried tomato
    & cumin dressing
2-3 tsp cumin seeds
150ml extra-virgin olive oil
Juice of 1½ lemons
1 red chilli — *chopped roughly*
75g sun-dried tomatoes

Preheat the oven to 200°C. Soak the sun-dried tomatoes in boiling water for 15 minutes to rehydrate them, then drain and set aside.

Chop the aubergines into medium cubes. In a bowl toss them in a little olive oil, salt and pepper. Transfer to a baking tray, two if necessary, and roast until tender, turning occasionally (about 20 minutes). While the oven is hot, toast the cumin seeds for the dressing for 3 or 4 minutes. You can spread them on a little piece of foil beside the aubergines. Set both aside to cool.

Make the dressing by blending the olive oil, chilli, lemon juice, sun-dried tomatoes and toasted cumin seeds with a stick blender or in a food processor. The dressing will be quite a thick tomato purée, not a pourable liquid.

Drain and rinse the chickpeas and place in a large bowl. Chop the feta into 1cm cubes. When the roast aubergines are cool, place them in the bowl with the chickpeas and feta. Spoon over the dressing and combine gently, trying not to break up the feta cubes. Just before serving, mix in the baby spinach, so that it stays nice and fresh.

Cook's notes

Borlotti bean, roast butternut squash & courgette in lemon & tarragon   *v gf wf yf cn*

Picture the colours that perform together in this salad. Magnificent pinky-maroon borlotti beans. Bright orange chunks of squash, tinged at the edges with oven-roast rustic brown. Forest-green courgette slices and golden flakes of almond. All illuminated by a glistening herb oil. This treasure trove of hypnotic hues is truly a sight to behold.

And it tastes great too. The tarragon lends a sweet, aniseedy undertone, which seeps into the flesh of the courgette, whilst the lemon and basil lighten the whole salad, cutting through the starchiness of the beans and squash. And in case it might have been lacking bite, there are crunchy flaked almonds in every mouthful.

A word about shopping for this salad: borlotti beans, popular in Italian cooking, are a relatively recent arrival to Irish shores and have not yet become as readily available as other, more established beans. They are stocked by most health food shops and some specialist food stores. They are about the same size as a kidney bean and are easily recognisable by their uniquely dappled exterior: maroon-speckled marbling on a light-pink background, rather like a beautiful bird's egg. If, however, you cannot lay your hands on borlotti beans, pinto beans are a perfectly satisfactory alternative. Similarly tarragon, though 'king of herbs' in France, where it has a revered position as the essential herb in Béarnaise sauce, has not yet fully infiltrated the Irish marketplace. If you have difficulty finding fresh tarragon, don't despair, the dried herb will work okay in this recipe (use 2 level teaspoons), as long as the basil is fresh. If you do succeed in buying fresh tarragon and have some left over after making this salad, it combines well with carrots, mushrooms or spinach. See opposite for suggestions.

Preheat the oven to 180°C.

Chop the butternut squash into medium chunks (about 1½cm) and the courgettes into 1cm-thick half moons. Keeping the two vegetables separate, toss them in a little olive oil, salt and pepper and transfer to baking trays.

Roast until tender, turning occasionally. The courgette will take about 20 minutes, the squash about 30 minutes. While the oven is hot, toast the flaked almonds until golden (about 5 minutes), tossing once. Set aside to cool.

1 large butternut squash
   (about 900g)
2 courgettes
150g flaked almonds
2x400g tins of borlotti beans
   (or pinto beans) or 200g dried
   beans soaked overnight &
   cooked as per page 38
Extra-virgin olive oil
Salt and pepper

Lemon & tarragon dressing
150ml extra-virgin olive oil
Juice of 1 lemon
25g *(small bunch)* tarragon
25g *(small bunch)* basil
Salt and pepper

Make the dressing by blending the oil, lemon juice, tarragon and basil with a stick blender or in a food processor. Season lightly with salt and pepper, bearing in mind that the roasted vegetables have already been seasoned.

Drain and rinse the borlotti beans and place them in a bowl with the roasted vegetables and most of the toasted almonds, all of which should be cool. Pour the dressing into the bowl and combine gently, taking care not to break up the chunky vegetables. Serve with a sprinkle of the remaining almonds.

Tarragon

If you buy a bag of tarragon for this salad and are wondering how else to use it, try one or two of the following:

Carrot, lentil & tarragon soup
Make as the carrot and basil soup on page 66, replacing basil with a handful of tarragon, stalks removed. Garnish with a swirl of pouring cream and a few whole tarragon leaves.

Mushroom, spinach & tarragon
  cream sauce for tagliatelle
Wilt 200g spinach and then remove from the pan. Fry 2 shallots (or 1 onion) and 2 cloves of garlic, both finely chopped, for 5 minutes. Add 200g mushrooms (wild if possible), cook until soft and then remove from the pan. Deglaze the pan with a splash of vegetarian white wine and cook for 1 minute. Stir in 300ml pouring cream and reduce for 3 minutes. Finally, add the spinach, shallots

Cook's notes

and mushroom, as well as some finely chopped tarragon to the cream. Season to taste. Spoon over some fresh tagliatelle. For a homemade pasta recipe, see page 244.

Pan-fried courgette & tarragon omelette
Slice the courgette into ½cm rounds and pan-fry on both sides in a minimal amount of extra-virgin olive oil. Allow 2 large, free-range eggs per person. Whisk the eggs with some salt and pepper. Heat a non-stick pan with a little oil or butter and, when hot, pour in the omelette mix. As the egg sets, use a spatula to push it towards the centre and tilt the pan so the still runny egg flows towards the edges to cook. When almost all the egg has set, cover one half of the omelette with courgettes and a sprinkling of finely chopped tarragon. Fold the other half over, turn off the ring and leave to cook in its own heat for a minute. Serve with a fresh tomato salad.

Butter bean, roast fennel, pepper & rocket in garlic & lemon   *v gf wf yf*

This bean salad has a lovely combination of sweet vegetables and spicy rocket. As the peppers roast in the oven they become shrivelled and jammy and their natural sweetness is intensified. Roasted, the anise-flavoured raw fennel mellows into mild, juicy wedges, beautifully golden brown, and tinged with caramel. The garlic pays a visit to the oven too and, when it re-emerges, its pungent sharpness is transformed into a deep, nutty, almost creamy flavour, central to the dressing.

To counterbalance the sweet peppers, caramelised fennel and roast garlic, there is a generous quantity of fresh, crispy rocket, which, as a member of the mustard family, is packed with peppery punch. Rocket has enjoyed its time in the spotlight over the past decade — it experienced a rapid rise from relative obscurity to culinary centre-stage in the 1990s, when its pungent tang was extolled by excited foodies. But as soon as every self-respecting restaurant and gourmet foodhall integrated rocket into its menu, it was branded trendy and over-used by some high-brow critics, who found its mass availability rather vulgar.

Nevertheless, flash-in-the-pan popularity and the inevitable price hike that ensued do not change the fact that rocket is a great ingredient, combining the fresh crispness of lettuce with the spicy tanginess of a herb. These are perfect qualities for use in a bean salad, as beans, not being the most aromatic or textured of ingredients, are greatly enhanced by a flavourful and crunchy side-kick such as rocket.

If you are cooking your own butter beans for this salad, be sure to drain them as soon as they are soft, and before they get in any way mushy, otherwise the salad risks becoming soggy and starchy. One hour should be plenty for butter beans, but check them regularly throughout cooking, as each batch varies slightly.

When used as a raw ingredient in salad, fennel should be chopped into thin, delicate slices. To do this, trim the stalks, chop the fennel in half through the root, discard the core, then, cut-side down, slice it thinly.

However, for roasting fennel, as it is soft and juicy, larger wedges are preferable. Chop the bulb in half and leave the core intact. Place flat side down and cut each half into 6-8 wedges, being sure to slice through the core each time, leaving some of it attached to each wedge to hold it together.

2 red peppers
2 yellow peppers
4 small/3 large bulbs of fennel
2x400g tins of butter beans
    (standard tins) or 200g dry
    beans soaked overnight &
    cooked as per page 38
200g rocket — *rinsed &*
    drained if not pre-washed
Extra-virgin olive oil
Salt and pepper

Roast garlic & lemon dressing
100ml extra-virgin olive oil
Juice of 2 lemons
2 bulbs of garlic
Salt and pepper

Preheat the oven to 180°C.

Chop the fennel into wedges and the peppers into medium strips. Keeping the peppers separate from the fennel, toss the vegetables in a little olive oil, salt and pepper and transfer to two baking trays. Chop the top off the two bulbs of garlic, toss them in olive oil and place them, open top up, in the corner of the baking tray with the fennel. Pour a little extra olive oil into the centre of each bulb. Roast all the vegetables until tender, turning occasionally. The peppers will take about 20 minutes and the fennel and garlic 30-40 minutes. Set aside to cool.

When the garlic is cool, hold it at the uncut end of the bulbs and squeeze the soft flesh out through the cut end. Using a stick blender, or in a food processor, blend together the olive oil, garlic and lemon juice. Season lightly with salt and pepper, bearing in mind that the roasted vegetables have already been seasoned.

Drain and rinse the butter beans and place them in a bowl with the roasted fennel and peppers. Pour over the dressing and combine gently. Just before serving, chop the rocket roughly and add it to the salad, so that it stays nice and crisp.

Bulghar wheat, roast butternut squash & baby spinach in mint & lemon   *v yf*

Of all wheat products commonly used in cooking, bulghar wheat is the nutritional champion, a far cry from energy-rich but low-nutrient white flour. Bulghar is derived from wholewheat grains, which have simply been steamed (par-cooked), dried and hulled, retaining much of their natural goodness.

Each grain on a head of wheat is actually a seed ready to go where the wind takes it, find a fertile patch of soil, take root and grow. Like all seeds, wheat berries, in their original state, are full of nourishment to feed the seed along its journey. In the case of 95% of wheat grains, modern agriculture intervenes long before the seed ever embarks on its wind-swept journey, instead whisking it off to the mill to turn it into flour, bulghar, couscous, semolina, bran and cracked wheat. Each of these wheat products involves varying degrees of processing, resulting in a greater or lesser loss of the rich nutrients contained within the grain. From a health-based, wholefood perspective, it's preferable to use wheat products that retain as much of the original kernel as possible, whilst still being palatable, digestible and delicious.

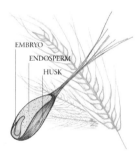

A grain of wheat, just like most grains, has three distinct parts. The outside layer is the *husk*, which, if removed, becomes what we know as bran. It is famously rich in fibre. Beneath the husk lie the *endosperm* and the *embryo*. The embryo is the tiny part of the grain that will grow into a new plant. As the centre of reproduction, the embryo is a hub of nutritional excellence, high in protein, natural oils, vitamins and minerals. Removed from the grain, it is known as wheat germ.

The endosperm makes up 80% of the wheat kernel and consists of energy-yielding carbohydrate upon which the embryo, if left to its own natural devices, would feed. It is from the endosperm that white flour is milled for transformation into bread, cakes, pastry and a thousand and one other consumer products. White flour is light, fine and high in bakers' beloved gluten — and it performs impressive transformations, from thickening white sauce to rising into towering yeasty buns to twirling into pasta fusilli. However, almost all the nutrients are lost in milling this versatile powder, as both the husk and the germ are discarded for being too fibrous and unwieldy. So foods that contain a lot of white flour should be combined with lots of fresh vegetables and pulses to ensure a balanced meal.

Bulghar wheat needn't be tarred with the same brush, however. It is significantly less processed than flour, semolina or even couscous. Only the husk is removed, leaving the embryo and the endosperm, making bulghar not only an energy-rich starch, but also an excellent source of fibre and a good source of protein, iron and vitamins B1, B3 and E. It is lower in fat and calories than brown rice and comes with the added advantage of being extremely quick and easy to throw together – it just needs to be soaked in boiling water for ten minutes, making it a top-quality, child-friendly fast food that can be eaten warm with a little olive oil and seasoning or transformed into a nutty, wholesome salad such as the one described below.

1 large butternut squash
    (about 900g)
2 large red onions with a squeeze
    of lemon*
400g bulghar wheat
    (dry weight)
200g baby spinach — *washed &*
    drained if not pre-washed
50g flat-leaf parsley *(big bunch)*
Extra-virgin olive oil
Salt and pepper
400ml boiling water

Mint & lemon dressing
100ml extra-virgin olive oil
Juice of 2 lemons
    *(*including a little squeeze for*
    the red onions)
50g *(medium bunch)* fresh mint
1 tsp ground cinnamon
Salt and pepper

Preheat the oven to 180°C.

Toast the teaspoon of cinnamon in the oven for 5 minutes on a small tray or a piece of tinfoil. Chop the butternut squash into medium chunks (about 1cm), toss in a little olive oil, salt and pepper and transfer to a baking tray. Slice the red onions thinly, toss in a little olive oil, salt and pepper and place on a separate baking tray. Roast the vegetables until tender, turning occasionally. The red onion will take 15-20 minutes and the squash 30-40 minutes. When the red onion is done, stir in a small squeeze of lemon juice to revive its pigmentation, which dulls in the heat of the oven. Set the roast vegetables aside to cool.

While the vegetables are roasting, place the bulghar wheat in a large bowl and stir in a pinch of salt and a tablespoon of olive oil. Pour 400ml of boiling water over the bulghar and leave for 15 minutes, fluffing occasionally with a fork.

Next, make the dressing by blending the olive oil, lemon juice, mint and cinnamon with a stick blender or in a food processor (reserving a couple of sprigs of mint to garnish if desired). Season with salt and pepper. When the bulghar wheat is cool, add the roast vegetables to the bowl, pour in the dressing and fold together gently. Just before serving, chop the flat-leaf parsley roughly. Stir the parsley and the baby spinach into the salad and serve with a sprig of mint.

Wheatgrass

The same wheat berries that make bulghar wheat (as well as all other wheat products) are the source of the popular super-booster that is wheatgrass.

Wheat berries (seeds) store the dormant potential to sprout and grow into wheat plants. Once exposed to water, the embryo (nerve centre) unlocks that growth potential. Each wheat berry contains all the nutrients necessary to begin plant life. Once small roots have formed, the shoots take further nourishment from the soil.

The young grass shoots that develop from the wheat berries are full of vitamins, minerals, protein, amino acids, oxygen, enzymes and chlorophyll. Chlorophyll is the green blood of plants and is very similar in chemical make-up to human haemoglobin. Wheatgrass has been identified as having wonderful detoxifying, cleansing and antiseptic properties. It is associated with improved digestion, increased energy, high spirits, physical healing and an overall sense of well-being.

The grass juiced fresh in Cornucopia is grown by Morna Lynn of Living Green Enterprise, Donard, County Wicklow, who grows tray upon tray of organic wheatgrass in specially constructed sheds for sale in health food shops, juice bars and health food restaurants.

It is also possible to grow wheatgrass at home: you will need seed trays, soil mix, organic wheat berries, a mister (spray bottle) and a bottle of sea vegetable extract (if available). The seeds should be soaked overnight in clean water, then drained. Spread them over the soil in a seed tray and sprinkle with a top layer of soil. Cover the tray with newspaper and leave it in a cool, airy place. Every day remove the newspaper, spray some water on the soil and replace the newspaper. If you have sea vegetable extract, add a drop to the water each day. When shoots begin to appear, discard the newspaper and continue to water lightly daily. When the grass is about 20cm high (about 7 days), cut it 2cm from the soil. Store the cut grass in the fridge. With continued watering, a second harvest of grass will grow from the same tray, after which the soil should be tossed out, the roots broken up, a bit of fresh soil mix added, and a new tray of seeds started.

Drink small quantities of this potent juice at a time (one shot glass). Wheatgrass should be juiced immediately before drinking, as it will begin losing nutrients as soon as it is juiced. Drinking a shot of wheatgrass on an empty stomach will enable maximum absorption of nutrients.

Wheatgrass juicers are a bit of an investment but, if you drink wheatgrass regularly, will save money in the long-term. They are available directly from Morna of Living Green (www.livinggreen.ie) as well as, at time of writing, Nourish health food shops and a selection of farmers' markets, juice bars and numerous independent health food shops.

Japanese-style rice with marinated tofu & sea vegetable in tamari and ginger   *v gf wf*

Japanese-style rice is an old-time favourite comfort food in Cornucopia – a filling, flavourful mouthful of chewy dressed rice, salty sea vegetable and tamari- and ginger-marinated tofu. It is not actually the kind of food you would ever find in Japan, where the venerable rice is more often than not served plain, separated from other elements of a dish, to be savoured in its simplicity. However, it does make use of many specifically Japanese ingredients, bringing them together into a Western-style creation.

This salad is not one that can be thrown together at the drop of a hat. There are several stages to its preparation, from cooking the brown rice to marinating and frying the tofu, to toasting the seeds and soaking the sea vegetable, so allow yourself a good hour to complete all the elements. The finished product, however, is worth the extra effort – it is outstandingly delicious. As this is a starchy, deeply flavoured recipe, it is best served with lightly dressed raw vegetables. To continue the Japanese theme, try coupling it with the carrot and daikon salad on page 166.

The novel ingredient in this salad, for most Irish cooks at least, is arame – a black, stringy sea vegetable that grows on rocks beneath the sea around the Ise Peninsula in Japan. It is available dried in health food shops. As an alternative to flying boxes of sea vegetable halfway around the world, there are some Irish sea vegetables that work really well in this salad, also available from health food shops. Try dulse, Atlantic wakame, kelp or sea spaghetti: break into small pieces, boil for 10 minutes, drain and incorporate into the salad.

Sea vegetables (edible seaweed) play an important role in many Eastern dishes and medicines. Their health and healing properties are due to a remarkably high concentration of bio-available (usable by the human body) vitamins and minerals, much higher than any land plants. Sea vegetable is rich in vitamins A, B, C and E as well as calcium, potassium, chloride and sodium. It contains a high level of vegetable protein and its plentiful non-soluble fibre makes it a great cleanser as it passes through the digestive tract. Sea vegetable is still quite an exotic taste for Westerners. If you like to challenge your taste buds, some other simple uses for the honourable sea vegetable are: add a few pieces to your soup stock or stir some pieces into a broth about ten minutes before it's finished simmering. If you have wakame, kelp or dulse, you can immerse it in simmering water for ten minutes, drain and toss it with a little Japanese vinaigrette (toasted sesame oil, rice vinegar, mirin and salt) with some daikon radish and cucumber as an unusual and highly nutritious salad.

200-250g firm tofu
  (1 standard block)
400g *(uncooked weight)*
  long-grain brown rice
50g dried arame *(or Irish
  alternative, see above)*
2 carrots
3 tbsp sesame seeds
1 bunch of spring onions
  (about 12)
100g bean sprouts
Unrefined sunflower oil

Tofu marinade
2 cloves of garlic
1 thumb-size piece of ginger
  — peeled
100ml tamari *(or shoyu if not
  required to be gluten-free)*

Tamari & ginger dressing
50ml tamari *(or shoyu if not
  required to be gluten-free)*
30ml unrefined sunflower oil
30ml toasted sesame oil
30ml mirin
1 clove of garlic
1 thumb-size piece of ginger

First, marinate the tofu, so that it has plenty of time to absorb the flavours. Chop the tofu into 1½cm cubes and place in a small, flat-bottomed dish. Blend all the marinade ingredients together with a stick blender or in a food processor and pour it over the tofu, ensuring each cube is coated with liquid. Set aside for one hour.

Rinse the brown rice in cold water and then place it in a pot and cover with about 2½ times its volume in water. Bring to the boil, turn down the heat, cover and simmer for about 30 minutes, or until tender but still chewy. Drain, rinse several times in cold water, drain again and place in a large mixing bowl. See page 184 for the step-by-step method of perfect brown rice cooking.

Next, fill a small pot with water and bring to the boil. Plunge the arame (or Irish sea vegetable, broken into small pieces) into the boiling water for 10-12 minutes. Drain and rinse under cold water immediately, then add it to the rice bowl. Do not discard the cooking water from the arame — keep it to use in a soup stock or pour it as a nutrient-rich fertiliser over house- or garden plants.

Next, grate the carrots on the coarsest side of the grater, or chop into very fine juliennes (matchsticks). Place a wok over a high heat with a splash of sunflower oil. When the oil is hot, flash the carrot in the pan for two minutes, just long enough to soften it. Add the carrot to the rice bowl and wipe out the wok, ready to use again.

Rather than turn the oven on to toast such a small quantity of sesame seeds, toast them in the wok. Place the clean, dry wok over a medium heat and push the sesame seeds around for about three minutes, until they turn a shade darker, but not approaching brown. Throw them in on top of the rice, arame and carrot mix.

When the tofu has marinated for an hour, drain off the liquid, but do not discard it, as it will be used later. Return the wok to a high heat with 50ml of sunflower oil (about 3 tablespoons). Once the oil is very hot, carefully add the tofu and fry for about 10 minutes, turning each piece occasionally so that all sides are browned, reducing the heat if necessary.

When the tofu has been evenly browned, remove it from the oil using a slatted spoon and transfer to a sheet of kitchen paper. Pat the top with a second sheet of paper to remove excess oil.

Chop the spring onions and add them, the beansprouts and the tofu to the rice mix. Stir gently to incorporate all the elements.

Next, make the dressing by peeling the garlic and ginger and then combining all the dressing ingredients with a stick blender or in a food processor. Pour this dressing over the rice mix and fold it in until it has been evenly distributed. Taste the salad and, according to your preference, add some or all of the reserved marinade to deepen the flavour. Alternatively, place it in a serving jug for people to help themselves.

Glass noodles, mangetout peas & peanuts in a chilli & lime dressing   *v gf wf cn* ♡

In China and Japan, noodles are a symbol of long life and are eaten at important celebrations such as weddings, birthdays and Spring Festival (New Year). The longer the noodle the better, and much care is taken not to break them during the cooking process, for that would be inauspicious. As noodles are quite a standard part of the Asian diet, their length does not prove a major challenge during the eating process — etiquette allows for a level of slurping and a style of ingestion that would be considered rather unusual by Irish standards. So, in recognition of any inexpert noodle-eating gracelessness out there, this recipe suggests cutting the noodles into more manageable lengths. If however, you are well versed in the art of the noodle, then leave them long and lucky and, 长命百岁 *chang ming bai sui* (may you live to be a hundred).

These particular noodles wouldn't be a bad place to start on that centenarian journey. Glass noodles, or cellophane noodles as they are sometimes called, are made from green mung beans and are, as a result, a much better source of protein and iron than a wheat- or rice-based noodle. They are also wheat- and gluten-free, which makes them easy on the stomach as well as a useful option for wheat-intolerant and coeliac people. Glass noodles can be found in dried bundles at your local Asian food shop and some specialist food halls. Some have an almost invisible string holding the bundle together; take care to remove this before plunging them into hot water. When cooked they are transparent, chewy and quite slippery. They easily take on the flavour of the deliciously zingy lime and chilli dressing in this salad, and their soft texture contrasts perfectly with the fresh and crunchy vegetables and nuts.

Preheat the oven to 180°C. Place the peanuts on a roasting tray and toast them for about 8 minutes, shaking once or twice. Set aside to cool, rub them between your hands to remove loose skins and chop them roughly.

Bring a pot of salted water to the boil and plunge the glass noodles in for 2 minutes. Drain and rinse in cold water immediately. Holding the noodles aloft with one hand, use a knife or kitchen shears to cut them in half for easier eating. Place them in a mixing bowl and stir through a tablespoon of toasted sesame oil to stop them sticking together. Again, bring a pot of salted

150g peanuts
  (organic if possible)
200g pack of glass noodles
200g mangetout beans
  (or sugarsnap peas)
1 bunch spring onions
200g beansprouts
75g *(large bunch)* fresh
  coriander
1 tbsp toasted sesame oil

Chilli & lime dressing
Juice of 2 juicy limes *(or 3 not
  very juicy limes)*
50ml tamari *(or shoyu if not
  required to be gluten-free)*
25ml toasted sesame oil
25ml apple concentrate *(or 1 tsp
  brown sugar if not required
  to be sugar-free)*
1 red chilli — *chopped roughly*

Cook's notes

water to the boil and blanch the mangetouts for 2 minutes. Drain and rinse in cold water. Slice the spring onions. Place them, along with the mangetouts, beansprouts and peanuts, into the mixing bowl with the noodles.

Next make the dressing by blending all the ingredients with a stick blender/food processor. Pour this over the noodles and toss to distribute evenly. Just before serving, chop the fresh coriander roughly and stir it into the salad. Check the seasoning and add a dash more sesame oil and tamari if desired.

Sprouted bean salad with ginger, lemon & coriander

v gf wf yf ♡

From the opening of Cornucopia in 1986, there were four standard daily salads as well as a selection of variables. The original four were garlic potato with hazelnuts, coleslaw, fresh fruit salad and leafy garden salad. Until 2002, no other salad was elevated to the lofty ranks of 'so consistently popular that it simply must be made every day'.

Then in 2002, this sprouted bean salad was introduced. It had long been the intention of our proprietor Deirdre to offer her customers the vitamin-, mineral-, protein- and enzyme-packed wonders of freshly sprouted beans. But Cornucopia being such a limited physical space, we simply could not add shelf-loads of sprouting jars to the already tightly packed kitchen, nor secure stable environmental conditions for successful, hygienic sprouting. To solve our dilemma, along came David Ashe in the guise of his one-person Kildare-based Living Foods enterprise, and, with him, the possibility of a regular supply of freshly sprouted beans, hand-delivered to our kitchen by the basin-load. When Deirdre first came across David Ashe, she took a sample of his wares to the then head chef, Cathy Maguire. 'See what you can do with these,' she said. The very next day she was presented with the salad described below. She knew immediately that she was onto a winner, that this salad would wow staff and customers alike. Shortly afterwards, Cathy left Cornucopia to become a vegetarian chef, with a degree of television celebrity, in Melbourne, Australia.

Initially the sprouted bean salad was made every Monday, Wednesday and Friday. Most customers, when offered a choice of ten salads, ordered it, and many returned to the counter after their meal to buy a take-away portion too. Not only did it sell out long before evening, but every Tuesday, Thursday, Saturday and Sunday we were inundated with disappointed sprouted bean fans who were anything from mildly discombobulated to irrationally incensed to find their favourite pick-me-up unavailable. The punters had spoken – before long, sprouted bean salad became the fifth daily standard.

This salad tastes of health, in a totally yummy way. It's crunchy and leafy and gingery. It's colourful and textured and fun. You can actually feel it doing you good from the first chew. Small packs of sprouted beans are available from health food shops and some progressive food stores. Home-sprouting, if you have time, is inexpensive, easy and hugely satisfying, because the results are so immediate. For some tips on embarking upon your home-sprouting journey, see overleaf.

Bring a small pot of salted water to the boil. Chop the green beans in half and blanch them for 2 minutes in the boiling water. Refresh them immediately in cold water. Drain and place in

200g green beans
2 small heads of two different
    lettuces *(or 1 large head
    of lettuce)*
1 red pepper
1 yellow pepper
1 red onion
400g sprouted beans *(purchased
    in health food shop or
    home-sprouted; see overleaf)*

Gingery lemon
    & coriander dressing
Juice of 1 lemon
25ml apple juice concentrate
50ml extra-virgin olive oil
50g *(medium bunch)*
    fresh coriander
1 thumb-size piece of ginger
    (about 25g) — peeled
Salt and pepper

Cook's notes

a large mixing bowl. Wash the lettuce in salted water, drain it thoroughly and chop roughly. Slice the red onion into thin moons. Dice the peppers finely. Place all of these ingredients in the mixing bowl with the green beans and add in the sprouted beans.

To make the dressing, peel the ginger, then blend it with the lemon juice, olive oil, apple concentrate and coriander until smooth, using a stick blender or a food processor. Add a little salt and pepper to taste. Just before serving, pour the dressing over the salad and toss to distribute evenly.

The joys of home-sprouting

Why eat sprouted beans?

In brief, sprouted beans are a low-fat, low-calorie, animal-free source of protein, enzymes, anti-oxidants and a broad range of vitamins and minerals – pretty much a perfect food source. At a slightly more technical level, sprouted beans are a living food, seeds which are just beginning to grow into adult plants, filled with the potential of new life. Every plant seed contains enough energy and nourishment to feed on during the earliest stages of its life, before it has developed roots to feed from the soil. This food to grow lies in wait until the seed has found suitable conditions to embark on its life. By soaking seeds, nuts or beans, the enzymes in them become active, unlocking all the goodness that lies within, and the young plant begins to grow. It is this living, growing mini-plant that we recognise as a cute little sprout. Eaten raw and fresh, all of its goodness can be enjoyed by the human body. In addition, the live enzymes that stimulate the sprout to grow work alongside the enzymes in the digestive tract to extract maximum nutritional benefit from other food passing through the body.

A head of broccoli is, without a doubt, a healthy choice. However, unlike a newborn sprout, it represents the end of the growing process. It is severed from the plant and transported, now lifeless, from field to kitchen, separated sometimes by several hundred miles and several days of storage, all the while losing both nutrients and flavour. It will then, more often that not, be steamed or boiled at a temperature that destroys any remaining enzymes in the plant. By the time this broccoli is eaten, it has lost some of its natural goodness. By sprouting a jar of broccoli seeds, you can enjoy live food which has suffered no loss of nutrients, is delicious raw and which adds a big fat zero to your carbon print. Give it a go!

Your sprouting kit

- A large, see-through, wide-mouthed jar with a good rim
- A piece of muslin or cheesecloth about 20cm square (enough to generously cover the mouth of the jar and secure down with an elastic band)
- A strong rubber band or length of string
- Some dried beans or seeds to sprout

What to sprout

Basically any seed or bean can be sprouted, depending on the flavour and texture that you want. As different kinds of seeds and beans sprout at different rates, it is best not to mix your base seeds, but rather to have several jars on the go at once until you figure out which ones take approximately the same length of time. Sprouting seeds should be bought from a health food shop and not a garden centre, as seeds for planting may have been treated with pesticides. Almost any seed you can think of and many varieties of beans can be sprouted successfully and consumed. For intense flavours that enhance a green salad, try mustard seeds, onion seeds, fennel seeds or radish seeds. For a nutty, substantial sprout that will form the basis of a salad itself, try chickpeas, mung beans, aduki beans, lentils, black-eye beans or split peas. For a light and airy addition to salads and sandwiches, alfalfa sprouts are a winner. The Cornucopia sprouted bean salad consists of a mixture of sprouted chickpeas, azuki beans, green lentils and mung beans.

Chickpea (2-3 days' sprout time)
A crunchy and nutty addition to green salads, rice salads and bulghar wheat salads.

Alfalfa (4-6 days' sprout time)
A tender, crispy fresh addition to green salads, tomato salads and sandwiches.
Fantasic with hummus and pita bread.

Radish (4-6 days' sprout time)
A spicy, peppery kick to sprinkle onto quiches, into omelettes and any kind of salad.

Lentils (2-3 days' sprout time)
A sweet and crunchy lively addition to stirfrys and sprinkled into soups. Mix with
lemon juice, olive oil and cherry tomatoes for a delicious summer salad.

Azuki (2-3 days' sprout time)
A mild-flavoured, colourful (red) addition to salads, soups and stir-frys. Add to
bulghar salad/brown rice salad to create a whole protein.

Method

Place the seeds or dried beans in the bottom of the jar up to about one fifth full. Fill the jar up to the top with room temperature water and leave to soak overnight (12-15 hours). Next day, cover the mouth of the jar with muslin and secure it tightly with an elastic band or string. Pouring through the muslin, drain all the water from the jar. Put the jar in a warm place to start sprouting. It is vital to rinse the seeds/beans once or twice a day by filling the jar up to the top with water and draining it off through the muslin. Without this regular rinsing, the sprouts will taste bitter and risk getting mouldy. The sprouting process takes one to three days, depending on the size and quality of the seeds/beans and the temperature of the room. It is also a matter of taste, as the sweetness levels vary throughout the sprouting process, so you can nibble at them as you rinse them and decide when they taste most delicious. When ready, if not all eaten immediately, the sprouts can be stored in an uncovered bowl in the fridge for up to three days.

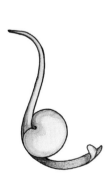

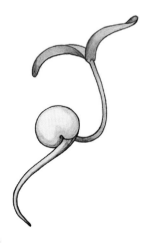

Carrots

The humble carrot is such a wonderfully hardy salad vegetable — even after it has been grated and dressed, it stays fresh, sweet and crunchy, doesn't wilt, doesn't turn brown; in fact it gets brighter and glossier.

If you can source and afford organic, locally grown carrots, the difference in taste is quite noticeable. Farmers' markets offer a relatively inexpensive year-round supply of sweet, organic carrots. If you buy a big bunch to keep for several days, they should be stored in a manner that minimises the amount of moisture they lose. Trim the leaves (if intact), as they rob the carrots of moisture and nutrients once out of the ground. Store in the fridge, wrapped in a plastic bag or in a paper towel, where they will keep for up to two weeks without withering or losing their trademark sweet crunch.

Organic carrots don't need to be peeled; they can just be scrubbed under cold water and topped. One portion of carrot salad will provide more than the recommended daily amount of vitamin A and is a good source of fibre, vitamins C and K and potassium. The anti-oxidant carotenes in carrots help the body heal and protect against infection and disease. Cornucopia serves some form of raw grated carrot salad nearly every day, and below are two of the most popular.

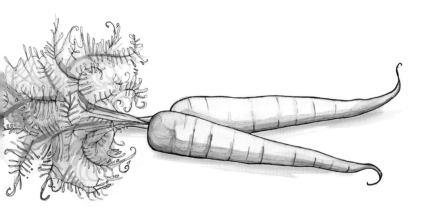

Gujarati carrot with toasted mustard seeds
v gf wf yf ♡

Gujarati carrot is a true testament to the 'simple is best' adage of many food-lovers — it is literally just carrots, mustard seeds, a dash of lemon and a splash of oil. The result is deeply flavourful, keeps really well and combines deliciously with almost any other food, from Indian curries to mashed potato pies. The fun and flavour of Gujarati carrot derives from popping the mustard seeds in boiling oil before pouring them, hot oil and all, over the carrots, giving the salad a smoky, nutty undertone, which is lightened by the splash of lemon juice. It's a brilliant last-minute salad, as it can be prepared in about ten minutes with minimum mess and maximum satisfaction.

Gujarati carrot (or gajar ka) salad is named after the westernmost state of India, which borders the Arabian Sea and Pakistan. The traditional cuisine is almost entirely strictly vegetarian, though many foreign influences have gradually altered that reality. This salad was placed on the world stage by Madhur Jaffrey, the famous Indian actress-cum-cookery writer, who has almost single-handedly taught the Western world the basics of authentic Indian home cooking over the course of the last thirty years. Her best-selling cookbooks and charismatic BBC television cookery series introduced simple and healthy recipes, which demystified Indian cooking and introduced many people to new spices, techniques and exciting vegetarian recipes that have stayed in their repertoire for decades.

10 medium carrots
50g *(3 tbsp)* black mustard seeds
Juice of 1 lemon
100ml refined sunflower oil*
Salt

in this recipe we exceptionally recommend using a refined oil which is more suitable for this kind of high heat cooking

Peel and grate the carrots and place in a large mixing bowl.

Heat the oil in a very small pot over a medium heat. When the oil is smoking hot, carefully add in the mustard seeds. Don't stand with your face over the pot as stray seeds sometimes rocket out of the oil. As soon as the mustard seeds begin to pop and turn a slightly grey shade (about one minute), remove the pot from the heat and pour the entire contents over the carrots.

Add the lemon juice and a pinch of salt and toss well to distribute evenly.

Carrot, daikon & sesame seed in a Japanese-style dressing
v   gf   wf   ♡

This carrot salad is a colourful mix of carrot, pepper, spring onion and the rather more unusual ingredient that is daikon radish. Daikon is a long white radish about five to ten times the size of a carrot, popular in Asian cuisine. It is milder in piquancy than the small red radishes more familiar to the Western kitchen. It is a very commonplace ingredient in Japan, where it is grated and dressed with shoyu and ginger (daikon oroshi) as an accompaniment to tofu, pickled in rice vinegar and sake as a side dish to be eaten with oily foods (tsukemono), and used rather like a turnip in slow-cooked winter soups and stews (oden).

In Ireland, daikon is available in Asian food shops and some specialist food stores, but rarely outside of them. While you are shopping for your daikon, the dressing on this carrot salad may require you to invest in a few new cupboard condiments, especially if Japanese cuisine is not part of your normal repertoire, namely mirin and rice vinegar. Both are available from health food shops and Asian food shops. Mirin is a kind of Japanese rice wine, sweeter and lower in alcohol than sake and used only in cooking. Rice vinegar, as the name suggests, is made from fermented rice. It is milder and mellower in taste than the cider vinegar and white wine vinegar popular in Western vinaigrettes.

To integrate this carrot salad into a Japanese-style lunch, serve it with a portion of hot sticky Japanese rice and a bowl of miso soup. Chop some firm tofu into 1½cm cubes, marinate them for an hour in soy sauce, ginger and garlic (and a little honey or brown sugar if you like), then drain them and fry on all sides in a hot pan with a couple of millimetres of sunflower oil. Finally drizzle with a teaspoon or two of marinade and sprinkle with some toasted sesame seeds. A meal worthy of a Shinto monk!

50g *(3 tbsp)* sesame seeds
5 medium carrots
1 small or ½ large daikon radish
 (400-500g)
1 bunch of spring onions
1 red pepper

Japanese-style dressing
30ml mirin
50ml brown rice vinegar
75ml toasted sesame oil
Salt

If you happen to have the oven on already for something else, place the sesame seeds on a small oven tray and toast until golden, tossing once or twice (about 5 minutes). Otherwise use a small pan placed over a medium heat (with no oil). Simply push the seeds around the pan for about 3 minutes, until they turn a shade darker, making sure they don't burn. Set aside to cool.

Peel and grate the carrots and daikon and place in a large mixing bowl. Chop the spring onion into diagonal rounds and the red pepper into

very thin strips. Add them, as well as the toasted sesame seeds, to the mixing bowl. Sprinkle in a little salt and then mix together all the ingredients. Combine the mirin, vinegar and sesame oil and pour over the salad. Toss well to distribute the dressing evenly and season with extra salt if necessary.

Fennel, rocket, tomato & olives in a balsamic vinaigrette
v gf wf ♡

It should, of course, be said of all food that good-quality ingredients are crucial. However, this is truer of some recipes than others. None more so than this salad, which absolutely requires delicious ripe vine tomatoes and as-good-as-you-can-afford black olives, as well as rich extra-virgin olive oil and a well-aged (over five years if possible) thick and musky Italian balsamic vinegar: *aceto balsamico di Modena*. Served at room temperature so that all the flavours can sing, this is a simple but exquisite combination of some of the best elements of the Italian kitchen. Have a few hunks of crusty bread on hand to mop up the dressing from the plate. And prepare yourself for instant gustatory transportation to a sun-drenched terrace in Tuscany.

When choosing olives, the question of whether to buy pitted or unpitted may arise. Pitted olives, *oliva senza nocciolo*, are conveniently unthreatening to loose fillings and oblivious children, and there's none of that awkward spitting out of half-chewed pits. However, the pitting process affects both the intensity of flavour and firmness of flesh of the olive, as well as removing, not only the pit, but a portion of the fruit too. The gourmet choice is definitely unpitted olives, along with ample warning to anyone eating the salad and provision of a side dish to delicately dispose of the pits!

The delicious balsamic vinaigrette for this salad can be used to dress many other salads. Try it on any of the following:

- *Mixed leaves, cherry tomatoes & toasted bread croutons*
- *Grilled asparagus or braised artichoke hearts*
- *Beef tomatoes with vegetarian mozzarella cheese*
- *Puy lentils with wilted spinach*
- *Dressed radicchio with toasted pine nuts topped with vegetarian goat's cheese crostini*

Slice the tomatoes in quarters and place them in a large mixing bowl. Sprinkle them immediately with salt and pepper and leave them to absorb the seasoning. Next, slice the red onion and fennel thinly and roughly chop the rocket. Drain the black olives. Add all of these to the mixing bowl with the tomatoes.

To make the dressing, simply blend together all the ingredients. Just before serving, pour this

8 good-quality ripe vine tomatoes
2 red onions
2 bulbs of fennel
200g rocket — *washed &*
drained if not pre-washed
150g good-quality black olives

Balsamic vinaigrette
100ml extra-virgin olive oil
50ml good-quality vegetarian
balsamic vinegar
2 cloves of garlic
1 tsp apple concentrate (*or*
unrefined brown sugar)
Salt and pepper

vinaigrette over the salad and turn gently to distribute all the ingredients evenly, being careful not to bruise or break up the tomatoes. Check the seasoning and add a dash more balsamic vinegar or a pinch more salt if necessary.

Note: If using unpitted olives, warn anyone eating the salad to watch out for their teeth.

Beetroot, watercress, orange & pumpkin seed in a citrus dressing *v gf wf yf* ♡

On days when this salad is on the menu, several glasses of mysterious red liquid are to be found stored safely in corners frequented by staff, giving the impression that a drinks reception for thirsty vampires may be about to take place. The glasses are actually full of a most delicious combination of beetroot juice, citrus juice and apple concentrate. As containers of this beetroot salad sell out, some of the staff pounce on them and drain any excess dressing into a glass for later — an energy-boosting, detoxifying, blood-enriching treat.

If the juice is that popular, the salad must be good. And it is — a rather wonderful colour explosion of deep purple grated beetroot, glossy orange flesh and lush watercress, with the added interest of a generous portion of crunchy toasted pumpkin seeds. This is a really low-calorie and totally fat-free salad, which still delivers on flavour and texture. Beetroot, especially raw, has much to recommend it from a healthy-eating perspective. The sweet-tasting root is rich in folic acid and potassium, as well as detoxifying properties. If you buy beetroot with the leaves still on, wash them, chop them roughly and add them to the salad with the cress; they are as rich in iron, calcium and vitamin C as spinach leaves.

Pigment warning: the betalain pigment in beetroot will stain anything porous — your hands, your wooden chopping board, and, more catastrophically, your clothes. If the disaster of 'beetroot juice meets white shirt' does occur, soak a slice of white bread in cold water and place it on the stain. Do this on both sides of the affected area. Most of the pigment will be absorbed by the bread. Then wash as normal.

For most individuals who eat beetroot, the bright red betalain pigment is neutralised as it passes through the body. However, about 10-14 per cent of digestive systems do not neutralise the pigment, resulting in the harmless, but sometimes shocking, occurrence of the condition known as Beeturia, or pink pee. Be prepared!

Preheat the oven to 180°C. Place the pumpkin seeds on a baking tray and toast them for about 8 minutes, tossing once or twice and removing them at the slightest hint of browning. Set aside to cool.

Peel and grate the beetroots and transfer to a large mixing bowl. Peel the oranges and remove the flesh from each segment, trying to keep the shape intact. If the watercress is nice and small,

150g pumpkin seeds
6 large *(8 medium)* beetroots
2 oranges *(or 2 grapefruit)*
200g watercress — *washed &
    drained if not pre-washed*

Oil-free citrus dressing
Juice of 1½ lemons
Juice of 1 orange
30ml apple concentrate
    (or 1 tbsp runny honey)*
Salt and pepper

** If you use honey the salad will
no longer be vegan.*

it can be added as is. If it is a little ungainly, chop it roughly first. Add the orange segments, cress and toasted pumpkin seeds to the mixing bowl.

Combine the lemon juice, orange juice and apple concentrate. Add a little salt and pepper. Just before serving, pour the citrus dressing over the salad and combine gently to distribute it evenly, trying not to break up the orange segments. Check for sweetness and salt, adding a dash more apple concentrate or seasoning if necessary.

Roasting beetroot

This delicious salad should go some way to convincing beetroot sceptics that beetroot is not the enemy, nor does it occur solely as boiled, pickled slices in jars. Another dramatically delicious way of serving this vegetable, sure to win over the most uncertain beetroot eater, is to roast it. As with roasting any vegetable, roasting intensifies the natural sweetness of the beetroot and it develops a lovely musky depth of flavour.

Plain roast beetroot

Peel the beetroots and chop them into quarters. Toss them in a little extra-virgin olive oil, salt and pepper. Place them in a roasting try. Cover with foil and roast in a medium oven until soft (approximately one hour), removing the foil twenty minutes before the end.

Honey roast beetroot

This is an absolute treat. Prepare as for plain roast beetroot above, but this time toss the chunks of beetroot in extra-virgin olive oil, a drizzle of organic runny honey (or a sprinkling of unrefined brown sugar), a dash of good-quality vegetarian balsamic vinegar and a few sprigs of thyme. The result: smoky, caramelised, deep-coloured wedges of flavour sensation.

Crunchy Thai-style salad in a peanut & chilli dressing
v gf wf cn

For those who do not always enjoy 'healthy' salads, this is a delight. Folk who generally avoid bowls of raw vegetables like the plague will happily tuck into a portion of this crunchy Thai-style salad because the dressing is so irresistibly tasty – like a very posh peanut butter dressed up with lime, chilli and fresh coriander. The recipe includes a single chilli pepper, but that can be increased to two for a really spicy kick.

Should acquiring a daikon radish be problematic (they are available at most Asian food shops), replace with some chopped fennel, celery or white cabbage, or simply increase the quantities of the other components to compensate. This salad keeps quite well compared to most raw salads, as the dressing is not too juicy and the particular vegetables used are not prone to wilting, so you can pack any leftovers into a lunchbox for the next day.

Peanuts, in moderation, are a healthy and wholesome snack – they fill you with energy and make you feel satisfied for several hours. They contain a higher proportion of protein than any other nut (27%). They provide a good source of fibre and are packed with vitamins and minerals. Although peanuts have a high fat content, they are monounsaturated, or 'good' fats. Peanuts, being a plant food, contain zero cholesterol and have anti-oxidant benefits. Still in their shells, they can be boiled or steamed; out of their shell, they can be eaten raw, roasted or as peanut butter (see page 177).

Preheat the oven to 180°C. Place the peanuts on a roasting tray and toast them for about 8 minutes, shaking once or twice. Set aside and, when cool, chop them thoroughly.

Slice the baby corns in half lengthways. Bring a small pot of salted water to the boil and blanch the baby corn and the mangetout for 2 minutes. They should remain *al dente*. Refresh them immediately in cold water. Drain and place in a large mixing bowl.

Peel the daikon, chop it in half lengthways and slice it into thin half discs. Peel the cucumber (or leave it unpeeled if you prefer) and slice it into thin rounds. Slice the spring onions into thin diagonal slices. Add all these vegetables, as well

200g baby corn
200g mangetout beans
1 small daikon radish *(or about
    500g)*
1 cucumber
1 bunch of spring onions
200g beansprouts

Peanut & chilli dressing
200g peanuts *(organic if
    possible)* — *half of these are
    for the salad itself*
Juice of 2 limes
50g *(medium bunch)* fresh
    coriander
1 red chilli — *chopped roughly*
100ml toasted sesame oil
25ml apple concentrate (*or 1 tsp
    unrefined brown sugar*)
Salt

as the beansprouts, to the mixing bowl. Take half of the roasted peanuts. Chop them roughly and add them to the bowl too. Toss to combine.

To make the dressing, blend the lime juice, sesame oil, red chilli and fresh coriander using a stick blender or in a food processor. Next blend the remaining half of the peanuts into the dressing until smooth, forming a paste. Spoon this dressing over the salad and fold it in gently to distribute evenly.

Homemade peanut butter
with option for almond or hazelnut butter *v gf wf yf cn*

Peanut butter is really easy to make at home. It tastes great, contains no preservatives and you are in complete control of how much (if any) salt or sweetener goes in. The quantities below make about half a jar. Stored in the fridge, homemade peanut butter will keep for two weeks. Enjoy on toast, crackers, bread, rice cakes, oat cakes, etc.

For those who prefer to avoid peanuts, use a nut of your choice, for example roasted hazelnuts or almonds, blended respectively with hazelnut oil or almond oil (or vegetable oil).

225g raw, shelled peanuts *(organic if possible)*
1-1½ tbsp peanut oil *(or unrefined vegetable oil)*
Pinch salt

Preheat your oven to 180°C. Roast the peanuts on a baking tray for 8 minutes. Set aside to cool. Rub to remove any loose skins.

For smooth peanut butter
Place all the peanuts, along with the oil and a pinch of salt into a food processor and blend until smooth. Start with the smaller quantity of oil and add a little extra if necessary to achieve a nice texture. Different peanuts contain different levels of oil, so each batch will require a slightly adjusted amount of oil.

For crunchy peanut butter
Roast the peanuts as above. Place ⅔ of the peanuts into the food processor, along with the oil and salt. When completely smooth, add in the final ⅓ of the peanuts and, using the pulse function, blitz until the peanuts are of a suitably crunchy consistency.

For sweet peanut butter
If you like your peanut butter slightly sweet, add a teaspoon of runny honey or apple concentrate.
Note: by adding honey, the peanut butter will no longer be vegan.

Cook's notes

Main courses

Casseroles & curries (served with rice) ...

Spanish chickpea casserole	196
Moroccan chickpea tagine	200
Thai green curry with chickpea, squash & tofu	204
Sweet potato, broccoli & lentil sambar	208
Potato, pea & mushroom curry	212

Some enduring favourites ...

Vegetable, noodle & marinated tofu stirfry	214
Creamy cauliflower, broccoli & leek gratin	218
Leek, spinach & lentil nut roast	222

Mashed potato dishes ...

White bean & roast Mediterranean vegetable pie, basil mash	232
Pumpkin, courgette & green lentil pie, mustard & dill mash	235
Baked Portobello mushrooms on leek mash with onion gravy	238

Pasta ...

Spinach & hazelnut cannelloni in tomato sauce with basil oil	246
Butternut squash & regato cannelloni in tomato sauce	250
Roast squash, courgette & spinach lasagne	252

Polenta ...

Polenta square with roast summer vegetables & olive tapenade	260
Roast garlic polenta bake with leek, mushroom & spinach in a red pepper sauce topped with goat's cheese	266

To Greece & beyond ...

Vegetable & lentil moussaka	274
Wild rice & mushroom dolmades, garlic cream & pepper purée	278
Spanakopita	284
Wild mushroom, leek & spinach filo parcels	288
Couscous-filled aubergine halves, roasted cherry tomato sauce	294

Quiche ...

Basic quiche	300
Courgette, blue cheese & pine nut quiche	304
Cherry tomato, feta, spinach & olive quiche	308

Winter festive ...

Sweet potato, spinach & hazelnut en croûte on parsnip mash with red wine & juniper gravy	310

Introduction to main courses

The daily menu in Cornucopia includes five hot dishes: a combination of rice dishes (stews, casseroles, curries), bakes (pastas, pies, polenta) and quiches. Of the five main courses, generally two are vegan and two are gluten-free. Our aim is always that each dish be wholesome, satisfying and tasty – that every customer leaves feeling they have had a delicious and filling feed.

By 7.30am every morning the main chef of the day has arrived, donned his/her work clothes and is focusing intently on today's menu. By 7.45am all the prepared vegetables, chopped by the prep chef the previous day, have been brought up from the cold room and sorted out. By 8.00am at least eight pots are already up and running on cookers, starting to steam and hiss. Around this time, the front shutter (at half-mast as the restaurant is not yet open) is pushed open and the delivery men from our vegetable produce supplier in Smithfield (Dublin's fruit and vegetable wholesale market) start wheeling in trolley after trolley of fresh fruit and vegetables – almost a van-ful in total. As soon as everything has been checked in, the chefs grab whatever they need most urgently before the rest is carried, box by box, down to the cold room. Over the course of the morning, both large ovens are constantly full of roasting vegetables, most of the fourteen kitchen rings are flaming away under bubbling pots and the main chef's bench is a busy workshop of chopping, slicing, mixing, stirring, sieving, blending, sprinkling, rolling, assembling, testing and tasting. From boxes of raw vegetables and fresh herbs, from bins of dried beans and lentils, from containers of spices and blocks of cheeses, from pots of water, bottles of milk and trays of eggs, start to emerge two forty-litre pots of soup and the recognisable makings of five sizeable and promising main courses, as well as the rice and garnishes to go with them. It is quite a daily feat of strength, focus, organisation and clever use of space. Not to mention the skills of flavouring, creativity, spontaneity and affability under extreme time pressure, with lunchtime service approaching 'faster than a speeding bullet,' as our chef Eddie used to say. Starting a

casual conversation with the mains chef at 11.45am is about as likely to elicit a polite response as poking him/her firmly with a newly sharpened pitchfork. It is no time for idle gossip as countdown to the notorious noon deadline begins.

It never ceases to wow me: at 11.59 the hotplate is empty; at 12.00 it is a steaming arrangement of four hot dishes, one quiche, two soups, rice and, depending on the menu, mashed potato, bulghar wheat or couscous. At precisely the same time as the hot food emerges from the kitchen, the lunchtime waiting staff arrive at the counter and there is a momentary buzz of excitement as everyone plans what they'll be having on their first break, based on what they see before them. And then they glance up and see that they are not alone in admiring the chef's wares – a queue of lunchtime earlybirds has already approached the hot-food counter, peering through the slanted glass, taking a moment to relate each dish to the freshly chalked inscriptions on the board and then pointing out or naming what they've decided to go for. And thus a day of hot-food service begins. Depending on the weather or the day of the week or other unknown cosmic permutations and combinations, one day the creamy cauliflower and broccoli gratin flies out, the next day roast vegetable ragout with herbed spaghetti hits the spot and the next day it's almost impossible to keep up with demand for potato, pea and mushroom curry.

Having filled the hotplate, the mains chef breathes a momentary sigh of relief, nibbles at a selection of his/her morning's hard work and, without much further ado, starts up two new thirty-litre pots of soup in anticipation of at least one, if not both, of the lunchtime soups running out sometime mid-afternoon. Soon a head pops into the kitchen, 'Chef, can I call curry please! And rice is halfway. And the potato Lyonnaise has two portions left. How long on the next quiche?' One thing that's a near certainty in a Cornucopia chef's life: once the food is made, selling it never presents a problem.

I remember years ago identifying a certain category of customer in Cornucopia that hadn't quite make sense to me yet. This particular genre of person usually came in around 6 o'clock in the evening. They were male, from the countryside and very decent. They ordered a main course with two salads and, more often than not, a slice of brown bread and butter and a glass of milk. They were on their own or in pairs. They did not readily fit the profile of some of the more discernible groups that frequent Cornucopia – vegetarians (of course), fans of health food, special diet adherents, artists and bohemians, shoppers (we are, after all, located just off Dublin's main shopping street), politicians, musicians, hippies, holistic lifestyle followers, academics (Trinity College is just around the corner), staff from local businesses, radicals, punks, travellers following their guidebooks. I often wondered who all these single men were and why they chose to eat in Cornucopia. Over the course of time, I realised they are simply hungry boys who want a decent plate of homemade food. They want to tuck in, eat up and feel full and satisfied. They like Cornucopia because it reminds them of food their mother used to cook at home, not because their mother was a vegetarian, but because she whipped up tasty meals from scratch with fresh ingredients and served hearty platefuls that filled them up and fuelled them through their days.

Cornucopia main courses are, in general, substantial, unfussy plates of 'grub' and, much as we also strive constantly towards refinement of flavours and textures, we have never lost sight of the primary goal, which is to provide good-quality, tasty meals made with wholefood ingredients. In September, when the university term starts up, we often sell gift vouchers to mothers for their first-year college student children, a parting gift to launch their offspring into third-level life. A way of feeding them from afar that is safer than giving them cash (which might be more likely to be spent on beer and late-night battered chocolate bars than dinner). I've often felt proud of the 'mothering' vibe about our food, for what greater act of humanity is there than the provision of nourishment

for one's family. As customer after customer peers into the hot-food counter and their
eyes alight upon what their stomach really wants, there is enormous satisfaction in
being a member of the team providing that. Here we present some of the recipes that
have rendered such pleasure over the years to us as staff and to hungry customers alike.

And so came the question of which of our many, many main course recipes should
be included in this book. All the chefs and waiting staff had an opinion. The ones
they like to eat, the ones they like to cook, the ones they introduced to the restaurant
themselves, the ones that look great on the hotplate, the ones that they remember
with nostalgia, the ones that suit their special diet, the ones that have crispy cheese
on top, the ones that don't contain chillies, the ones in which they particularly
like the chunks of marinated tofu, the ones invented by their favourite chef and,
of course, the ones that they ate on their first lunch break in Cornucopia when it
dawned on them that they could eat such fantastic food for free for the duration of
their working life in the restaurant. Oh joy! Between staff opinion, a month-long
customer survey and a few gut instincts on the part of the book team, we settled upon
a selection of dishes, heavy on the old favourites that have survived the test of time,
with a sprinkling of newer recipes. Of the 23 recipes, 12 are vegan (or have vegan
options) and 11 are gluten-free. Many recipes include variations to show how the
basic technique introduced in that dish can open the door to experimentation and
imagination. Most require only some pots, pans and baking dishes, and occasionally
a food processor and a hand-held blender. All of the recipes serve 4-8 people,
depending on how hungry they are and what side dishes (if any) are on offer.

Main courses: some basic information

Cooking brown rice

Most stews and curries in Cornucopia are served on a bed of organic brown rice. Good-quality long-grain and short-grain brown rice are available from health food shops. Allow about ⅓ cup of dry rice (75ml) per person, if serving with a main course.

· First, wash the rice in cold water.
· Place the rice in a sufficiently large pot and cover with at least two and a half times its volume of cold water and a pinch of salt.
· Place on a high heat and bring to the boil, then cover with a lid and reduce to a low heat to simmer for 35 minutes. Stir once or twice to avoid the rice sticking to the base of the pot, but don't over-stir or the rice will become sticky and starchy. When it is cooked, the rice should be soft, but still nice and chewy.
· Never let the rice pot dry out. This is unlikely to happen if you start with plenty of water and keep a lid on during simmering. If, however, the water does run low, top it up during cooking with some boiling water.
· Remove from the heat and transfer to a colander to drain. Pour a kettle of boiling water over the rice to remove the starch released in cooking. Serve immediately.

Stock recipe   *v gf wf yf*

Several of the recipes in this chapter require vegetable stock, to add depth of flavour to sauces and gravies. Vegetable stock is basically water flavoured by vegetables and herbs and there is no definitive recipe for it, rather a great freedom to use up odds and ends that are lying around the kitchen. Your stockpot should consist of about half vegetables/herbs and half water.

It's always useful to have stock in the freezer, so, if a recipe calls for 500ml of stock, you might as well make a litre or two and freeze the leftover in small batches (a handy way to reuse yoghurt tubs or mineral bottles) for the next time you need some. Below is a recipe for 1½ litres of stock, which can be varied to suit the contents of your larder. Depending on what you will be using your stock for, you can make it a little more interesting by adding strips of lemon zest, some porcini mushrooms or some roasted garlic skins.

1 onion
3 cloves of garlic
2 carrots
    (or plenty of carrot tops)
2 sticks celery, including the leaves
1 leek *(or plenty of discarded
    dark-green leek ends)*
5 bay leaves
10 whole black peppercorns
A few sprigs of thyme
    (or rosemary, oregano, sage)
Extra-virgin olive oil
2½ litres of water

Chop all the vegetables roughly. Coat the base of a large pot with olive oil and place over a medium ring. Add the onion, carrot, garlic, celery and leek, stir briefly, cover with a lid and sweat over a low heat for 10 minutes.

Add the water, bay leaves, thyme and peppercorns, bring to the boil and simmer for 45 minutes. Strain the stock using a colander or sieve. Use the back of a spoon to press through as much liquid as possible. Discard all the vegetables and herbs and retain all the liquid.

Béchamel

Béchamel is one of the mother sauces of French cuisine. Also known as white sauce, it is basically scalded infused milk whisked into a butter and flour roux, or paste. Béchamel appears in many guises: as the white sauce on top of lasagne and moussaka, as the cheese sauce in gratins and as the parsley sauce on the steamed carrots and mashed potato at Sunday dinner.

The recipe below is just a guideline. Increase or decrease the quantity as required. Once you have mastered the art of the béchamel, the flavour can be varied both at the point of infusing the milk (by including cloves, garlic, peppercorns, onion, bay, thyme, etc) and also after the sauce is complete (nutmeg, vegetarian cheese, mustard, chives, parsley, basil, etc). The thickness of the béchamel depends on the ratio of flour and butter (roux) to milk. For a standard sauce, use an equal weight of flour and butter and add a zero to that weight for millilitres of milk (ie 30g flour, 30g butter, 300ml milk). For a thinner sauce, increase the amount of milk slightly. If you would like your béchamel to set a little (for example for lasagne), stir in one free-range egg yolk per 500ml of milk after the sauce is cooked.

Béchamel sauce

- ½ onion studded with 3 cloves
- 3 bay leaves
- Few sprigs of thyme
- 5 peppercorns
- 500ml milk
- 50g butter
- 50g plain flour
- Nutmeg *(freshly grated)*
- Extra-virgin olive oil
- Salt and pepper

Infuse the milk by bringing it to a very slow boil with the onion, cloves, bay leaves, thyme and peppercorns. Remove it from the heat, leave it to infuse for 20 minutes and then strain the milk into a jug, discarding the solid matter. Place the butter and a small dash of olive oil over a low heat. When melted, sprinkle on the flour and cook for 3 minutes, stirring constantly.

Now start adding the milk, bit by bit, ensuring each batch is fully incorporated before you add more. Be very patient in adding the milk and never stop stirring. When all the milk has been added, cook for a further 5 minutes (still stirring). Remove from the heat, season with salt and pepper and grate in a little nutmeg. Use plain or flavour with grated vegetarian cheese or finely chopped herbs.

Tomato sauce   *v gf wf yf* ♡ *(cs)*

Where would we be without the ubiquitous tomato sauce? Starving, I'd say! Certainly, this Main courses chapter would be only half as long without tomato sauce in one form or another: as a base for stews and as a sauce for pasta and bakes. Below is a recipe for a very basic tomato sauce, a building block to so much more. Add roasted vegetables for a delicious ragout, add roast mushrooms and olives as a pasta sauce, reduce it down, spread it on a pizza base and top with cheese, enrich it with red wine, paprika, chilli, roast garlic ... With a good tomato sauce, the possibilities are endless. Tomato sauce can be made from either tinned or fresh tomatoes. If using fresh tomatoes, choose ripe, red, vine-ripened tomatoes. If using tinned tomatoes, try to source organic ones. Some people like to add a touch of sweetener to balance the tartness of the tomatoes, although this is a matter of personal taste.

1 onion
1 carrot
2 stalks of celery
3 cloves garlic
25g *(small bunch)* oregano
2x400g tins of plum tomatoes *(organic if possible)* or 1kg *ripe plum tomatoes*
Pinch of unrefined brown sugar *(or dash of apple concentrate)* — *optional*
Extra-virgin olive oil
Salt and pepper

If you are using fresh tomatoes, they must first be deskinned. Cut an X into the skin of each, place them in a suitable bowl and pour boiling water over them. After one minute, drain the tomatoes and the skins can now be removed with ease. Quarter them and set aside.

Roughly chop the onion, carrot, celery and garlic. Cover the base of a large pot with olive oil and add the chopped vegetables. Cover with a lid, reduce to a low heat and sweat for 15 minutes, stirring regularly. After 15 minutes, add the oregano and freshly skinned (in which case add 200ml water) or tinned tomatoes. Bring to a simmer and cook gently on a low heat for 30 minutes. Stir regularly to prevent sticking and burning. When the sauce has cooked fully and the juices have reduced, use a stick blender to blend it to a smooth consistency. Season with salt and pepper. Add a pinch of brown sugar (or drop of apple concentrate) to sweeten slightly if you like.

Roasting vegetables

Of all the basic cooking techniques for vegetables, roasting produces the biggest, boldest flavours. In the hot, dry environment of the oven, much of the moisture evaporates from the vegetables, so they shrink and their flavour is concentrated into a small space, making it more intense. The touch of oil (or butter) in which the vegetables are tossed encourages the outside to become golden and crispy in places, making for lovely colouration and a delicious lightly charred flavour. Meanwhile, the interior becomes soft and tender and a little sweet, as the natural sugars caramelise in the heat.

Eaten just lightly seasoned, or incorporated into dishes, roast vegetables are rich and satisfying and deep in flavour. The difference in taste and texture between a steamed red pepper and a roasted red pepper, for example, is remarkable. That roasted pepper can turn run-of-the-mill tomato soup into an opulent, melodious treat. The same roasted pepper brings life to a simple lemon and olive oil butter bean salad with delightful strips of colour and flavour. And the roasted red peppers found in the stews and bakes in the chapter that follows don't tend to get lost within the dish, for the roasting process locks in the flavour and allows each vegetable a little individuality within the overall recipe.

A few tips for roasting vegetables:

- The oven should be hot, at least 200°C.
- Chop the vegetables into even pieces, so they roast at a consistent rate.
- Place the chopped vegetables into a mixing bowl, drizzle on a little olive oil, add a pinch of salt and pepper and toss to distribute. This allows you to use as little oil as possible, and avoids pools of oil building up in the corners of the roasting tray.
- If using large quantities, roast the different vegetables in separate roasting trays, to allow you the freedom to remove the trays from the oven one by one as the vegetables take different lengths of time to cook.
- If, however, you are cooking a small quantity of a few different vegetables, roast them all together in one tray but compensate for their different roasting times by chopping them into different sizes. Chop quick-roasting ones quite large (aubergines, courgettes, peppers, mushrooms, leeks, etc), medium-roasting ones medium (butternut squash, sweet potato) and slow-roasting ones quite small (parsnip, carrot, baby potato, etc). Don't chop tomatoes, shallots or garlic cloves, just add them whole.

· Toss vegetables once or twice while roasting to prevent them burning or sticking, but don't move them around too regularly, as you want them to develop some light charring, for flavour, texture and colour.

Blanching

Quite a number of the main course recipes require you to blanch some of the vegetables in advance. Blanching involves plunging the prepared vegetables into boiling salted water until just *al dente* and then draining and rinsing immediately in cold water to prevent the heat of the vegetable continuing the cooking process. The main concern in blanching is not to overcook the vegetables, and a matter of one minute can make all the difference between a broccoli floret with a pleasant bite and a broccoli floret that is soggy and sad. Remember that blanched vegetables for main courses will be reheated within the stew or bake and will cook a little more at that stage, so don't worry if they still retain a slight crunch after blanching.

· Chop the vegetables into even pieces, so they cook at a consistent rate.
· Bring a suitably large pot of salted water to boiling point before throwing the vegetables in, and return to the boil before reducing the heat.
· Ideally, if blanching several different vegetables, cook them in separate batches, as they will all soften at different rates.
· Blanching times will depend on how large or small the vegetable is chopped; for example, rounds of carrots take 10-12 minutes, but finely sliced juliennes take only 2-3 minutes.
· Spinach: 1 minute. Green beans, baby corn, mangetouts, sugar snaps:
· 2 minutes. Broccoli, courgette: 3 minutes. Cauliflower: 5 minutes.
· Carrots: 8-12 minutes (unless chopped very finely into juliennes).
· As soon as the vegetables have reached an *al dente* texture, arrest the cooking process by draining immediately and running them under cold water. This is to prevent them continuing to cook in their own heat.
· If you have several different vegetables to blanch, lift each batch out with a slotted spoon and reuse the boiling water for subsequent batches.

Lids on pots

Placing a lid on a pot makes an enormous difference to the type of cooking that occurs within that pot. A lid is required, for example, for sweating vegetables. This is a cooking technique used extensively in cooking soups and sauces. The idea of sweating the starter vegetables (mirepoix), usually onion as well as carrot, celery and leek, is to soften them and draw out their flavours relatively slowly. Were you to try this without a lid, the moisture would quickly evaporate from the vegetables and they would start to crisp and burn long before they became soft. If you place a lid on the pot, however, the water that evaporates from the vegetables cannot escape, and the vegetables remain moist enough to soften slowly without browning or burning.

When cooking a sauce or a stew, placing a lid on the pot allows the elements within the pot to cook without the liquid reducing and also without too much fear of the base of the pot sticking and burning. In order to reduce a sauce or stew, to intensify its flavour or to achieve a suitably thick texture, remove the lid from the pot, allowing the moisture to evaporate. Stir regularly, as the thicker a sauce becomes, the more likely it is to catch on the base of the pot.

Another reason for using lids is for the environmental benefits. A pot of potatoes will cook perfectly happily without a lid, as long as there is plenty of water covering the potatoes. However, more energy will be required for the water to both reach and maintain boiling point without a lid than with a lid; by using a lid, the pot will come to the boil more quicly and then simmer steadily at a very low heat. The environmental impact seems negligible, but it definitely falls into the every little bit helps category.

Around the world on a chickpea

The first three recipes in this chapter involve chickpeas, a long-time favourite for both salads and main courses in Cornucopia. The three dishes in question hail from three different continents and three different cooking traditions, for the mighty chickpea, having started life on a plant in the Middle East, has travelled far and wide along many trade routes – east into India and Sri Lanka, west into the Mediterranean countries of Northern Africa and Southern Europe and all the way to Mexico and South America via Spanish migration. It has taken on many shapes and forms on its journey round the world: boiled and roasted, whole and blended, ground and sprouted.

In Spain, and anywhere Spanish-influenced, the chickpea is called *garbanzo*. In France, *pois chiche*. In Italy, *ceci*. In Indian dishes, you'll recognise it as *chan(n)a*. Whatever the name, chickpeas have two great benefits: they hold their firm, nutty texture well for cooking (unlike some beans which can turn mushy in the blink of an eye) and they are full of nutritional goodness. Chickpeas contain over 20% protein. They should ideally be combined with a whole grain to produce a whole protein, meaning a source of all eight essential amino acids required by the body for building and repairing human tissue. Examples of chickpea-based whole proteins are hummus on brown bread, falafel in a brown pita pocket, chickpea tagine on bulghar wheat (as per this chapter) and Spanish chickpea casserole on brown rice (also in this chapter). Like all beans and pulses, chickpeas are a very good source of cholesterol-lowering dietary fibre. As one clove of garlic per day is also believed to have cholesterol-lowering effects, hummus would seem to be a perfect food for anyone watching their cholesterol. Chickpeas are also low in fat and provide a steady, slow-release source of complex carbohydrate energy. They are remarkably high in folic acid and provide a good source of iron. Sprouting chickpeas increases their nutritional value further (see page 161 for tips on sprouting).

Chickpeas are called *cicer arietinum* in Latin, which means 'ram-like bean', because the gnarly surface of the chickpea, with its tiny suggestion of a tail, somewhat resembles the head of a ram. It also somewhat resembles the shape of a pebble, which has slightly more relevance to modern-day cooks. Although all dried chickpeas sold commercially have been checked for stones, a few sometimes manage to slip through, so it is advisable, before soaking chickpeas, to lay them out on a clean, dry tray and search for any foreign bodies that would cause an unpleasant crunch in your stew or an irreversible mechanical failure in your blender. Although it is a rather strange start to the chapter on 'main courses', while on the subject of chickpeas I have included a recipe for hummus, as a little hummus with crudités is a perfect precursor to any main course!

Cornucopia hummus   *v gf wf yf*

- 2x400g tins of chickpeas
  *(standard tins) or 200g dry
  chickpeas soaked overnight
  & cooked as per page 38*
- 100ml extra-virgin olive oil
- 130ml lemon juice
  (juice of 2-3 lemons)
- 1-1½ tbsp light tahini
- 2-3 cloves of garlic
- 1 tsp salt
- Pinch of pepper

Blend all the ingredients together in a food processor until smooth. In the case of the lemon, garlic and tahini, start with the smaller of the quantities suggested and add extra after tasting. If the hummus seems a little thick, add a splash of water. Serve in a toasted pita pocket or on brown bread or as a salad accompaniment.

Hummus also makes a delicious dip for crudités: serve it in a bowl, drizzled with olive oil, garnished with lemon wedges and surrounded by batons of raw chilled carrot, celery, cucumber, red pepper and florets of broccoli (see overleaf). Hummus can be stored in the fridge, covered, for up to 3 days.

Chickpea plant

Spanish chickpea casserole

v   gf   wf   yf   ♡   (cs)

When considering what recipes to include in the cookbook, we ran a month-long survey amongst customers asking for their suggestions and requests. Spanish chickpea casserole topped the main courses poll by a long shot, which came as a great surprise to some of the staff, who considered it 'just a simple ragout with chickpeas'. But simple is often best, of course, and Spanish chickpea casserole has enjoyed years of popularity in Cornucopia, whilst some other seemingly more adventurous stews have come and gone.

This dish appeals on many levels. Firstly, it is the good-looker of Cornucopia casseroles. On days when it appears on the menu, one is left in no doubt as to how much we really do eat with our eyes. Like a peacock in full mating display, it is impressively colourful and arrogantly self-assured. Customers approach the hot-food counter and, long before they've deciphered what dish is what, their eyes have been irresistibly drawn to the deep tomato red, the myriad roast vegetables and the dots of chickpeas in the Spanish casserole.

On top of its visual magnetism, for the creatures of habit amongst us, Spanish chickpea has all the familiar comfort of a tomato-y roast vegetable ragout, but with the novel addition of protein-packed chickpeas and a distinctively Spanish twist of oregano.

This dish is served in Cornucopia on brown rice. It is also delicious accompanied by roasted baby potatoes: allowing 5 or 6 baby potatoes per person, halve them and, in a bowl, toss them in a little olive oil, salt and pepper, a few sprigs of thyme and a pinch of paprika (optional). Transfer to baking trays and roast for 30-40 minutes or until golden brown and cooked through. An efficient system would be to roast the vegetables for the casserole (see step 1 below) and then use the baking trays and the hot oven to roast the potatoes, which, if the winds of fortune blow your way, will result in potatoes and casserole reaching completion at the same time!

First roast the vegetables. Preheat the oven to 200°C. Chop the courgette, aubergine and peppers into medium-size pieces and, keeping each vegetable separate, toss them in a bowl with a little olive oil, salt and pepper. Transfer to three separate baking trays and roast in the oven until soft, agitating once. The different vegetables will cook at different speeds.

When ready, set aside. If very oily, place the vegetables on kitchen paper to absorb some of the

1 courgette
1 aubergine
1 yellow pepper
1 red pepper
3 red onions
2 fennel bulbs
½ bulb garlic
50g *(medium bunch)* fresh
     oregano
2x400g tins of plum tomatoes
     (organic if possible) or 1kg
     ripe plum tomatoes
1x400g tin chickpeas
     (standard tin) — drained and
     rinsed or 100g dry chickpeas
     soaked overnight and cooked
     as per page 38
Juice of 1 lemon
Extra-virgin olive oil
Pinch of unrefined brown sugar
     (or dash of apple
     concentrate) — optional
salt and pepper
200ml water

Basil oil
Juice of ½ lemon
100ml extra-virgin olive oil
25g *(small bunch)* fresh basil
Pinch of salt

oil. Turn off the oven or, if making baby potatoes (see above), pop them in now.

While the vegetables are roasting, slice the onion, fennel and garlic thinly. Cover the base of a large pot with olive oil and heat over a medium ring. Add the onion, fennel and garlic. Stir to coat them with oil, cover with a lid, turn down to a low heat and sweat for 15 minutes, stirring occasionally.

Meanwhile, prepare the tomatoes. If you are using fresh tomatoes, they must first be deskinned. Cut an X into the skin of each, place them in a suitable bowl and pour boiling water over them. After one minute, drain the tomatoes and the skins can now be removed with ease. Chop them into quarters.

Now place the freshly skinned (in which case add 200ml water) or tinned tomatoes in a bowl and, removing the main stalks, add the oregano. Use a stick blender to blend the tomatoes and oregano to a smooth consistency. When the onion mix has sweated, add the herbed tomatoes to the pot, bring to gentle simmer and cook for 30 minutes, stirring occasionally. The sauce will reduce and thicken.

Finally, stir in the chickpeas and roast vegetables. Bring back to a simmer, add the lemon juice and season with salt and pepper. Add a pinch of brown sugar (or apple concentrate) to sweeten slightly if you like. Serve on a bed of rice or with roasted baby potatoes.

Basil oil

For an impressive finishing touch to your Spanish chickpea casserole, drizzle each dish decoratively

with a little basil oil. Blend the ingredients with a hand blender until smooth. This can be stored in the fridge for three days, but take it out an hour before use as it goes a little solid when chilled.

You can double the quantity of ingredients and thereby have some extra herb oil on hand for adding to pastas, drizzling over salad, swirling into soups or livening up a sandwich.

Cook's notes

Moroccan chickpea tagine
with orange-scented bulghar wheat

v yf cn (gf and wf if desired, see below)

This is a classic North-African spiced casserole with slow-cooked vegetables and dried fruit, served up on a bed of aromatic bulghar wheat. Tagines are traditionally served with couscous, but in Cornucopia we often use bulghar wheat, as it is a whole grain and therefore contains more nutrition, as well as adding a nice nutty texture. Chickpeas replace the traditional meat ingredient. From the moment you start cooking, the seven spices that go into this dish give off aromas so suggestive you may find yourself momentarily transported to a night market in Marrakech or to a sumptuously described scene from Paulo Coelho's *The Alchemist*.

The word 'tagine' refers to the special earthenware pot in which this dish is cooked, a wide-based, glazed pot with a tall conical lid, which ensures that the sauce does not lose too much moisture. The tagine is traditionally brought to the centre of the table with the lid removed, scattered with fresh herbs. As few of us have a traditional Moroccan earthenware pot at our disposal, a successful means of recreating this cooking method is to use a good-quality cast-iron pot with a heavy lid, which will allow you to cook the tagine really slowly, at a gentle simmer, without it drying out or sticking to the base of the pot.

This tagine is quite amenable to accommodating whatever fruit and vegetables you have in your kitchen. For example, try supplementing the dried apricots with prunes, dates or sultanas. Equally, try broccoli instead of courgette, butternut squash or baby potato instead of sweet potato, any colour pepper you can find rather than sticking to red pepper – as long as the balance of spices is about right, the results will be similarly delicious. On the subject of spices, there is one ingredient in this recipe that may prove a little difficult to source, that is sumac – a tangy, slightly citrusy, red-coloured spice. If you can't find it in your nearest Middle-Eastern or Asian food store, don't despair; proceed without it, as both the dried apricots and orange zest in the bulghar bring tanginess to the dish too.

The recipe for bulghar wheat to accompany the Moroccan tagine is remarkably tasty and definitely worth the extra effort. The zest of the orange marries wonderfully with the tang of the apricot in the casserole. And the toasted almonds add a pleasing crunch – an unexpected surprise.

Note: should you be cooking for anyone who cannot eat wheat or gluten, serve the tagine on rice instead.

For the tagine
2x400g tins of plum tomatoes
    (organic if possible) or 1kg
    ripe plum tomatoes
1 onion
1 carrot
2 courgettes
2 medium - large sweet potatoes
1 yellow pepper
150g green beans
25g *(small bunch)* fresh mint
8-10 dried apricots
2 tbsp ground cumin
1 tbsp ground coriander
½ tsp cayenne pepper
1 tsp sumac *(available in Middle*
    Eastern food stores)
5 crushed cardamom pods
2 quills of cinnamon
1 heaped tsp turmeric
1x400g tin of chickpeas
    (standard tin) — or 100g dry
    chickpeas soaked overnight
    and cooked as per page 38
25g *(small bunch)* fresh parsley
Unrefined sunflower oil
Salt and pepper

For the bulghar
400g *(dry weight)* bulghar wheat
400ml boiling water
1 tbsp extra-virgin olive oil
Zest of 2 oranges
100g flaked almonds
Salt and pepper

If you are cooking bulghar wheat to accompany the tagine, preheat your oven to a medium temperature and toast the flaked almonds until golden brown. Turn off the oven and set the almonds aside.

Now prepare the vegetables. If you are using fresh tomatoes, they must first be deskinned. Cut an X into the skin of each, place them in a suitable bowl and pour boiling water over them. After one minute, drain the tomatoes and the skins can now be removed with ease. Chop them in quarters.

Place the freshly skinned (in which case add 200ml water) or tinned tomatoes in a bowl and blend until smooth with a stick blender. Dice the onion and chop the carrot quite small. Chop the courgette into half moons about ½cm thick. Halve the green beans. Chop the sweet potato into medium-size chunks and the yellow pepper into medium squares. Quarter the dried apricots and chop the fresh mint finely. Keep all the vegetables separate.

Measure the seven spices into a bowl. To crush the cardamom pods, push down on them with the flat side of a chef's knife, or roll over them with a rolling pin. Coat the bottom of a large saucepan generously with sunflower oil and place over a medium heat. Add the spices and cook for five minutes, stirring very frequently to ensure they don't stick or burn. Next add the chopped onion and carrot and sauté for another five minutes, stirring occasionally.

Finally add the chopped tomatoes and about 300ml of cold water and bring to a gentle boil.

Turn down to a low heat, cover with a lid and simmer for 15 minutes, until the carrots start to soften.

While the tomato mix is simmering, bring a small pot of salted water to the boil. Blanch both the green beans (2 minutes) and the courgettes (2-3 minutes), ensuring that both retain a pleasant bite, as they will cook further in the heat of the stew. Refresh in cold water immediately after blanching, drain and set aside.

When the tomato mix has simmered for 15 minutes, add in the yellow pepper, sweet potato and chopped apricots. Leave the pot on a low heat, still lidded, for a further 15-20 minutes. Meanwhile, prepare the bulghar wheat. Place it in a suitable container and add a pinch of salt and pepper and a tablespoon of olive oil. Stir to distribute evenly, and then pour 400ml of boiling water over it. Cover and set aside, fluffing with a fork occasionally. When the bulghar is soft (10-15 minutes), stir in the zest of two oranges and the toasted almonds. Check the seasoning.

When all the vegetables in the tagine are almost soft, add in the chickpeas (if using tinned, drain and rinse them first), the blanched courgettes and green beans and the chopped mint. Season to taste and return to a simmer. Serve the tagine on bulghar wheat or brown rice scattered with a little chopped parsley.

Cook's notes

Thai green curry with chickpeas, squash & tofu

v   gf   wf   cn   (coconut)

It caused great amusement to some of us waiting staff when, a couple of years ago, a Chinese colleague, who was teaching us a few words of his mother tongue, informed us that a very typical way to say hello in his part of China was 'Chi le ma?' which translates directly as 'Have you eaten yet?' Now there's a country where food replaces weather as the central point of conversation, we noted. It reminded me that, when I visited Thailand a couple of years before that, my phrase book explained that a polite form of hello in southern Thailand is 'Gin gang ry wahnee?' – literally, 'What kind of curry are you eating today?' – an indication of just how many subtleties and variations exist within what we call Thai red, Thai green and Thai yellow curries. This is a Cornucopia deluxe vegetarian version of the basic Thai green curry, packed with protein from both chickpeas and tofu, loads of fresh vegetables, and a rich, spicy coconut broth. Using two green chillies will make a mild curry. If you prefer a spicier kick, use three, or maybe even four.

The typical Thai curry is cooked for a much shorter time than curries in India. They also use more fresh herbs and fewer dry spices. This dish, for example, requires a bunch each of Thai basil and coriander, which are blended and added to the broth not long before serving, turning it an attractive, fresh green hue. As is commonly known, leafy herbs lose their colour and flavour when exposed to heat for a prolonged period, so, once they've been added, bring the rest of the ingredients together quickly in the pot and, as soon as everything is hot, blow your whistle or bang your gong or ring your bell or do whatever is necessary to get the hungry hordes to the table NOW!

Preheat your oven to 200°C. Chop the butternut squash into chunky cubes. Toss them in a dessertspoon of sesame oil and a little salt and pepper and roast in the oven until soft (about 30 minutes), agitating once or twice. Turn off the oven and set the roast squash to one side.

Next, prepare the other vegetables. Dice the shallots (or onion) small. Chop the chillies and galangal (or ginger) finely. Chop the green pepper into medium pieces. Slice the carrot and courgette into delicate long diagonals. Separate the broccoli into bite-sized florets. Slice the babycorn in half lengthways.

½ butternut squash *(about 500g)*

2 shallots *(or 1 onion)*

1 green pepper

1 carrot

1 head of broccoli

1 courgette

100g mangetout

100g baby corn

2-3 green chillies

1 tbsp coriander seeds

1 thumb-sized piece of galangal
   (or ginger)

8 lime leaves

2 stalks of lemongrass

1 block *(200g)* creamed coconut

200g tofu

1x400g tin of chickpeas
   *(standard tin) or 100g dry
   chickpeas soaked overnight
   & cooked as per page 38*

25g fresh coriander

25g fresh thai basil *(or normal
   basil if unavailable)*

1 tbsp apple concentrate *(or 1
   dessertspoon of unrefined
   brown sugar)*

1 lime *(for garnish)*

1-2 tbsp tamari *(or shoyu/soy
   sauce, if not required to be
   gluten-free)*

Unrefined sunflower oil

Sesame oil

Salt and pepper

Bring a pot of salted water to the boil and, one by one, blanch the carrots, courgettes, broccoli, baby corn and mangetout, ensuring that they each retain a pleasant bite. Refresh each vegetable under cold water immediately. Approximate blanching times: carrots: 6-8 minutes; courgette, broccoli, mangetout, babycorn: 3 minutes.

With all the vegetables ready, coat the base of a large pot generously with half sunflower oil, half sesame oil and place over a medium heat. Add the shallots, chillies, galangal and coriander seeds and fry for 3 minutes, stirring constantly. Next add the green pepper and fry for another 3 minutes, continuing to stir. Finally, add about 200ml of cold water, cover with a lid and turn to a low heat to simmer.

Meanwhile, place the bruised lemongrass (hit it hard with the base of a saucepan to crush it slightly, which allows the flavours to emerge) and lime leaves into a pot with 500ml of water. Bring to the boil and leave to bubble vigorously until it has reduced by about half. Remove it from the heat and use a sieve to strain it into a bowl, discarding the lemongrass and lime leaves. Chop the creamed coconut into chunks and add it to the strained liquid, stirring to mix it in.

Next, pour the coconut infusion into the large pot with the spices and green pepper. Add 1 dessertspoon of apple concentrate (or 1 dessertspoon of unrefined brown sugar) and all the fresh coriander and basil (no need to chop them). Using a stick blender, blend this mixture until smooth. Chop the tofu into bite-sized chunks. Drain and rinse the tinned chickpeas.

Add both to the coconut and spice mix. Add all the blanched vegetables to the pot too and bring the whole lot back to a low simmer. Season with 1 or 2 tablespoons of tamari or shoyu, to taste.

This curry must be served immediately if it is to retain its bright, fresh green colour. Serve it in a bowl spooned over rice, garnished with a wedge of lime on the side, for those who want to add an extra zing.

Cook's notes

Sweet potato, broccoli & lentil sambar
v gf wf yf ♡

No other dish in Cornucopia achieves quite the same red-sky-at-night glow as the sambar. The meeting of turmeric with tomato and whatever other alchemy takes place produces an orange hue quite unique to the sambar, instantly recognisable by staff and regular customers alike.

Inside Cornucopia 'sambar' refers to this specific recipe, made with specific ingredients. However, outside of Cornucopia, 'sambar' refers more generally to a type of food preparation common in Southern India and Sri Lanka: cooking peas (*toovar dal*) and a variety of vegetables in a tamarind broth flavoured and thickened with 'sambar powder' (made of mixed spices and ground lentils). The basic Indian sambar is more soup-like than the Cornucopia one, as it tends to be one of several dishes at the table, whereas our recipe is a more Western-style meal unto itself, so it's packed with more vegetables and lentils.

This is about as healthy a hot dish as you are likely to find. It has plenty of protein (lentils are 26% protein), is high in fibre (lentils, sweet potatoes), low in fat and contains plenty of lightly cooked green vegetables (broccoli) and chunks of the highly nutritious and energy-rich sweet potato. Consider this for a journey: the sweet potato is native to Central America, where it is one of the oldest-known cultivated vegetables. It was tasted, enjoyed and brought back to Europe by Christopher Columbus in 1492, whereupon it began its integration into Mediterranean and North-African cuisine. It was brought east into Asia by Portuguese traders in the 16th century and established itself firmly in the cooking traditions of China, Japan and India. And sometime between the 16th century and the end of the 20th century, it made its way back from India to Ireland in the guise of a sambar, and entered the doors of Cornucopia, where it has remained ever since – a firm favourite of the I-like-stuff-that-goes-on-rice brigade.

If you are using fresh tomatoes, cut an X into the skin of each, place them in a suitable bowl and pour boiling water over them. After one minute, drain the tomatoes and the skins can now be removed with ease. Chop them into small chunks and set aside.

Next, prepare the vegetables. Dice the onions finely and chop the carrots quite small. Separate the broccoli into florets and chop the sweet potato into bite-sized chunks, not too small, as they will

1 onion
3 carrots
5 medium sweet potatoes
    (about 800g)
1 large or 2 small heads of
    broccoli
2x400g tins chopped tomatoes
    (organic if possible) or 1kg
    ripe plum tomatoes
150g red lentils
1 tbsp ground cumin
½ tbsp ground ginger
1½ tbsp fenugreek leaves
1 tbsp ground coriander
½ tbsp turmeric
½ tsp cayenne pepper
1 cinnamon quill, broken in half
Fresh coriander to garnish
    (optional)
Unrefined sunflower oil
Salt and pepper

structure the dish. Cover the sweet potato with cold water until you are ready to use it, to prevent it turning brown. Measure out all the spices and place them in a bowl, ready for use. Place the freshly skinned (in which case add 200ml water) or tinned tomatoes in a suitable bowl and, using a stick blender, blend until smooth.

Bring a pot of salted water to the boil. Rinse the lentils in a sieve, then add them to the pot. Stir to prevent them clumping together. Simmer for 8-10 minutes, stirring occasionally, until they have just turned yellow. Drain immediately and set aside. While the lentils are cooking, blanch the broccoli florets for 3 minutes in boiling water. Drain and refresh under cold water immediately.

Now cover the base of a large pot generously with sunflower oil and place over a medium heat. Add the spices, stirring constantly to prevent them sticking. After 2 minutes, add the diced onions and continue stirring for 3 minutes. Next add the carrots, fresh or tinned tomatoes and 500ml cold water. Cover with a lid, bring to a gentle simmer and reduce to a low heat, stirring occasionally. After 10 minutes, add the sweet potatoes and continue simmering for a further 15 minutes, or until the sweet potatoes and carrots are soft. Check them with the tip of a knife. Remove the cinnamon quill.

Finally, stir in the lentils and the broccoli. Season to taste. Bring back to a simmer and serve on rice. Garnish with some roughly chopped fresh coriander leaves, if desired.

Cook's notes

Ode to a sweet potato

The sweet potato, though relatively new to our shores, is beginning to establish itself as a staple of the Irish kitchen. One sweet potato provides stable, slow-release energy (about 80 calories) in the form of complex carbohydrates, is an excellent source of vitamin A, a very good source of vitamin C and a good source of dietary fibre and vitamin B6. Sweet potatoes are great vegetables for children, as not only are they nutritious and delicious, but they pack them up with energy too.

Sweet potatoes should be stored in a cool dark environment, but not in the fridge. They should be peeled and chopped just before cooking, as they will turn brown. Alternatively, after chopping, cover them in cold water until you are ready to use them.

I first encountered sweet potatoes when I lived in Japan. From late autumn, all through the cold winter months, sweet potato hawkers came up from the country and pushed their trolleys of hot coals out onto the streets of my town shouting 'Yaki-imo, ishi yaki-imo, oishii yaki-imo dayo' ('Baked sweet potato, baked on coals sweet potato, delicious baked sweet potato!'), with wafts of smoky, caramelised smells drifting on the breeze. The vendors simply wrap each sweet potato in foil and place it into the smouldering coals until soft, then remove them to cool a little before selling. To eat, you just unwrap the foil, tear open the skin of the potato and devour.

Baked sweet potato is so simple yet indescribably divine. To make it at home, wash the sweet potatoes, pierce the skin a few times with a fork and place on a baking tray. Bake in a 200°C oven for 45-70 minutes, depending on size. Alternatively, wrap in tinfoil and place over a barbecue. When cooked, they will be really soft and possibly oozing a little sticky liquid. Eat as is (skin and all if you like) or with a knob of butter and a hint of pepper or a tiny pinch of cinnamon.

Potato, pea & mushroom curry
gf wf ef cn

This is a creamy, mild curry, enriched by ground almonds and somewhat like a vegetable korma in colour, texture and taste. It is also level 1 in simplicity – a one-pot wonder with minimal preparation required, but rendering a fulsome and hearty dish, which requires nothing more than a bed of rice or a hot naan bread to complete it.

The ingredient that brings the recognisable yellow glow to this recipe is turmeric, which is used in Indian cuisine for both its taste and its dramatic colour. Closer to home, it provides the yellowness of English mustard, certain cheeses and many seemingly unnaturally yellow cakes, biscuits and sweets. It is also a spice that seems to have signed a pact of destruction with Murphy's Law – the law that states that whatever can go wrong, will go wrong. Turmeric is very, very yellow. The kind of yellow that might look out of place on a white tee shirt or an eggshell floor or a light pine table. Which is exactly where it has a terrible tendency to end up, if you're not careful. One of our much-loved chefs, Eddie Bates, was a demon with the turmeric. Korma was a staple on his repertoire, a dish which, in catering quantities, requires a good hearty cupful of turmeric. Somehow Eddie regularly managed to miss the pot, but showered himself, his workstation and the light blue floor in yellow dust, creating an artistic luminosity about the kitchen and bringing amusement to all but the evening chef who'd be cleaning up after him! So, beware the wandering turmeric.

As the evening chef who was faced once or twice with the fall-out of Eddie's famous turmeric tornadoes, I can only recommend hot sudsy water for the stained surfaces, followed by a few days ignoring the remaining yellow glow, at which point it seemed to forget itself and go away. As for clothing, a squeeze of lemon mixed with baking soda rubbed in then rubbed off, followed by regular washing, seems to remove most of the offending blotch.

Similar to all the stews and curries in this section, this recipe will feed four to eight people, depending on their size, hunger and the availability of other dishes. If you intend to hold some over until the next day, keep the frozen peas separate for that amount. Only add them in at the end of reheating, or they will lose their vibrancy and turn grey.

Firstly, prepare the vegetables. Dice the onion finely. Quarter the baby potatoes and halve the button mushrooms. Peel the garlic and ginger, chop them as well as the chillies (finely) and place them in a bowl with the turmeric, cardamom, cinnamon stick and bay leaves.

1 onion
2 cloves garlic
15 baby potatoes *(about 800g)*
30 button mushrooms
    (about 400g)
1 or 2 red chillies
1 thumb-size piece of ginger
¼ tsp ground cardamom
1 tbsp turmeric
1 cinnamon stick
3 bay leaves
400ml cream
400ml natural yoghurt
    *(preferably a thick
    Greek-style one)*
75g ground almonds
200g frozen peas
Unrefined sunflower oil
Salt and pepper

One red chilli will make a very mild curry; two will add a bit more kick.

Cover the base of a large pot generously with sunflower oil and place over a medium heat. Cook the diced onion in the oil for 5 minutes. Next, add the bowl of garlic, ginger and spices and cook for a further 3 minutes, stirring constantly to ensure the spices don't stick or burn.

Remove the pot from the heat and stir in the cream, yoghurt and 200ml cold water. Return to a medium heat and bring to a simmer, still stirring regularly. Now gently add the chopped potatoes, cover with a lid, reduce to a low heat and cook for 30 minutes. Remove the cinnamon stick and bay leaves. Add the mushrooms and cook for a further 5 minutes, or until they are tender.

When the potatoes and mushroom are cooked, stir in the ground almonds, season to taste and finally add the frozen peas. Bring back to a gentle simmer and serve on rice.

Cook's notes

Vegetable, noodle & marinated tofu stirfry

v ♡

Pretty much everyone who knows the basics of cooking has made a stirfry. So we did debate whether there was a place for stirfry in our cookbook. The answer came when we referred back to the aim of this book – to publish the tried and tested recipes that customers have favoured over the years. By which measure, this stirfry is one of the first past the post. When a big dish of it arrives out onto the counter, hot and steaming, straight from the wok, it immediately attracts attention and regularly sells out in a couple of minutes.

The key ingredient in this stirfry, that sets it head and shoulders above many others, is the marinated tofu: little mouthfuls of intense flavour hiding amongst the vegetables and noodles. It is essential to marinate the tofu first and then proceed with the other preparation, so that it has time to absorb as much of the shoyu, ginger and chilli as possible. In fact, if you can do this a couple of hours before making your stirfry, all the better.

Tofu is the major source of protein in the vegetarian diet of Buddhists in China and Japan and has become popular in the west as a low-fat, zero-cholesterol source of protein (it contains about 10% protein). It is also a good source of iron, calcium and magnesium. Tofu comes from the Japanese word *tou fu* which means bean curd. It is produced from milk pressed from soybeans in much the same method that cheese is produced from dairy milk. Unlike cheese, tofu has very little taste or smell and is therefore suitable for use in both sweet and savoury cooking. In order to taste delicious, it must be imbued with other flavours, such as the marinade in this recipe or the sweet ingredients in the tofu cheesecakes on pages 414-423.

Note: if you would like to make this recipe suitable for a gluten-free diet, replace the wheat noodles with rice noodles and replace the shoyu with tamari.

As mentioned above, if you can marinate the tofu a few hours before cooking, it will have plenty of time to absorb all the wonderful flavours. Peel the ginger and garlic and chop roughly. Chop the chillies roughly too. If you like only a hint of chilli, use one; if you prefer a spicy kick, use two. Using a stick blender or food processor, blend the shoyu, 50ml of sesame oil, ginger, chilli, garlic, star anise, cloves and fennel seeds until smooth. Chop the tofu into 1½cm cubes, place

1 pack *(400g)* firm tofu
1 red onion
1 carrot
75g baby corn
6 baby choi
75g green beans
75g mangetout
1 red pepper
1 small head broccoli
1 pack *(340g)* wheat noodles
    (or rice noodles)
Fresh coriander leaves to garnish
Handful of beansprouts to
    garnish *(optional)*
Sesame oil
Unrefined sunflower oil

For the marinade
200ml shoyu *(or good quality
    soy sauce or tamari)*
50ml sesame oil
1 thumb-sized piece ginger
1 or 2 red chillies
3 cloves garlic
1 star anise
3 cloves
1 tsp fennel seeds

in a suitable bowl and pour the marinade over them. Set aside to infuse.

Next, prepare the vegetables. Slice the red onion into thin moons. Slice the carrot into delicate batons. Halve the baby corns lengthways. Chop the baby choi into quarters and separate out the leaves. Slice the red pepper into thin strips. Separate the broccoli into small florets.

Bring a pot of salted water to the boil and blanch the broccoli, baby corn, mangetout and green beans (2-3 minutes) and carrots (5-6 minutes). Drain and refresh under cold water immediately. They should be quite *al dente*, as they will cook further in the wok. Make sure they are very well drained, as excess water will turn the stirfry into a stirbath.

Bring a fresh pot of water to the boil and cook the noodles according to the instructions on the packet. Stir them several times after plunging them into boiling water, to ensure they don't clump together. Take care not to overcook them, as they will make the stirfry mushy.

Now take your wok. All the stirfry ingredients should be within easy reach of the cooker, so you can add them easily and quickly. There are too many vegetables to successfully fry this off in one batch, so it will be done in two identical batches. Place the wok over a high heat and add a splash of both sesame oil and sunflower oil. Move the wok to coat all sides with oil. When the oils are beginning to smoke, throw in half the onion, carrot and pepper. Stir quickly with a wooden spoon for 2 minutes. Next, add half of all the other vegetables and stir for 2 minutes. Now spoon in half of the tofu and half of the marinade and stir again to incorporate. Finally add half of the noodles and, with a wooden spoon in each hand, fold all the ingredients together until heated through. Check the seasoning and add a splash extra shoyu or sesame oil if necessary. This recipe doesn't require salt and pepper.

Cover the first batch to keep it warm for the few minutes it takes to fry off the second batch. Alternatively, set the second batch aside for tomorrow. Serve garnished with chopped coriander and, if you fancy, a handful of fresh, crunchy beansprouts.

Creamy cauliflower, broccoli & leek gratin
ef

We make many kinds of creamy gratin in Cornucopia: the vegetables vary according to season, the breadcrumb topping varies according to the whim of the chef and the herbs vary according to what would best suit the other ingredients. The white sauce, or béchamel sauce, remains the same throughout and, once you've mastered that, you are equipped to make as many different gratin permutations and combinations as the contents of your kitchen and your imagination can conjure up.

Making a smooth, tasty béchamel sauce requires little more than patience. The milk is scalded with herbs and spices in advance and left to infuse for half an hour. When you make the sauce itself, measure the butter and flour out in advance and have the milk close by, ideally in a jug. Make sure to stir the flour in the melted butter for a full 3 minutes, so that it is fully cooked and, once you start to add the infused milk, do not be tempted to pour more than a little drop at a time, especially at the beginning: the more slowly you add the milk, the less likely your sauce is to develop lumps. Never stop stirring/whisking throughout, or the sauce will stick to the base of the pot and start to burn. If you do have the misfortune to produce a lumpy béchamel, all is not lost – you can push it through a sieve or blend it with a hand-held blender and no one but you will know the difference.

Imagine a cold winter's day. You fancy a good feed but are loath to leave the house to battle with whatever climatic misery pervades outdoors. This gratin is one which should not require a shopping trip, presuming you have butter, flour, milk, a few slices of bread and some vegetables, however disparate, at your disposal. The recipe can be adapted to whatever vegetables you have available – steam, boil, fry or roast them in advance. Make a plain or cheesy béchamel. To the breadcrumbs, add any seed, any herb. Your cupboards will provide you with the possibilities; your instincts will guide you as to what will taste good. Within an hour, you'll have a hot, creamy meal emerging from the oven, without having put your nose outside the door (unless you grow thyme in your back garden).

Preheat your oven to 180°C.

Start by infusing the milk for the béchamel sauce. Peel the onion and stud it with the 5 cloves. Place it in a small pot with the thyme, bay leaves, peppercorns and milk. Bring it to a gentle simmer, being very careful not to let it boil over – milk has a habit of leaping out of the pot rather suddenly.

For the béchamel sauce
850ml milk
½ onion
3 bay leaves
5 cloves
10 peppercorns
Few sprigs of thyme
70g butter
70g plain flour
Nutmeg *(freshly grated)*
150g vegetarian strong cheddar
   (use half of this in the sauce)
50ml extra-virgin olive oil
Salt and pepper

For the breadcrumbs
100g plain yeast bread
   (ensure bread does not
   contain E920)
75g pumpkin seeds
25g *(small bunch)* **fresh dill**
50ml extra-virgin olive oil
Salt and pepper

For the vegetable base
1 small or ½ large cauliflower
2 small or 1 large head
   of broccoli
2 carrots
3 leeks
Pinch of freshly grated nutmeg
Splash of vegetarian white wine
   (optional)
Extra-virgin olive oil
Salt and pepper

Turn off the heat and set the pot aside for at least 20 minutes to infuse.

Now make the breaded crust. Using a food processor, reduce the bread to fine crumbs. Chop the dill finely and place it in a bowl with the breadcrumbs, pumpkin seeds, a little salt and pepper and a splash of olive oil. Mix it all together.

Next, prepare the vegetables. Separate the cauliflower and broccoli into good chunky florets (to structure the gratin). Slice the carrots into delicate matchstick-like batons. Halve the leeks lengthways and then chop into medium squares. Wash them thoroughly in a big basin of water, rinsing several times. Set aside to drain.

Bring a large pot of salted water to the boil and, one by one, blanch the cauliflower, broccoli and carrots. They should take about 3-4 minutes each. Make sure they retain a pleasant bite, to avoid a mushy gratin. Refresh each vegetable in cold water immediately and set aside.

Next fry off the leeks in two batches. Coat the base of a frying pan with olive oil and place over a medium heat. When it is hot, add half of the leeks and, agitating regularly, fry until soft. Add a pinch of salt, pepper and a grating of nutmeg while they are frying. If you are feeling extra luxurious, add a splash of white wine to the pan about halfway through and allow the moisture to evaporate. Repeat for the second batch of leeks. Set aside.

Now make the béchamel sauce (white sauce). Remove all the bits from the infused milk by

Variations
Vegetable alternatives
Baby potato, mushroom
& baby spinach
Boil potatoes, pan-fry mushrooms,
pan-wilt spinach

Butter bean, leek & squash
1 tin butter beans, pan-fry leeks,
oven-roast squash

Celeriac, potato & red onion
Thinly slice and boil celeriac and
potato, oven-roast red onion

Some other vegetables that work
wonderfully well in gratins:
Courgettes (blanched or pan-fried),
asparagus (blanched or roasted),
fennel (blanched or roasted),
green beans (blanched) *& savoy*
cabbage (blanched or pan-fried),
red pepper (roasted)

Topping alternatives
(if using commercial bread,
ensure it has no E920)

Breadcrumbs, flaked almonds &
chopped chervil/parsley

Breadcrumbs, poppy seeds &
basil (blended into the olive oil)

Breadcrumbs with crumbled
vegetarian feta & thyme

pouring it through a sieve (you might like to transfer the milk to a jug, to make it easy to pour bit by bit into the sauce). Put the butter and a good splash of olive oil into a medium pot and place over a low heat. When the butter has melted, sprinkle in the flour, stirring constantly with a wooden spoon for 3 minutes to cook out the flour. It will come together into a paste.

Now, gradually add the infused milk. Start with a very small amount and stir until fully incorporated. Add a little more milk and, again, stir until fully incorporated. Repeat this procedure with great patience, always ensuring the sauce is of an even consistency before adding more milk. Initially, the sauce will keep thickening, but gradually it will take on the form of a creamy béchamel. When all the milk has been added, cook for a further 5 minutes (still stirring) and then remove from the heat.

Grate the cheddar and sprinkle half of it into the white sauce, stirring until it is fully melted. Add a grating of fresh nutmeg and season with salt and pepper. Next, assemble the gratin. Lightly butter the inside of a large casserole dish. Arrange the cauliflower, broccoli, carrot and leeks evenly inside. Pour the béchamel sauce over and smooth a little. Scatter the remaining cheddar cheese over the sauce and finally top with the breadcrumb mix. Bake in the oven for 25-30 minutes until the crust is golden. Serve with a crisp green salad, lightly dressed.

Leek, spinach & lentil nut roast
v   gf   wf   yf   cn

This recipe is a little piece of Cornucopia history, for it is no longer to be found on the hotplate in the restaurant. To introduce new recipes into our repertoire, so that the menu remains dynamic and adventurous, some old recipes have to be put into retirement. The nut roast is perhaps associated with 'old school' vegetarianism, or 'beard and sandals' cooking – quite earnest and unrefined and a little dated. As a result, it received its golden handshake five years ago in full recognition of many wonderful years' service to hungry lentil-lovers, in whose hearts it will live on, though they may have moved on to savouring more contemporary creations.

We believed for a long time that no original written recipe existed for the leek, spinach and lentil nut roast; that it had gone to the grave with its creator, Eddie Bates, on whose Saturday menu it made a regular appearance. Eddie's Saturday workbench permanently had a half-chopped leek floating around on it, ready to be thinly sliced onto his nut roasts as he assembled them over the course of the day. He took enormous pride in decorating the top of his roasts, sometimes simply with leeks and chopped nuts, sometimes with the colourful addition of rounds of red pepper or tomato.

Recently, Deirdre, our boss, was leafing through dusty folders of scraps of paper. I studiously ignored most of them until, lo and behold, there before me lay two sheets of jotter paper decorated by Eddie's hand with the coveted recipe for leek, spinach and lentil nut roast. Being a traditionalist by nature, I sequestered the relic to copy it down for my own reference. As I ran my eye over the simple ingredients and straightforward method, I recalled several devoted customers who used to smile broadly as soon as they spotted the nut roast on the counter. It may have been passed over by some customers in favour of a creamy lasagne, but those who liked Eddie's nut roast, boy did they like it! So for any fans out there of the leek, spinach and lentil nut roast, here it is, in all its nostalgic glory.

As I was cycling from home to the location of our recipe-testing early one day, equipped with the ingredients to cook and test this recipe in a domestic environment, a young man at a bus stop interrupted my pre-morning-coffee daze with a bellow of 'Here missus, you're leaking!' 'Hardy har' I muttered, presuming he was referring to the fact that a bunch of leeks was protruding from my sports bag, too long to fit in properly. Some hours later, having first made a couple of batches of bread, I reached for the leeks to start prepping the roast and was perplexed to discover only two leeks where once there were seven. With no vegetable shops in the vicinity and a time schedule to adhere to, I reprimanded the only imaginable culprit, Paco the dog, as I searched for leek scraps around his hangout zone. Then the witticism from the young man at the bus stop replayed itself in my head and the penny dropped. Back on my bike, I retraced my journey and found, scattered along the way, a trail of the missing five leeks.

Well-scrubbed, they did eventually find their way into a delicious nut roast, which, upon tasting, asserted itself as eminently worthy of inclusion in our book, a blast from the past perhaps, but a glorious blast from a valuable past.

For the nut roast
500g red lentils
300g nuts *(hazelnuts, cashew nuts, almonds, brazil nuts etc.)*
1 onion
2 medium carrots
2 stalks of celery
2 cloves of garlic
A few sprigs of fresh thyme
6 bay leaves
6 leeks
400g spinach or baby spinach
Freshly grated nutmeg
A few sprigs of fresh basil
Extra-virgin olive oil
Salt and pepper

For the lemon & parsley sauce
150g cooked red lentils *(from main batch)*
1 bulb of garlic — *roasted*
Juice of 1-1½ lemons
200ml vegetable stock — *(see page 184) or 200ml boiling water with ½ tsp of bouillon*
50g *(medium bunch)* fresh parsley
Extra-virgin olive oil
Salt and pepper

Preheat your oven to 180°C. Start by cooking the lentils. Bring a large pot of salted water to the boil. Add 2 bay leaves and the lentils and reduce to a simmer. Stir occasionally to prevent the lentils clumping together or sticking to the base of the pot. Cover with a lid and cook for 8-10 minutes, until soft and yellow. Drain in a sieve, remove the bay leaves and set aside. Do not be alarmed that the lentils are quite mushy.

When the oven is hot, spread the nuts out on a baking tray and toast in the oven for 8 minutes, tossing once or twice. Set aside to cool, rub them briskly to remove any loose skins and then chop them roughly.

Chop the top off the bulb of garlic (for the lemon and parsley sauce), toss the whole bulb in olive oil and place it in a small baking tray. Pour a little extra olive oil into the top to coat the cloves inside. Roast in the oven for 30 minutes, then set it aside to cool.

Next, chop the onion, carrot, celery and garlic (2 cloves) really finely. Coat the base of a large pot generously with olive oil, place over a medium heat and add the onion, carrot, celery, garlic, the sprigs of thyme and two bay leaves. Cover with a lid, reduce to a low heat and sweat for about 20 minutes, stirring regularly, until the vegetables are all just soft. Transfer to a large mixing bowl and remove the thyme and bay leaves.

While the vegetables are sweating, prepare the spinach and leeks. If using regular spinach, remove the stalks and wash and drain it thoroughly. Baby spinach generally comes pre-washed. Keep ½ of a leek separate and unchopped to be used later as a garnish. Slice the rest of the leeks in half lengthways and then into medium pieces. Wash well in a big sink of water and set aside to drain.

Now coat a frying pan sparsely with olive oil and place over a high heat. Add half the spinach and some salt, pepper and a grating of nutmeg and cook until the spinach is soft and most of the moisture has evaporated from the pan. Repeat with the second batch of spinach, or use two pans simultaneously. Add the cooked spinach to the mixing bowl. Again, coat the pan with oil, a little more liberally this time, and reduce to a medium heat. Throw in half the leeks and some salt, pepper and a bay leaf and fry until soft, stirring regularly. Repeat with the second batch of leeks. Add the cooked leeks to the mixing bowl and remove the bay leaves.

Next, mix all the ingredients for the nut roast. Keep aside 150g (about a cupful) of cooked lentils for the lemon and parsley sauce, then add the remainder to the mixing bowl. Keep aside about 50g of chopped nuts (for garnish) and add the rest of them to the mixing bowl. Finally chop the fresh basil finely and put that in too. Now, using a gentle touch, fold everything together and season with salt and pepper. Transfer the mix to a suitable baking dish and smooth it down.

To garnish, take the leek and slice into thin rounds, but at an angle so that they are oblongs.

Arrange them into lines on top of the bake and drizzle all over with a little olive oil. Scatter chopped nuts between the lines of leeks. Bake in the oven for 30 minutes.

While the nut roast is baking, make the parsley and lemon sauce. Place the 150g of cooked lentils into a suitable bowl and add 200ml of vegetable stock (see page 184) or water and bouillon, the squeezed out flesh from the roasted garlic and a dash of olive oil (use the oil from the garlic roasting if available). Use a stick blender to blend until smooth and then pass through a sieve (the finer the better) to make for a smooth sauce.

Finally add the lemon juice and parsley and blend again. Season with salt and pepper, place in a small pot and bring to a low simmer, ready to spoon over each portion of the nut roast when it emerges from the oven.

Potatoes

Three recipes involving mashed potato follow: two mashed potato pie recipes and one recipe for stuffed mushroom on mash with gravy. It's sort of the comfort food section, at least for Irish people, who tend to view nicely seasoned mashed potato as less like baby food and more like a grown-up's occasional right to the simple life — to food that only requires transfer from plate to mouth, at which point it kind of finds its own way into your tummy, no chewing necessary — a perfect antidote to the complications of modern life.

The modest mash must not be taken for granted, however, as I discovered years ago when I worked for a family in France as an au pair. On top of learning the language, as a city kid I hoped to pick up a few rustic cooking tips from this nature-based family, whose nearest neighbour was the bachelor dairy farmer several large fields away (from whom I collected a pail of warm, yellowish milk each evening). Our garden was bursting with vegetables all summer: big healthy lettuces and cabbages, spinach, courgettes, tomatoes, beans and peas of every shape and form, broccoli and carrots … And fine, boisterous chickens muscled their way around their extensive stomping ground, clucking with delight at each culinary treasure that they plucked from the earth and laying the most delicious eggs in exchange for their room and board. To add to our wealth of resources, the papa, a forest ranger, gathered fresh herbs and wild mushrooms during his woodland patrols, and the fields behind our house were replete with blueberries, whilst the cousins up the road ran a strawberry farm. We enjoyed fresh, delicious food every day and drank a tisane of forest leaves before bed every night.

Imagine my surprise when one day the maman, as usual, informed me of what I was to prepare for lunch. Salade verte from the garden, omelette aux herbes and pomme purée (mashed potato). I asked her where the potatoes were. She handed me a box of powder, to be reconstituted according to the instructions on the back. Even bearing in mind my possibly imperfect comprehension of the instructions, the resultant salty gloop was as far from mashed potato as orange squash is from a glass of freshly pressed juice. It was actually strangely satisfying in its own exotic way, but it also made me appreciate just how wholesome and hearty good old-fashioned mashed potato is.

When buying potatoes for mashing, go for floury (also described as starchy) as opposed to waxy varieties. Floury potatoes are quite dry, soft and crumbly and are best for baking, mashing, frying, chipping and roasting. Waxy potatoes are firmer and hold their shape, making them suitable for serving as boiled potatoes, for cooking in stews, as ingredients in gratins or as salad potatoes. Below are listed some of the popular potato varieties on the Irish market, as a guide for selecting a suitable potato for a particular dish.

	Floury		Waxy
	Desiree		Baby potatoes
	Golden wonder		Cara
	Kerr's pink		Cultra
	King Edward		Cyprus
	Maris piper		Homeguard
	Queens		Marfona
	Record		New potatoes
	Rooster		Pink fir apple
			Premier
			Saxon

When boiling potatoes for making a mash, always start them in cold salted water, bring to a boil and reduce to a gentle simmer, so they are not bashed about too violently. Steaming or pressure-cooking are useful for this. As soon as the potatoes are soft, drain in a colander and then return the potatoes to the now empty pot and place over a very low heat to allow as much moisture as possible to evaporate. Mash the potatoes with a little butter or olive oil while they are on the heat, encouraging further evaporation, so you get a light, fluffy mash. Simply add salt and pepper for a simple, classic, please-all mash. Alternatively, add further flavour and texture to your mashed potato with members of the onion family (pan-fried leeks, roast garlic, sautéed shallots, finely chopped spring onions), herbs (finely chopped dill, basil, parsley), mustard (wholegrain, Dijon) or even cheese (grated strong or smoked cheddar). Potatoes can also be combined with other mashed vegetables for delicious mashes: try combining two parts potato with one part boiled parsnip, celeriac or carrot.

White bean & roast Mediterranean vegetable pie with basil mash   *v gf wf yf* ♡ *(cs)*

A rich tomato sauce, replete with roasted vegetables and pearly white beans, topped with a crispy on top, soft in the middle mash, flavoured with basil and olive oil, spooned with ease from a hot pie dish, steaming and oozing flavour. The only problem we have ever had with this recipe is how to prepare enough of it to last the whole day in the restaurant. No matter how much is made, it stands up and walks off the hotplate at a rate of knots, selling out before evening. This is quite understandable: it contains delicious flavours of the Mediterranean combined with the familiar appeal of mashed potato — a lovely meeting of cultures.

If you are serving this for a more formal occasion than the average family dinner, try baking it in small individual ramekins — one per guest — and decorate each with a sprig of basil. Equally if you are preparing food for a household of one or two, freeze however many individual ramekins you don't require immediately and bake them one by one. If baking from the freezer, make sure the mini pie is fully defrosted first (this will take several hours). Cover with foil and bake in a medium oven for 30 minutes, then remove the foil and bake for a further 30 minutes, to ensure that the beans and vegetables have been exposed to a high temperature.

Preheat your oven to 200°C. Firstly, prepare the vegetables for the pie base. Chop the onion, carrot, celery and (peeled) garlic roughly and set aside (they will later be blended, so no need to be fussy). Chop the peppers, courgette and aubergine into medium-size pieces. Keeping each vegetable separate, toss them in a little olive oil, salt and pepper, transfer to three baking trays and roast in the oven until soft, turning once or twice. They will take different lengths of time to roast. While the vegetables are roasting, bring a small pot of salted water to the boil. Chop the fennel into medium pieces and blanch in boiling water for about 10 minutes, until soft. Drain and refresh immediately in cold water. Place the roasted peppers, courgette and aubergine and the blanched fennel in a bowl and set aside. Reduce the temperature of the oven to 180°C.

For the base
1 large onion
1 carrot
2 stalks of celery
3 cloves garlic
2 red peppers
1 large courgette
1 aubergine
1 fennel bulb
2x400g tins of plum tomatoes
*(organic if possible) or 1kg
ripe plum tomatoes*
1x400g tin butter beans *or
cannellini beans (standard
tin) or 100g dried
butter beans soaked
overnight and cooked as per
page 38*
25g *(small bunch)* fresh oregano
A few sprigs of rosemary
Pinch of unrefined brown sugar
*(or dash of apple
concentrate) — optional*
Extra-virgin olive oil
Salt and pepper

For the mash
6 large floury potatoes *(such as
roosters)* — about 1.6kg
25g *(small bunch)* basil
½ lemon
75ml extra-virgin olive oil
Salt and pepper

Next, make the red sauce. If you are using fresh tomatoes, they must first be deskinned. Cut an X into the skin of each, place them in a suitable bowl and pour boiling water over them. After one minute, drain the tomatoes and the skins can now be removed with ease. Chop them in quarters.

Remove the leaves from the stalks of rosemary and oregano. Cover the base of a large pot with olive oil and place over a medium heat. Add the roughly chopped onion, carrot, celery and garlic, as well as the rosemary and oregano leaves, to the pot, stir briefly, cover with a lid and reduce to a low heat to sweat for 15 minutes. Stir occasionally. Then add freshly skinned (in which case add 200ml water) or tinned tomatoes and simmer for a further 20 minutes, or until all the vegetables are really soft. Continue to stir occasionally. When the vegetables are cooked, blend the red sauce until smooth using a stick blender. Stir in all the roast vegetables and fennel. Drain and rinse the butter beans (or cannellini beans) and mix them in too. Season with salt and pepper. Add a dash of brown sugar or apple concentrate if you'd like to sweeten the sauce slightly.

Meanwhile, peel and quarter the potatoes. Place them in a large pot of salted water and bring to a boil. Reduce to a low heat, cover with a lid and simmer until soft. Drain in a colander, and then return the potatoes to the same pot over a very low heat to release as much moisture as possible. Remove from the ring and mash.

Place the fresh basil, juice of lemon, about 75-100ml of olive oil and a pinch of salt and pepper into a small container and, using a stick blender, blend until smooth. Pour this over the mashed potato and mash it in until evenly distributed. Check the seasoning.

To assemble the pie, place the tomato sauce with beans and vegetables into the base of a large and deep ovenproof dish. Spoon the mash on top, then use a spatula to smooth it over. Use the back of a knife to mark out a lattice on the smooth surface. Alternatively, use a piping bag to pipe the mash in an up and down motion onto the top of the pie. Or go for a more rustic look by simply crumbling the mashed potato over the tomato mix with clean hands.

Now place the pie in the preheated oven for about 30 minutes, or until the mash is a crispy, light-brown colour and the tomato juice is bubbling around the edges. Serve with some lightly cooked greens or with a crisp green salad.

Pumpkin, courgette & green lentil pie with mustard & dill mash   *v gf wf ♡*

This is basically a vegetarian shepherd's pie. Although you may not have been wandering the hilltops tending woolly livestock all day, this is definitely a dish best enjoyed with a hearty appetite — at the end of a day's hiking or after a match or a marathon, or to celebrate the end of a 24-hour fast. If you've got a mighty hunger on you, this pie will go all the way to filling you up. It's packed with pumpkin and courgette, complete with green lentils, immersed in a flavour-loaded brown sauce and topped with a tangy mash; all you need is a big glass of milk or soymilk to wash it down!

Ideally, source local pumpkins for your pie, available in Ireland from about October to January, especially in colourful stacks at farmers' markets. Alternatively, butternut squash are available all year round. A tip for peeling pumpkins is to cut them into eight or ten moon-shaped wedges first, trying to follow the natural indentations in the vegetable. It's far easier to peel each wedge one by one than to tackle the undulating and delightfully gnarled surface of a sizeable pumpkin. As for what to do with the unused half of the pumpkin, try combining it, and your leftover stock (see below), in a top-class version of the roast squash soup on page 70. Simply replace the butternut squash with your half pumpkin and some of the water with stock and proceed directly to heavenly soup.

The recipe requires half a litre of vegetable stock, but provides for an alternative of hot water and a spoon of bouillon. If buying bouillon, try to source a low-salt (low-sodium), additive-free, vegan bouillon (organic if possible), which can be found in health food shops. Of course, if you have the time, preparing your own vegetable stock is preferable (follow the recipe on page 184, use 500ml in your pie base and freeze the rest or use it immediately for a delicious soup) substituting it for some of the water in any of the soup recipes in this book to add an extra dimension of flavour.

Preheat your oven to 200°C.

Start by preparing the vegetables for the base. Chop the onions, carrots and garlic very finely and set aside. Chop the pumpkin (or squash) into medium-size cubes, toss in a little olive oil, salt and pepper, and roast in the oven for about 30 minutes or until soft, agitating once during roasting. When fully cooked, set aside. Reduce the oven to 180°C. Meanwhile, slice the courgettes into ½cm-thick rounds. Heat a little olive oil in a pan

For the base
2 onions
2 carrots
3 cloves garlic
½ medium pumpkin *(or 1 medium butternut squash)* — about 700g
3 courgettes
300g green lentils *(or puy lentils)*
4 bay leaves *(2 for lentils, 2 for sauce)*
A few sprigs of fresh thyme
2 heaped tsp paprika
150ml vegetarian red wine
2 tbsp tomato purée
300ml vegetable stock *(see page 184) or 500ml boiling water plus 1 heaped tsp good-quality bouillon*
4 tbsp (60ml) tamari *(or shoyu if not required to be gluten-free)*
Extra-virgin olive oil

For the mash
6 large floury potatoes *(such as roosters)* — about 1.6kg
25g *(small bunch)* fresh dill
1-2tbsp wholegrain mustard
Pinch of freshly ground nutmeg
Extra-virgin olive oil
Salt and pepper

and place over a medium heat. Place a single layer of courgettes into the pan and top with a little salt and pepper. When slightly browned on one side, turn and brown the other side. Repeat with a second batch of courgettes if necessary.

Next, prepare the lentils. Bring a small pot of salted water to the boil. Add 2 bay leaves and the lentils and reduce to a simmer. Stir occasionally to prevent the lentils clumping together or sticking to the base of the pot. Cover with a lid and cook for 15-20 minutes, or until tender but not mushy. Rinse well under cold water, drain, remove the bay leaves and set aside.

Now make the sauce for the base. Coat the base of a large pot generously with olive oil and place over a medium heat. Add the finely chopped carrots, onions and garlic, as well as the other 2 bay leaves and the sprigs of thyme. Stir briefly, cover with a lid and turn down to a low temperature to sweat for 15 minutes. Next, add the paprika and red wine and reduce until almost all the liquid has cooked off. Finally, add the tomato purée, tamari (or shoyu) and vegetable stock (or bouillon and water). Simmer the sauce until it is well reduced and all the vegetables are cooked (about 15 minutes). When the sauce is ready, stir in the pumpkin, courgette and lentils. Check the seasoning — a twist of pepper would be nice, but, due to the tamari, it may not require any salt. Set aside.

While the sauce is cooking, peel and quarter the potatoes. Place them in a large pot of salted water and bring to the boil. Reduce to a low heat, cover with a lid and simmer until soft. Drain in a colander, and then return the potatoes to the same pot over a very low heat to release as much moisture as possible. Remove from the ring and mash.

Place the mustard, roughly chopped dill, nutmeg and about 75-100ml of olive oil into a small container and, using a stick blender, blend until smooth. Pour this over the mashed potato and mash it in until evenly distributed. Season with salt and pepper.

To assemble the pie, place the lentil and roast vegetable sauce into the base of a large, deep ovenproof dish. Spoon the mash on top and smooth it over with a spatula. Use the back of a knife to mark out a lattice on the smooth surface. Alternatively, use a piping bag to pipe the mash in an up and down motion onto the top of the pie. For a simpler method and more natural look, simply crumble the mashed potato over the base with your hands.

Now place the pie in the preheated oven for about 30 minutes, or until the mash is a crispy, light-brown colour and the base juice is bubbling around the edges. Serve with some lightly cooked greens.

Variations
Here are two alternative versions of this tasty pie to try:

Mushroom, leek & green lentil pie
Omit the pumpkin and courgette. Replace with similar quantities of pan-fried (or oven-roasted) mushrooms and leeks. Proceed with the rest of the recipe as normal.

Spinach, cauliflower
& puy lentil pie
Omit the pumpkin, courgette and green lentils. Replace with cauliflower (blanched in boiling water), spinach (wilted in a pan) and puy lentils. Follow the rest of the recipe as normal.

Baked Portobello mushrooms on leek mash with onion gravy *ef cn cs*

This meal of meals was created in recent years by Tony Keogh, our present head chef and culinary leading light, who considers it 'mash and gravy heaven'. It bears many hallmarks of his favourite ingredients: good-quality cheese, chunky mushrooms, a dash of tamari here, a generous knob of real butter there. The result is a big, wholesome plate of grub – unashamedly rustic, not an air of refinement about it.

Portobello mushrooms are large, brown, musky-scented mushrooms, perfect for stuffing, as their thick flesh holds firm in the oven. They are called *cappellone* in Italian, meaning big hat, for their elegant domed cap is a cut above the average mushroom. As you will be paying rather more than the average mushroom price, make sure you choose your Portobellos carefully – they should be plump, earthy and bone-dry. Avoid any that appear shrivelled or in any way slippery (they're starting to go off). Store them in the fridge with a free flow of air around them. As with all mushrooms, Portobellos should not be washed, but rather tapped free of any debris and then wiped clean with slightly damp kitchen paper or a clean cloth.

As is visible from the ingredients, this recipe falls simply into three parts: stuffed mushroom, gravy, mash. However, making them one by one would result in two parts being cold when the third part is finally ready. So the method below is laid out to have all three elements reaching a hot, table-ready state at approximately the same time. As the ingredients are listed separately, it's quite easy to make just the mushrooms (perhaps for a fancy breakfast) or just the gravy (should you require some juice for a veggie burger) or just the mash (as a side-dish for a Sunday dinner) – just glance through the method for the relevant bits.

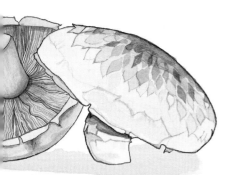

Preheat your oven to 180°C.

Gravy
Start by slicing the onions and garlic for the gravy very finely (they will not be blended). Into a large pot, put 50g butter and 50ml olive oil and place over a high heat. When the butter has melted, add the onions, stirring continuously for 3-4 minutes. Now add the spoon of sugar, garlic and bay leaves, reduce to a very low heat, cover with a lid and sweat for 20 minutes, until the onions are translucent and very soft. Stir the pot occasionally to prevent the onions sticking

For the onion gravy
3 onions
3 cloves garlic
1 tbsp unrefined brown sugar
2 bay leaves
400ml vegetable stock
    (see page 184) or 400ml
    boiling water and 1 heaped
    tsp good-quality bouillon
50ml tamari *(or shoyu)*
50g butter
50ml extra-virgin olive oil
Pepper

For the mushrooms
6 large Portobello mushrooms
200g Gubbeen cheese *(or any*
    vegetarian Irish farmhouse
    cheese, strong cheddar
    or regato)
200g plain yeast bread *(ensure it*
    does not contain E920)
200g walnuts
25g *(small bunch)* fresh parsley
50ml extra-virgin olive oil
Salt and pepper

For the mash
6 large floury potatoes
    (such as roosters)
    — about 1.6kg
2 leeks
100g butter
100ml hot milk
Pinch of freshly grated nutmeg
Salt and pepper

or burning. Next, add the stock (or water and bouillon) and a good twist of black pepper, bring to the boil, then reduce to a simmer. To thicken the gravy slightly, remove one ladleful of the mix and, in a small bowl, use a stick blender to blend it to a smooth consistency. Return this to the pot and stir it in. Finally add the tamari and check the seasoning. Turn off the heat and set aside.

Mushrooms
Next prepare the mushrooms. Wipe the Portobellos clean with some slightly damp kitchen paper, remove the stalk and brush them with a little olive oil on both sides and sprinkle with salt and pepper. Lay them cap-side down on an oiled baking tray, ready for stuffing.

Now, make the stuffing. Grate the Gubbeen cheese and place it in a large mixing bowl. Using a food processor, blend the bread into fine crumbs and transfer to the mixing bowl. Next, place the walnuts in the food processor and, using the pulse setting, mill them until they appear roughly chopped (or roughly chop them by hand) and transfer them to the mixing bowl. Finally, place the fresh parsley and 50ml olive oil (3 tbsp) into the food processor, blend together and transfer to the mixing bowl.

Add a twist of black pepper and mix to combine. Fill the six mushrooms generously with this stuffing. Don't press down on the mix too firmly – leave it quite loose. Don't cook the mushrooms quite yet; set them aside until the potatoes are almost ready.

Mash

To prepare the mashed potatoes, peel and quarter the potatoes and place them in a large pot of salted water. Cover with a lid, bring to the boil, reduce to a low heat and simmer until soft. Drain in a colander, and then return the potatoes to the same pot over a very low heat to release as much moisture as possible. Remove from the ring and mash.

While the potatoes are cooking, slice the leeks down the middle, chop them into small pieces, rinse them in a big basin of water and drain thoroughly. Now, pan-fry the leeks. Place 100g of butter in a frying pan over a medium heat. When it has melted, add the leeks, reduce to a low heat and, stirring regularly, cook until soft.

Transfer the mushrooms to the oven. Bake them on the middle or bottom shelf for 15-20 minutes, until the mushrooms are soft, the breadcrumbs are golden and the cheese oozing. While they are cooking, return the mashed potato to a very low heat and add the leeks, nutmeg, hot milk and a little salt and pepper and fold it all together until evenly combined. Check the seasoning, remove from the heat and cover to keep warm. At the same, bring the gravy back to a simmer. As soon as the mushrooms are ready, serve each one on a bed of mash with a liberal ladle of onion gravy. For a slightly more stylish presentation, use a ring mould to shape a round of mash, top it with a mushroom and surround this island with a moat of gravy. Tuck in!

Delicious vegan gravy

To make a wonderful vegan gravy for serving on mashed or roast potatoes, vegetables, nut roasts, etc, follow the gravy instructions for this recipe, with the following changes:

Instead of starting with 50g butter and 50ml olive oil, start with 75ml olive oil.

At the same time as you add the stock (or water and bouillon), add 1 tablespoon of Dijon mustard.

Two cannelloni recipes

Two recipes for cannelloni are introduced in the next few pages. Both use vegetarian cream cheese as a basis for the filling and both are baked in a rich tomato sauce. The first recipe combines toasted hazelnuts with oodles of spinach. The second marries roast butternut squash with sage and regato cheese. Both require a stick blender, food processor and piping bag, so beware the washing up! These dishes enjoy a solid customer fan-base, particularly as aficionados know exactly when they are available ...

Sundays at Cornucopia have become synonymous with the word cannelloni. We are not a restaurant that usually builds its menu around the days of the week. However, over the past few years, ne'er a Sunday has gone by that we have not had cannelloni as one of the main courses. There is one quite simple explanation – cannelloni is really popular, so we truly want to feature it on the menu. But it's also rather fiddly and labour-intensive to pipe each individual tube of pasta. In a busy weekday kitchen, it's almost impossible for one chef to keep up with demand without abandoning all his other pots. In contrast, Sunday trade is both more leisurely and more evenly paced, making it a perfect day to serve up the time-consuming yet worth-every-minute cannelloni without causing the chef of the day to lose his mind with cannelloni-induced stress!

It turns out we weren't too far off the mark making Sunday 'cannelloni day'. This particular tubular pasta was invented in 1907 by Salvatore Colette, a chef in the Sorrentine (Sorrento, SW Italy) restaurant of O Parrucchiano. It was an instant hit and soon became known as cannelloni, meaning 'large reeds'. During World War II, many quite wealthy families moved to Sorrento from Naples to escape persistent bombing. Salvatore's cannelloni had a whole new audience and experienced an irreversible boom, especially on Sundays, as a rich and delicious family day out treat on the Roman Catholic day of rest. So following authentic Italian tradition, we have established cannelloni as a Sunday indulgence!

The most common phrase of communication between waiting staff and kitchen staff in Cornucopia is 'Can I call (add name of dish/soup)'. The counter staff are responsible for letting the chefs know what items are running low by calling the dish when it is about ten minutes away from selling out: 'Can I call tomato soup?', 'Sorry, I forgot to call the gratin, it's all gone', 'Could you call food for me while I'm on my break?' A seemingly unrelated fact is that counter staff are welcome to bring home any food that is left on the hotplate when the restaurant closes. It is not entirely unusual for cannelloni to be 'called' rather over-zealously on Sunday evenings, perhaps long before it is halfway sold, ensuring that a fresh cannelloni appears on the hotplate only minutes before closing time, thus increasing the likelihood that the many cannelloni enthusiasts working that day will be dishing a few portions into their Tupperware containers to enjoy at leisure when they go home. What better advertisement for the deliciousness of a dish than that the staff, having spent eight or ten hours serving it, still use every trick in the book to ensure that they'll be tucking into it themselves for their tea!

A few tips before you embark on your cannelloni voyage:

- This may seem obvious, but it's best to choose a square or rectangular oven dish for baking your cannelloni, as an oval dish doesn't lend itself kindly to lining up the pasta neatly.
- When you are blending the filling for the cannelloni, try to make it as smooth as possible to make it easy to pipe, otherwise the muscles in your hand and forearm will get an unexpectedly rigorous workout.
- To achieve optimum smoothness, divide your filling ingredients into two or three identical batches and blend in small quantities, allowing the food processor to do its job more thoroughly and without leaping wildly around due to overload.
- If you do not have a piping bag, it's entirely possible to stuff the cannelloni with a teaspoon, scraping it in bit by bit and using whatever means you like to advance the mixture along the tube.
- Should you enjoy dabbling in the art of homemade pasta (see overleaf for recipe), for cannelloni cut your rolled-out pasta into 10cm (4in) squares, spoon the filling along one length, slightly in from the edge, roll up and transfer to a baking dish, sealed side facing down. Reduce the cannelloni oven time to 25 minutes if using fresh homemade pasta.

The two cannelloni recipes that follow are both delicious and extremely filling. It may not seem like a lot, but allow 3 or 4 tubes of cannelloni per portion. Remember that the filling is dense with cream cheese and nuts in one recipe and cream cheese, regato and squash in the other, so a small quantity is actually very satisfying, especially with a crisp green salad to clean the palate between mouthfuls.

Homemade egg pasta

Making your own fresh pasta is a lot easier than you might imagine, and it is head and shoulders above dried pasta in taste. In addition, many commercial dried/fresh pastas are made with battery eggs; by making fresh pasta you can ensure free-range eggs are used. This same basic recipe can be used for all forms of pasta.

If you have a pasta maker or pasta extruder, you can use different machine fittings to turn out a variety of shapes, from penne to spaghetti (length of cord) and linguine (little tongues). If you are relying on rolling out and hand cutting your pasta, then cannelloni, farfalle (butterflies; we call them bow-ties), lasagne, ravioli and tagiatelli are most readily achievable.

This recipe uses '00' Italian flour, which is available from shops stocking speciality Italian foodstuffs. If you cannot lay your hands on some '00', then unbleached strong flour will do fine. You can also use half wholemeal brown flour and half strong white flour for wholemeal pasta; wholemeal pasta is more prone to crumbling, so handle with care. The ratio of flour to egg is 100g flour to 1 free-range egg, and this serves one person, so you can scale up or down the quantities below.

To serve 4 people
400g '00' Italian flour
(or strong white flour)
4 free-range eggs
Pinch of salt
Drop of olive oil

Sift the flour into a mixing bowl and stir in a pinch of salt. Whisk the eggs in a separate bowl. Form a well in the centre of the flour and pour in the eggs, as well as a small splash of olive oil. Bring the dough together into a soft ball, cover with a clean tea towel and let it rest for 5 minutes.

On a lightly floured surface, roll out the pasta until it is about 2mm thick. Use a sharp knife or a serrated roller to cut it into the desired shapes. To cut long ribbons, such as tagliatelle, cut a 30cm square, fold it over loosely several times and then slice the ribbons one by one — they'll open back out as soon as they are plunged into water.

Fresh pasta should be plunged into a large pot of boiling salted water for 2 minutes to be *al dente* (3 minutes for wholemeal) and then drained immediately. In the case of lasagne or cannelloni, it is baked in its sauce in the oven for 25 minutes.

Tagliatelle
6mm-wide long ribbons

....

Farfalle
4cm squares (pinched together in the
centre to form a 'bow-tie')
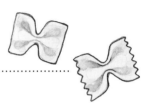
....

Ravioli
4cm squares (two sandwiched
together with filling)

....

Lasagne
10cmx20cm rectangles

....

Cannelloni
10cm squares (rolled around filling)

....

Spinach & hazelnut cannelloni in tomato sauce with basil oil *cn* *(cs)*

This recipe requires a piping bag with wide nozzle.

Note: some brands of cannelloni contain eggs. If so, make sure they are free-range. Alternatively, see page 244 for a recipe for fresh pasta.

Preheat your oven to 180°C. Start by preparing the cannelloni filling. Spread the hazelnuts out on a tray and toast them in the oven for 8 minutes, shaking once or twice. Set them aside to cool. When they are cool enough to be handled, rub them with your hands to remove the loose skins. No need to be too fastidious. Next, chop the cannelloni-filling onions quite small and finely slice the garlic. Coat the base of a medium pot generously with olive oil and place over a medium heat. Add the onions, garlic and bay leaves and stir briefly, cover with a lid and reduce to a low heat to sweat for 15-20 minutes, stirring occasionally, until the onions are translucent. Remove the bay leaves.

Meanwhile, prepare the spinach. If using regular spinach, remove the large stalks and wash and drain it thoroughly. Baby spinach usually comes pre-washed. Coat a frying pan sparsely with olive oil and place over a relatively high heat. When the pan is hot, add half the spinach, along with salt, pepper and a grating of nutmeg. Stirring regularly, wilt the spinach until it is cooked and the moisture has evaporated from the pan. Repeat for the second batch of spinach. Now leave the filling ingredients to one side to cool.

Next, make the tomato sauce. If you are using fresh tomatoes, they must first be deskinned. Cut an X into the skin of each, place them in a

For the cannelloni filling
150g hazelnuts
2 small onions
2 cloves of garlic
2 bay leaves
400g spinach *(or baby spinach)*
200g vegetarian cream cheese
300ml cream
Freshly grated nutmeg
Extra-virgin olive oil
Salt and pepper
16-20 cannelloni tubes *(less than
    1 standard box) or see page
    244 for fresh pasta recipe*

For the tomato sauce
1 onion
1 carrot
2 stalks of celery
3 cloves garlic
25g *(small bunch)* oregano
125ml vegetarian red wine
2x400g tins of plum tomatoes
    *(organic if possible) or 1kg
    ripe plum tomatoes*
Pinch unrefined brown sugar
    *(or dash of apple
    concentrate) — optional*
Extra-virgin olive oil
Salt and pepper

For the basil oil
50g *(medium bunch)* fresh basil
125ml extra-virgin olive oil
Juice of ½ lemon
Salt and pepper

suitable bowl and pour boiling water over them. After one minute, drain the tomatoes and the skins can now be removed with ease. Chop them in quarters and set aside.

Roughly chop the onion, carrot, celery and garlic. They will be blended, so no need to be too fussy. Cover the base of a large pot with olive oil and place over a medium heat. Add the onion, carrot, celery and garlic, cover with a lid, reduce to a low heat and sweat for about 15 minutes, stirring regularly. While the vegetables are sweating, remove the leaves from the stalks of oregano. After 15 minutes, add the oregano leaves and red wine to the pot and bring to a gentle simmer for 5 minutes. Finally, add the freshly skinned (in which case add 200ml water) or tinned tomatoes. Bring the sauce back to a simmer and allow it to cook gently on a low heat for 30 minutes to reduce. Stir regularly to prevent sticking and burning.

When the sauce has cooked fully, use a stick blender to blend it to a smooth consistency. Season with salt and pepper and set aside. Add a pinch of brown sugar (or apple concentrate) if you would like to sweeten the sauce slightly.

While the sauce is reducing, combine the cooled filling ingredients in a food processor. If you have a small food processor, this should be done in two identical batches. Blend together the hazelnuts, spinach, onions, cream cheese, 200ml cream (retain 100ml for later) and a grating of nutmeg. Make sure the mix is quite smooth, for ease of piping. Season with salt and pepper.

Line your cannelloni tubes up in an ovenproof dish. Fill a piping bag with some filling and pipe the cannelloni tubes full of cream cheese mix (see illustration), laying them down side by side in two rows in the baking dish. Continue until all the mix has been piped.

Now cover the cannelloni tubes with red sauce, so they are completely submerged. Drizzle the remaining 100ml of cream over the tomato sauce in a zigzag motion. Bake the cannelloni in the oven for 35-40 minutes. To check if the pasta is cooked, press with the tip of a knife and ensure it is soft. Let rest for 5 minutes before serving.

While the pasta is cooking, blend all the ingredients for the basil oil together until smooth. To serve, transfer 3 or 4 tubes of cannelloni and sauce to each plate, and drizzle each portion artfully with some basil oil. Serve with some lightly cooked greens or a crisp green salad.

Butternut squash & regato cannelloni in tomato sauce

cn   (cs)

This recipe requires a piping bag with wide nozzle.

Note: some brands of cannelloni contain eggs. If so, make sure they are free-range. Alternatively, see page 244 for a recipe for fresh pasta.

Preheat your oven to 200°C. Start by preparing the roast squash (or pumpkin). Chop the squash into medium chunks (random shapes are fine, as it will be blended). Toss it in a little olive oil, salt and pepper and transfer to two baking trays. Roast in the oven for about 40 minutes, until soft, turning once or twice. Set aside to cool. Reduce the oven to 180°C. Next, chop the cannelloni-filling onions quite small and slice the garlic finely. Coat the base of a medium pot with olive oil and place over a medium heat. Add the onions and garlic, stir briefly, cover with a lid and sweat for 15 minutes, until soft, stirring occasionally. While the onions are sweating, chop the 15 sage leaves roughly and add them to the pot too. Set both the butternut squash and the onions aside to cool right down, as they can't be blended with the cream cheese while still warm.

Next, make the tomato sauce, exactly as in the previous recipe. If you are using fresh tomatoes, they must first be deskinned. Cut an X into the skin of each, place them in a suitable bowl and pour boiling water over them. After one minute, drain the tomatoes and the skins can now be removed with ease. Chop them in quarters and set aside.

Roughly chop the onion, carrot, celery and garlic. They will be blended, so no need to be too fussy. Cover the base of a large pot with olive oil and place over a medium heat. Add the onion, carrot, celery and garlic, cover with a lid, reduce to a low heat and sweat for about 15 minutes, stirring regularly. While the vegetables are sweating, remove the leaves from the stalks of oregano. After 15 minutes, add the oregano leaves and red wine to the pot and bring to a gentle simmer for 5 minutes. Finally, add the freshly skinned (in which

For the cannelloni filling
1 large butternut squash *(about
     900g) or equivalent weight
     of seasonal local pumpkin*
2 onions
2 cloves of garlic
About 15 leaves of fresh sage
200g vegetarian regato cheese
200g vegetarian cream cheese
100-200ml cream
50g butter
Pinch of freshly ground nutmeg
16-20 tubes of cannelloni
     *(less than one standard box)
     or see page 244 for fresh
     pasta recipe*
Extra-virgin olive oil
Salt and pepper

For the tomato sauce
1 onion
1 carrot
2 stalks of celery
3 cloves garlic
25g *(small bunch)* oregano
125ml vegetarian red wine
2x400g tins of plum tomatoes
     *(organic if possible) or 1kg
     ripe plum tomatoes*
Pinch of unrefined brown sugar
     *(or a dash of apple
     concentrate) — optional*
Extra-virgin olive oil
Salt and pepper

case add 200ml water) or tinned tomatoes. Bring the sauce back to a simmer and allow it to cook gently on a low heat for 30 minutes so the sauce can reduce. Stir regularly to prevent sticking and burning. When the sauce has cooked fully, use a stick blender to blend it to a smooth consistency. Season with salt and pepper. If you would like to sweeten the sauce slightly, add a pinch of brown sugar or a dash of apple concentrate.

While the sauce is reducing, combine the filling ingredients in a food processor. If you have a small food processor, this should be done in two identical batches. Blend together the roast squash, onions and sage, cream cheese, nutmeg and 100ml of cream. Season with salt and pepper. If the mix seems too stiff to pipe, add a little more cream (it will depend on the consistency of the squash).

Now finely grate the regato cheese. Add about ½ of it to the cream cheese mixture (just stir it in), keeping the rest to one side. Line the cannelloni tubes up in an ovenproof dish. Fill a piping bag with some filling and pipe the cannelloni tubes full of cream cheese mix (see page 248), laying them down side by side in two rows in the baking dish. Continue until all the mix has been piped.

Cover the cannelloni tubes with all the red sauce, so they are completely submerged. Bake in the oven for 35-40 minutes. Halfway through cooking, scatter the remaining regato cheese evenly over the red sauce. To check if the pasta is cooked, press with the tip of a knife and ensure it is soft. Let it rest for 5 minutes and then serve with some lightly cooked greens or a crisp green salad.

Roast squash, courgette & spinach lasagne *(cs)*

Note: fresh lasagne and some dried lasagne contain eggs. If so, ensure that they are free-range. Alternatively, see page 244 for a fresh pasta recipe.

Lasagne. It's a nostalgic word for anyone who was a vegetarian in the eighties in Ireland when vegetable lasagne was the standard offering in every hotel, restaurant and dinner party for anyone who raised their hand tentatively to ask, 'What do you have for vegetarians?' It was usually served nestled up against a fine big portion of chips, to make up for what one was perceived to be missing out on. It's not that lasagne wasn't nice; it's just that it was rather predictable.

Cornucopia lasagnes strive to be anything but predictable. After all, lasagne would not be one of the Western world's favourite dishes if it did not have the potential to be both exciting and absolutely yummy. Start with a rich tomato sauce, fresh pasta (when possible) and a white sauce made with love and affection. To this add some well-selected vegetables, varying them to match the season or the contents of your pantry, and some tasty cheese, whatever your instincts tell you will taste best.

The lasagne recipe described here is a brilliant crowd-pleaser for both vegetarians and non-vegetarians alike. The great chunks of bright orange squash and juicy courgettes soak up the rich flavour of the red wine sauce and the spinach provides a pleasantly fresh surprise in the middle. The white sauce is no ordinary béchamel – it has the opulent addition of an egg yolk, to enrich and strengthen it, and has fresh basil blended through it for a unique and vibrant twist. And it does not require a portion of chips on the side! If you would like to make an egg-free lasagne, buy dry lasagne sheets made without egg (check the packet) and omit the egg yolk from the béchamel sauce.

Preheat your oven to 200°C. Start by preparing the vegetables for the lasagne. Chop the butternut squash and courgettes into neat, even, medium-size chunks. Keeping both vegetables separate, toss them in a little olive oil, salt and pepper and place them on baking trays. You may need two trays for the squash and one for the courgettes. Roast in the oven until soft, turning once or twice. The courgettes will take 25-30 minutes, the squash about 40 minutes. Set aside. Reduce the oven to 180°C. While the vegetables are roasting, prepare the spinach. If using regular spinach, remove the stalks and rinse and drain it thoroughly. Baby spinach generally comes pre-washed. Coat a frying pan with olive oil and place over quite a high heat. When the pan is hot, add half of the spinach and some salt and pepper. Stirring

For the lasagne
1 medium butternut squash
   (about 700g) or equivalent
   weight in seasonal pumpkin
2 large courgettes
400g spinach *(or baby spinach)*
1 packet of lasagne sheets
   (fresh if possible) or see page
   244 for fresh pasta recipe
150g vegetarian regato cheese
Extra-virgin olive oil
Salt and pepper

For the red wine sauce
1 onion
1 carrot
2 sticks of celery
3 cloves of garlic
About 15 leaves of fresh sage
200ml vegetarian red wine
2x400g tins of plum tomatoes
   (organic if possible) or 1kg
   ripe plum tomatoes
Pinch of unrefined brown sugar
   (or dash of apple concentrate)
Extra-virgin olive oil
Salt and pepper

For the béchamel sauce
50g butter
50g plain flour
500ml milk
1 free-range egg yolk *(optional)*
25g *(small bunch)* fresh basil
Pinch of freshly grated nutmeg
50ml extra-virgin olive oil
Salt and pepper

regularly, wilt the spinach until it is soft and there is almost no moisture left in the pan. Repeat for the second half of the spinach and set aside. When cool, chop the spinach roughly. Baby spinach does not need to be chopped.

Next, make the red wine sauce. If you are using fresh tomatoes, they must first be deskinned. Cut an X into the skin of each, place them in a suitable bowl and pour boiling water over them. After one minute, drain the tomatoes and the skins can now be removed with ease. Chop them into quarters and set aside.

Chop the carrot, onion, celery and garlic roughly – they will later be blended, so you don't need to be fussy. Coat the base of a large pot generously with olive oil and place over a medium heat. Add the carrot, onion, celery and garlic, stir briefly, then cover with a lid. Reduce to a low temperature and sweat for 15 minutes, stirring occasionally. When the vegetables have sweated, add the wine and sage and simmer for 5 minutes, so that some of the alcohol evaporates. Then add the freshly skinned (in which case add 200ml water) or tinned tomatoes and a little salt and pepper and simmer for a further 30 minutes, so the sauce can cook and reduce. Remove from the heat and, using a stick blender, blend until smooth. Check the seasoning. If you would like to sweeten the sauce slightly, add a pinch of brown sugar or a dash of apple concentrate. Set aside to cool and then stir in the roast squash and courgette.

Now make the béchamel sauce. Make sure you have everything to hand, as you need to stay at the cooker to stir the sauce. Using a medium pan,

Variations
Other Cornucopia lasagnes to try:
(Note: The red wine tomato sauce
and béchamel remain the same.)

*Roast Mediterranean vegetable
lasagne topped with flaked
almonds*
Roast aubergines, red and yellow
peppers, courgettes, red onions
and scatter flaked almonds and
vegetarian regato cheese over the
white sauce

*Mushroom, red onion & black
olive lasagne with goat's cheese*
Roast mushrooms and red onion,
cut four thin rounds of vegetarian
goat's cheese into eight half moons
and lay them onto the white sauce

*Fennel, leek & spinach lasagne
with vegetarian strong cheddar
cheese*
Parboil then roast fennel, pan-fry
leeks and pan-wilt spinach

melt the butter in the olive oil. Sprinkle in the flour
and, stirring constantly, cook it in the fat for about
3 minutes. It will come together into a paste.
Reduce to a low heat and very gradually begin
to add the milk, bit by bit. Don't add more milk
until the last batch has been fully incorporated.
As you add the first few batches of milk, the sauce
will keep returning to a paste, but it will eventually
start to take on the consistency of a creamy sauce.
Patience is important with a béchamel. That,
and constant stirring. When all the milk has been
added, cook for a further 5 minutes (still stirring)
and then remove from the heat. Season with salt,
pepper and a grating of nutmeg and stir in the egg
yolk (if using). The purpose of the egg is to set the
sauce slightly in the oven, but it is optional. Add the
fresh basil to the béchamel and use a stick blender
to blend it into the sauce.

Finally, build your lasagne. Use a deep, square
(or rectangular) oven dish. Ladle ⅓ of the red
wine sauce with vegetables into the base. Cover
with ½ the spinach and then a layer of lasagne.
Press securely into place. Ladle in another ⅓ of
the red wine sauce, cover with the second ½ of
the spinach and another layer of lasagne sheets.
Lastly, ladle in the remainder of the red wine
sauce, smooth it down a bit and cover with the
béchamel sauce. Grate the regato cheese and
sprinkle it over the top of the béchamel. Bake
in the oven for 30-35 minutes until golden and
bubbling. Check that the pasta is cooked by
inserting the tip of a knife to see if it is soft. Allow
to stand for 10 minutes before serving.

Polenta

Polenta is a bright yellow, gritty grain that, when cooked, takes on a consistency rather like semolina. It is a remarkably versatile grain, in that it can be served for breakfast or dinner, sweet or savoury, soft or set, baked or grilled. It is naturally quite bland tasting so lends itself well to being seasoned, sweetened or enlivened with herbs, spices, vegetarian cheeses or condiments. Polenta is coarsely ground cornmeal (cornflour), which has just had the hull removed, but the germ remains intact, complete with the protein, vitamins and minerals present in that growth centre of the grain. It is a good source of fibre, vitamin B12, vitamin A, vitamin C, magnesium and potassium.

Corn-based polenta is originally a South American creation, where corn is a native grass. Established as a staple peasant food of northern Italy in the 17th and 18th centuries, polenta has been integrated into the gourmet diet of the West in recent years, rather like the elevation of mashed potato and porridge from 'stuff your grandmother makes' to 'stuff you pay high prices for in restaurants'. Part of the reason for new-found interest in polenta is that it is a whole grain that contains neither wheat nor gluten, so is suitable for people with wheat intolerance or coeliac disease, and people who simply wish to reduce the amount of wheat-based products in their diet.

The recipes that follow are for set polenta: polenta that has been left in the fridge overnight to form a solid mass and then carved into squares or sheets. Set polenta is most suited to the style of service in Cornucopia, where we do not cook to order; rather customers choose their dishes from a hot-food display. Soft polenta, although not possible in our self-service restaurant, is well worth trying at home. In northern Italy, where polenta is a standard ingredient, a big pot of polenta is cooked and served soft for dinner, spooned hot onto the plate and topped with whatever sauce is on the menu. The leftover polenta is placed in the fridge overnight and then sliced and grilled for breakfast the next morning, topped with free-range eggs or vegetarian cheese or jam — so they enjoy the best of both worlds.

To make a pot of soft polenta, bring 1 litre of water to the boil. Stirring constantly with a large whisk, sprinkle in 200g of polenta. Reduce to a low heat and continue whisking until the polenta thickens to a porridge-like consistency. At this stage, add a good knob of butter, cover with a lid and cook for 30 minutes, stirring occasionally. For a vegan version, add 75ml olive oil instead of butter.

Savoury soft polenta

When the polenta is cooked, season with salt and pepper. This is delicious as an accompaniment for ragout or bean stew or roast vegetables with basil pesto. For a more flavourful polenta, try any of the following:

· Stir some pungent vegetarian grated cheese in at the end (regato, strong cheddar)
· Add some finely chopped herbs; stir basil or chives in at the end or add thyme or oregano earlier in the cooking (with the butter)
· Remove the pits from some good-quality black olives and fold them in
· Finely chop some oil-based sun-dried tomatoes (or rehydrate some dried ones) and stir them in

Sweet soft polenta

Serve as a hot breakfast to get the day off to a warm start (suitable as an alternative to porridge for coeliacs). When the polenta is cooked, add a tiny pinch of salt and sweeten with unrefined brown sugar or a squeeze of honey. Try any of the following serving suggestions:

· Top with a berry compôte made of mixed berries cooked with honey, a squeeze of lemon and a pinch of cinnamon
· Stir in some sultanas, cinnamon, nutmeg and toasted flaked almonds
· Top with a dessertspoon of crème fraîche and a teaspoon of your favourite homemade jam

The making of polenta always used to elicit a groan from the kitchen porters in Cornucopia. No matter how vigorously and diligently the chef stirs the polenta pot, a certain amount always sticks to the base. By the time the pot reaches the wash-up area, the polenta will have inevitably dried in, ready for battle to the death with anyone who tries to remove it. Top tip from our polenta-pot-cleaning-expert kitchen porters: there is no point fighting with a dry, crusty polenta pot. As soon as possible after the polenta has been served or transferred to another container, soak the pot in cold water for half an hour and the polenta will lift off surprisingly easily.

Regato polenta square with roast summer vegetables & olive tapenade   *gf* *wf* *ef* *(for vegan version, see next recipe)*

This is a really impressive dish and perfectly suitable for a dinner party, as you can do much of the preparation in advance and simply heat through and serve when the guests arrive. The base is a square of set polenta, strongly flavoured with regato cheese, which has been set in the fridge overnight and then grilled, so that it is crispy on the outside and soft in the middle. Layered on top of it are roasted and pan-fried vegetables, which have simply been seasoned with salt and pepper so that each one can been tasted and enjoyed in all its individual flavour. And riding high upon the vegetables is a delicious olive tapenade, a taste sensation of puréed olives, capers, herbs and lemon.

Tapenade is a condiment from Provence, derived from the Provençal word *tapéno*, meaning caper (as in the pickled Mediterranean plant bud, not the act of larking about). It has a salty, tangy full-on flavour. Should you fancy making a double batch of tapenade and reserving half of it in the fridge, it is lovely spread on fresh, crusty artisan bread or used, possibly alongside hummus (see page 193), as a dip for crudités (chilled batons of raw carrot, cucumber, celery, red pepper. etc).

A word of explanation as to why all the lovely vegetables for going on top of the polenta are oven-roasted, with the exception of the courgettes, which are pan-fried. Courgettes can be oven-roasted, but are far more delicious pan-fried or chargrilled. This is because courgettes have a high water content and they tend to release moisture and then stew in their own juices in the oven. Placed in a hot pan, their juices can quickly be sealed in and any moisture that they do release will evaporate off the pan. As this dish really celebrates the wonders of each individual vegetable, it's worth giving the courgettes the personal attention they deserve — they will emerge from the pan so wonderfully charred and tasty that you'll probably end up popping at least one or two slices directly into your mouth.

Note: advance preparation is necessary.

The day before, or eight hours in advance
Make the polenta in advance so it has time to set. Chop the garlic very finely. Place the butter and olive oil in a large, non-stick pot over a medium heat. When the butter has melted, add the garlic and bay leaves and cook for 3 minutes, stirring regularly. Now add 1 litre of cold water, increase the heat and bring to the boil. Turning vigorously with the largest whisk you have, rain in the polenta

For the polenta
3 cloves garlic
3 bay leaves
75g butter
200g coarse polenta
100g vegetarian regato cheese
50ml extra-virgin olive oil
Salt and pepper

For the vegetables
2 red onions
1 yellow pepper
1 red pepper
1 fennel
1 courgette
½ butternut squash *(about 500g)*
½ lemon
Extra-virgin olive oil
Salt and pepper

For the tapenade
3 cloves of garlic
1 lemon
25g *(small bunch)* oregano
200g good-quality black olives
30g capers
75ml extra-virgin olive oil
Pepper

and reduce to a very low heat. Continue whisking until the polenta thickens considerably (like a thick semolina) and starts to bubble lazily. Cover with a lid and cook for 40 minutes, stirring occasionally. While the polenta is cooking, grate the regato cheese. When the polenta is fully cooked, remove from the heat, stir in the regato and season with salt and pepper.

Pour/spoon the hot polenta into a roasting tray (23x23cm or equivalent) and smooth it with a spatula. Leave to cool and then refrigerate overnight or for at least 6 hours.

On the day of consumption
Preheat the oven to 200°C.

Start by preparing the vegetable topping. Chop the red onions into thin moons, the peppers and fennel into medium squares, the squash into medium chunks and the courgettes into ½cm-thick rounds. With the exception of the courgettes, toss each of the vegetables in a little olive oil, salt and pepper. Mix the red and yellow peppers and place them on one roasting dish. Mix the red onion and fennel and place them on another roasting dish. Place the butternut squash on a third roasting dish. Transfer them all to the oven and roast until soft, agitating once or twice. They will take different lengths of time to roast, between 20 and 30 minutes.

When the red onion/fennel tray is done, squeeze some lemon juice over and stir it into the vegetables. This will return vibrancy of colour to the red onions, which roasting tends to turn a little grey.

When the vegetables have finished roasting, set them aside and reduce the oven to 180°C. Meanwhile, pan-fry the courgettes. Coat the base of a frying pan sparsely with olive oil and place over a relatively high heat. When the pan is hot, fill it with courgette rounds and sprinkle them with a little salt and pepper. After a couple of minutes, check that the undersides of the courgettes are nicely golden brown, then turn them one by one and cook the other side. Repeat until all the courgettes have been cooked. Combine all the roast and pan-fried vegetables in a mixing bowl and set aside.

Next grill the polenta. Turn the tray of cold, set polenta upside-down onto a chopping board. Cut it into eight rectangles (4x2) or nine squares (3x3). Brush both sides of each piece of polenta with olive oil. Place the slices directly into a medium-heat grill and grill them on both sides until golden brown and a little crispy, then transfer them to a large oven dish. Distribute the mixed roast and pan-fried vegetables evenly between the slices of grilled polenta. Cover the dish with foil and bake in the oven for 20-25 minutes, until piping hot.

While the polenta slices are baking, make the tapenade. Carefully remove all the pits from the olives (unless you bought pitted ones). Destalk the oregano and peel the garlic. Place the olives, oregano, garlic, capers, the juice of the lemon and a twist of black pepper into a food processor and blend thoroughly. Keeping the machine running, pour in the 75ml olive oil gradually, until smooth. Serve the polenta slices hot from the oven with a generous spoonful of tapenade on top, accompanied by a crisp green salad.

Herbed polenta square with roast summer vegetables & olive tapenade   *v   gf   wf*

This is a vegan version of the last recipe. Only the ingredients for the polenta differ; the vegetable topping and the tapenade are identical. As polenta is naturally quite bland, it must be invigorated with flavour. In the case of the last recipe, the pungency of the regato cheese is quite sufficient. As the fresh herbs in this variation are not so dense in flavour, this polenta should be cooked in stock, rather than in water, to give it extra depth of flavour. For a recipe for vegetable stock, see page 184 (alternatively, though not quite as delicious, use 2 heaped teaspoons of good-quality vegan bouillon dissolved in 1 litre of boiling water).

Note: advance preparation necessary

For the herbed polenta
- **1 litre of vegetable stock** *(see page 184) or 1 litre of boiling water and 2 heaped teaspoons of good-quality vegan bouillon*
- **3 cloves garlic**
- **3 bay leaves**
- **200g coarse polenta**
- **50g** *(medium bunch)* **fresh basil**
- **75ml extra-virgin olive oil**
- **Salt and pepper**

The day before, or eight hours in advance

Make the polenta in advance so it has time to set. Chop the garlic very finely. Place the olive oil in a large, non-stick pot over a medium heat. Add the garlic and bay leaves and cook for 3 minutes, stirring regularly. Now add 1 litre of stock, increase the heat and bring to the boil. Turning vigorously with the largest whisk you have, rain in the polenta and reduce to a very low heat. Continue whisking until the polenta thickens considerably (like a thick semolina) and starts to bubble lazily. Cover with a lid and cook for 40 minutes, stirring occasionally. While the polenta is cooking, chop the fresh basil as finely as you can. When the polenta is fully cooked, remove from the heat, stir in the basil and season with salt and pepper.

Pour/spoon the hot polenta into a roasting tray (23x23x5cm, 20x25x5cm or equivalent) and smooth it with a spatula. Leave to cool and then refrigerate overnight or for at least 6 hours.

Now follow the previous recipe from the point of **'On the day of consumption'** onwards (see page 261).

Roast garlic polenta bake with leek, mushroom & spinach in a red pepper sauce topped with goat's cheese
gf   wf   ef   (vegan if desired, see variations)

The following bake could be viewed as a kind of lasagne-replacement therapy for anyone on a wheat-free or gluten-free diet. Just like lasagne, it is made up of layers of rich sauce, teeming with vegetables and thin slices of polenta, topped off with half moons of goat's cheese that melt and bubble and ooze in the heat of the oven. It serves wonderfully well, transferred to each plate with a lifter and finished with a colourful drizzle of basil oil.

This time the polenta is flavoured with white wine and roast garlic, which lends it a tanginess that contrasts pleasingly with the sweet roast red pepper sauce. This is simply a basic tomato sauce, enriched with three roasted peppers and a dash of red wine vinegar, which make a dramatic impact on the flavour. As for the mushrooms, leeks and spinach, the method laid out below suggests that they all be pan-fried rather than roasted or blanched, to really enhance their flavour and minimise unwanted moisture. However, should you be short of time, pan space or patience, while you are sautéing the mushrooms, roast the leeks in the oven and plunge the spinach into a pot of boiling water for one minute.

As with many recipes in this book, this particular version of the layered polenta bake is just a launch pad. Once you have mastered the idea of using layers of set polenta in a bake, all the elements of this dish can be experimented with. For different polenta flavourings, see page 257. Instead of the roast pepper sauce, try the red wine sauce (page 253), a simple tomato sauce (page 187) or a cheesy béchamel (page 186; note: the dish will no longer be gluten-free). Fill the sauce with whatever roasted or pan-fried vegetables you like and top off with grated cheddar or crumbled feta or a sprinkle of regato. The possibilities of the layered polenta bake are vast and varied.

Note: advance preparation necessary.

The day before, or eight hours in advance
Make the polenta in advance so it has time to set. Preheat your oven to 200°C. Chop the top off the bulb of garlic, toss it in olive oil and place it, open top up, in a small baking tray. Pour a little extra olive oil into the centre of the bulb. Roast for 40 minutes on the middle shelf. Set aside to cool. Melt the butter in a small pot until it turns brown and almost nutty-smelling. This is called a 'beurre

For the polenta
1 bulb of garlic
5 bay leaves
75g butter
200ml vegetarian white wine
200g coarse polenta
Extra-virgin olive oil
Salt and pepper

For the rest of the bake
3 leeks
400g field mushrooms
400g spinach or baby spinach
3 red peppers
1 onion
1 carrot
2 stalks of celery
3 cloves of garlic
1x400g tin plum tomatoes
    (organic if possible) or 500g
    ripe plum tomatoes
100ml vegetarian red
    wine vinegar
Freshly grated nutmeg
200g vegetarian goat's cheese log
Extra-virgin olive oil
Salt and pepper

For the basil oil
25g *(small bunch)* **fresh basil**
Juice of ½ lemon
100ml extra-virgin olive oil
Salt and pepper

noisette' and it will bring a lovely depth of flavour to the polenta. Place the white wine and bay leaves in a large pot over a medium heat. Allow to simmer for 5 minutes to burn off the alcohol. Remove the bay leaves. Now pour in 800ml of cold water and bring to the boil. Turning vigorously with the largest whisk you have, rain in the polenta and reduce to a very low heat. Continue whisking until the polenta thickens considerably (like a thick semolina) and starts to bubble lazily. Stir in the beurre noisette. Cover with a lid and cook for 40 minutes, stirring occasionally.

While the polenta is cooking, take the now cool roast garlic, hold it at the uncut end, squeeze the soft flesh out through the cut end, mash it with a fork and stir that into the bubbling polenta too. After 40 minutes' cooking, pour/spoon the hot polenta into a roasting tray (23x23x5cm, 20x25x5cm or equivalent) and smooth it with a spatula. Leave to cool for 30 minutes and then refrigerate overnight or for at least 6 hours.

On the day of consumption
Preheat your oven to 180°C. Start by preparing the vegetables for the bake. Halve the leeks lengthways, chop them into medium pieces, wash them thoroughly in a large sink of water, then set aside to drain. Wipe the mushrooms clean with damp kitchen paper and chop into thin strips. If using regular (not baby) spinach, remove the large stalks and rinse and drain it thoroughly. Baby spinach generally comes pre-washed.

As there is now a lot of pan-frying to do, if you have two pans available to you it will save time to use them simultaneously. If not, just put on some nice music and enjoy the frying. Coat the frying pan(s) sparsely with olive oil, place over a medium heat, add a small batch of mushrooms (do them in two or three batches, as an overcrowded pan will result in the mushrooms stewing rather than sautéing), a pinch of salt and pepper and fry them until they are soft and most of the moisture has evaporated from the pan. Repeat until all the mushrooms have been cooked.

Next, coat the pan a little more generously with olive oil and, still over a medium heat, add half of the leeks, a pinch of salt and pepper and a pinch of freshly grated nutmeg. Fry until soft. Repeat with the second batch of leeks. Finally, wipe out the pan, coat sparsely with olive oil and place over a relatively high heat. When it is hot, add half of the spinach, with salt, pepper and a grating of nutmeg and wilt until soft and most of the moisture has evaporated. Repeat with the second batch of spinach. When the spinach is cool enough, chop it roughly. This is not necessary if using baby spinach.

Next, make the red pepper sauce. First, halve the three peppers, toss them in a little olive oil, salt and pepper and place them in the oven to roast for about 30 minutes. As soon as they emerge from the oven, place them in a small bowl and clingwrap it tightly, so that no air can escape. After they have sat for ten minutes in their own steam, remove the clingwrap and the skins of the red peppers will peel off easily.

Meanwhile, make the sauce base. If you are using fresh tomatoes, they must first be deskinned. Cut an X into the skin of each, place them in a suitable

Variations

Vegan version

For a vegan version of this recipe, replace the butter in the polenta with 75ml of olive oil. Instead of finishing the bake with goat's cheese, bake it plain and then just before serving add a dollop of roasted yellow pepper purée to each portion (3 roasted yellow peppers skinned, 60ml extra-virgin olive oil, squeeze of lemon, salt and pepper), drizzled with basil oil.

Quick version

For a version of this recipe that does not require overnight setting, simply serve the polenta soft (about two serving spoonfuls per plate), with the roast pepper sauce and vegetables on the side, all drizzled with basil oil.

bowl and pour boiling water over them. After one minute, drain the tomatoes and the skins can now be removed with ease. Chop them in quarters and set aside.

Chop the onion, carrot, celery and garlic roughly. They will later be blended, so no need to be fussy. Coat the base of a large pot with olive oil and place over a medium heat. Add the onion, carrot, celery and garlic, stir briefly, reduce to a low heat, cover with a lid and sweat for 15 minutes. Then add the freshly skinned (in which case add 100ml water) or tinned tomatoes and the red wine vinegar and simmer gently for a further 30 minutes. Finally, add in the peeled roasted red peppers and, using a stick blender, blend the sauce until smooth. Stir the mushrooms, leeks and spinach evenly into the sauce and check the seasoning.

Retrieve the polenta from the fridge and turn it upside-down onto a chopping board. Chop it first into nine squares (3x3) and then, using a large slim knife, slice each square into three or four thin slices, rather like lasagne sheets. Select a large square or rectangular oven dish. First ladle ⅓ of the red pepper sauce with vegetables into the base of the dish. Cover this with a layer of half of the polenta sheets, pressed firmly into place and slightly overlapping if necessary. Ladle the next ⅓ of the red pepper sauce onto the layer of polenta and cover it with the rest of the polenta sheets. Top with the final ⅓ of the sauce and smooth it off a little. Chop the goat's cheese log into eight half moons and arrange them neatly on top of the bake. Transfer to the oven for 30 minutes.

While the dish is baking, make the basil oil. Combine the olive oil, fresh basil, juice of a lemon and a little salt and pepper in a small container and use a stick blender to blend until smooth. When the polenta bake emerges sizzling from the oven, allow it to stand for ten minutes before serving. Drizzle each portion decoratively with basil oil. Serve with a crisp green salad.

To Greece and beyond
– *the accidental Greek section*

When it came to organising the various main course recipes selected for inclusion in the book into a coherent chapter, there were some obvious groupings, the pastas, the polentas, the mash dishes, the rice dishes, the quiches and even the 'old reliables'. Surveying the motley bunch of recipes that remained, I noticed a completely unintentional ethnic theme – of the five random recipes, three were Greek: moussaka, dolmades and spanakopita. That left only two stragglers, so, in the interest of integration, they were extended honorary membership of the Greek section: wild mushroom filo parcels (a distant French cousin of the spanakopita, related on the 'filo' side of the family) and couscous-stuffed aubergine (Greek cuisine approves of stuffing aubergines, just not with couscous, but in the interests of integration ...) Thus was born the 'accidental Greek section': a collection of five Greek and non-Greek recipes.

Greek cuisine lends itself generously to vegetarianism, what with an abundance of sun-ripened fresh fruit and vegetables available year round. A key ingredient for most dishes is local olive oil, which can be mopped up with the crusty bread that makes its way to the table for most meals. Popular herbs are thyme, bay, oregano, dill, mint and parsley. Popular spices include cinnamon, clove, fennel seeds, cumin seeds and nutmeg. Add to that flavourful feta, thick creamy yoghurt, cheese filo pies, rice- and vegetable-stuffed vine leaves, fig leaves, peppers, aubergines, tomatoes, even stuffed courgette flowers, and a hungry vegetarian might just be hopping on the next flight to Athens.

If you do find yourself tucking into a plate of Greek delights, be it in your own kitchen or on a sun-drenched restaurant terrace in a mountain village outside Thessaloniki, perhaps the flavour will be enhanced by the knowledge that you are following in the footsteps of greatness, as the idea of vegetarianism in Western thinking was first introduced by the ancient Greek philosophers. For Socrates, Plato and Aristotle, a vegetarian society was more likely to be a peaceful society, as vegetables promoted health and took up less land than livestock, resulting in fewer tussles over land ownership. Pythagoras, an enlightened philosopher, pacifist and mathematician (the triangle man), believed that we should strive never to destroy life, as all life is equal (just like the square on the hypotenuse and the sum of the square of the other two sides). He considered vegetarianism a key factor in peaceful human co-existence, as slaughtering animals desensitised the heart to murder and cruelty, leading to crimes against fellow man. The first Western celebrity vegetarian, Pythagoras extolled the health virtues of a diet of vegetables for both the body and mind. He taught his students to eat the simple delicious foods offered by the nature around them, foods that did not require fire, foods that made life simpler rather than more complicated. Pythagoras essentially encouraged people to eat local vegetarian produce, plenty of raw or lightly cooked food and to eat in moderation. Doesn't that sound remarkably contemporary, considering he lived 2,500 years ago!

Back to the modern age, try the moussaka recipe for a truly hearty meal, the spanakopita for a quick and easy flavourful lunch or the dolmades as a starter that knocks the socks off the guests at your gourmet dinner party.

Vegetable & lentil moussaka

(gluten-free version included — see end)

There are so many versions of this traditional Greek layered dish. The basic components are aubergines, tomato sauce and an egg-enriched béchamel topping. Depending on the chef, the region and also on whether the moussaka is being served as an appetiser or a main course, further elements may be incorporated. The Cornucopia moussaka took several years to perfect — to retain enough of the classic elements of the dish, whilst creating a substantial, nutritious vegetarian meal. The definitive recipe, which we have settled on with much satisfaction, consists of a subtly spiced puy lentil, mushroom and tomato sauce onto which slices of potato and roast aubergine are neatly layered, all topped off with a rich and flavourful white sauce. A dish fit for hungry heroes after a busy day saving the world.

Many cookbooks suggest that aubergines should be sliced, salted, left for half an hour to ooze moisture and then wiped dry before cooking. This method of drawing out the juices is to remove the slight natural bitterness of the aubergine. However, most varieties of aubergine on the market today have been cultivated to be less bitter, and render this salting process unnecessary. Irish-grown aubergines are available from about May to September. Choose plump, firm specimens that feel heavy in the hand and have a healthy green stem.

To complete the Greek experience, serve the moussaka with tzatziki, a simple Greek cucumber salad. Grate (or finely dice) one large cucumber. For the dressing, mix a cup of yoghurt with half a clove of garlic crushed, a dessertspoonful of olive oil, a good squeeze of lemon and a few sprigs of fresh mint, very finely chopped. Season with salt and pepper and mix in the grated/diced cucumber. Refrigerate, so it is nice and cool when served. The clean freshness of the salad contrasts pleasantly with the spiced richness of the moussaka.

Preheat your oven to 180°C.

Start by preparing the milk for the béchamel sauce. Peel the onion and stud it with the cloves. Into a medium pot, place the onion, bay leaves, peppercorns and milk. Bring to the boil very gently and then set aside for 20 minutes to infuse.

Next, cook the lentils. In a sieve, rinse them thoroughly under cold water. Bring a medium pot with plenty of salted water and two bay leaves to the boil. Add the lentils and stir to stop them sticking

For the béchamel
½ onion
500ml milk
3 bay leaves
4 cloves
8 peppercorns
50g butter
50g plain flour
3 free-range eggs
Pinch of freshly grated nutmeg
Extra-virgin olive oil
Salt and pepper

For the base
200g puy lentils
4 bay leaves *(2 for lentils,
    2 for sauce)*
1 large onion
4 cloves of garlic
25g *(small bunch)* fresh oregano
2x400g tins plum tomatoes
    *(organic if possible) or 1kg
    ripe plum tomatoes*
1 tsp ground cinnamon
1 tsp ground cumin
2 large (3 medium) aubergines
300g *(about 16)* closed cap
    (regular) mushrooms
4 large waxy potatoes *(such as
    pink fir apple)* — about 1kg

together. Cover with a lid, reduce to a low heat and simmer for about 30 minutes, until the lentils are soft but not at all mushy. Drain and set aside.

Meanwhile, start the main sauce. If you are using fresh tomatoes, they must first be deskinned. Cut an X into the skin of each, place them in a suitable bowl and pour boiling water over them. After one minute, drain the tomatoes and the skins can now be removed with ease. Chop them in quarters and set aside.

Dice the onion and finely slice the garlic. Remove the stalks from the oregano. Place the freshly skinned (in which case add 200ml water) or tinned tomatoes in a suitable bowl, add the oregano and blend until smooth. Coat the base of a large pot with olive oil and place it over a medium heat. Add the onion and garlic, 2 bay leaves, cinnamon and cumin, stir briefly, cover with a lid and reduce to a low heat. Sweat for 15 minutes, stirring regularly to prevent the spices sticking and burning. Next, add the tomatoes with oregano and a little salt and pepper. Simmer for 30 minutes on a low heat, stirring occasionally. When the sauce is ready, stir in the cooked lentils, check the seasoning and set aside.

While the sauce is cooking, prepare the other vegetables. Peel the potatoes and slice them into ½cm discs. Place them in a large pot of salted water, bring to the boil, cover with a lid, reduce to a simmer and cook until soft. Be careful not to overcook the potatoes — they will soften quite quickly, as they are so thinly sliced. They need to be firm enough to be arranged in neat layers in the moussaka without crumbling in your hands.

Set aside. Slice the aubergines into 1cm-thick discs. Brush both sides of each disc with olive oil, lay them out in baking trays and sprinkle with a little salt and pepper. Roast in the oven until soft, flipping them over halfway through cooking, which takes 20-25 minutes. Set aside.

Chop the mushrooms in half, toss them in a little olive oil, salt and pepper and roast them too in the oven until tender, 15-20 minutes. When cooked, stir the mushrooms into the tomato sauce.

With everything else ready, make the béchamel sauce. Remove all the bits from the infused milk by pouring it through a sieve (you might like to transfer the milk to a jug, to make it easy to pour bit by bit into the sauce). Put the butter and a good splash of olive oil into a medium pot and place over a low heat. When the butter has melted, sprinkle into the flour, stirring constantly with a wooden spoon for 3 minutes to cook the flour. It will come together into a paste called a roux.

Now gradually add the infused milk. Start with a very small amount and stir until fully incorporated. Add a little more milk and, once again, stir until fully incorporated. Keep repeating this procedure, always ensuring the sauce is of an even consistency before adding more milk. Initially, the sauce will keep thickening, but gradually it will take on the form of a creamy béchamel. When all the milk has been added, cook for a further 5 minutes (still stirring) and then remove from the heat. Grate in a little nutmeg and season with salt and pepper. Whisk the three eggs in a small bowl and then stir them into the sauce.

Gluten-free moussaka

To make a scrumptious gluten-free version of this moussaka, replace the béchamel sauce with the following topping:

3 free-range eggs
500g Greek-style natural yoghurt
    (or any thick plain yoghurt)
25g *(3-4 sprigs)* **fresh mint**
A grating of nutmeg
Salt and pepper

Chop the mint finely. Beat the eggs. Combine all the ingredients and spread over the top of the moussaka instead of the béchamel sauce. Cooking time remains the same.

Choose a large rectangular (or square) oven dish. Ladle in half of the tomato and lentil mix and smooth it down. Cover with a neat layer of cooked potato slices, followed by a neat layer of roasted aubergine discs. Repeat with the second half of the sauce and the rest of the potatoes and aubergines. Finally, pour the béchamel sauce over the top. Bake in the middle shelf of the oven for 35-40 minutes, or until the top has set. Leave to settle for ten minutes before slicing and serving. Use a lifter to transfer each portion to the plate.

Wild rice & mushroom dolmades with garlic cream & red pepper purée   *gf wf ef cn*
Note: wild rice should be soaked overnight before cooking

This recipe was created by Tony Keogh (head chef) and Claire McCormick (pastry chef) for a gourmet vegetarian cookery demonstration in the stately setting of Farmleigh House, a Victorian house and garden in Dublin's Phoenix Park. They returned that evening to the rather more miniature environment of the Cornucopia kitchen with tales of galloping up and down long, majestic corridors from the kitchens to the entertainment quarters with arm-loads of ingredients and equipment and ones we made earlier, with our boss Deirdre in hot pursuit as their general purpose runner. Much to their relief, the demonstration was a great success, although, as soon as it ended, three exhausted Cornucopians collapsed straight onto the grass outside Farmleigh and a stiff drink was required to revive them!

These dolmades were demonstrated as a starter. A dolmade is essentially a stuffed leaf — typically, in Greece, a grapevine leaf stuffed with rice and vegetables. This recipe uses savoy cabbage leaves instead, which, though quite tough when raw, become wonderfully soft and malleable after five minutes of blanching. The filling has a rich mushroom flavour and the wonderfully chewy texture of wild rice. Elevating these cabbage rolls to gourmet heights are two magnificent sauces — a rich roast garlic cream and a sweet roasted red pepper purée — which are drizzled attractively over the cooked dolmades.

An artfully presented dolmade makes an impressive starter for a dinner party. Be aware that this is quite a labour-intensive recipe involving several processes and lots of washing up, so give yourself plenty of time. Once rolled, the dolmades can be set aside until you are almost ready to serve them. At that point, bake them for 20 minutes and reheat the roast garlic cream. The pepper purée does not need to be heated.

Having removed eight outer leaves from the savoy cabbage, quite an amount of vegetable remains. Savoy cabbage is delicious simply stir-fried with a little garlic, olive oil and seasoning. Alternatively, it is a wonderful ingredient for gratins (see page 218) and a key ingredient for the tomato, white bean and savoy cabbage soup (page 81).

The day before cooking
Soak the wild rice in a large pot of cold water overnight or for 8 hours.

The day of cooking
Preheat your oven to 180°C. Start by roasting the peppers for the purée and the garlic for the cream. Slice the red peppers in half and chop the

For the cabbage rolls
100g wild rice
    (uncooked, dry weight)
1 onion
1 tbsp ground cumin
1 tsp paprika
10 field mushrooms
    (about 800g)
100g walnuts
8 large savoy cabbage leaves
300ml vegetable stock
    *(see page 184) or 300ml
    boiling water with ½ tsp
    good-quality bouillon*
Extra-virgin olive oil
Salt and pepper

For the garlic cream
2 shallots
300ml vegetarian white wine
400ml cream
1 bulb garlic
Pinch of freshly ground nutmeg
30g butter
Extra-virgin olive oil
Salt and pepper

For the roast red pepper purée
4 large red peppers
A wedge or two of lemon
A few sprigs of fresh tarragon
A few sprigs of fresh dill
75ml extra-virgin olive oil
Salt and pepper

top off the garlic. Toss them all in olive oil, salt and pepper. Transfer to a baking tray. Pour a little extra olive oil into the open top of the garlic bulb. Transfer to the oven for about 30 minutes, turning the peppers once or twice. When soft, leave the garlic aside to cool and place the red peppers into a small bowl and clingwrap tightly, to steam in their own heat. This will make the skins easy to remove when making the pepper purée.

Next, make the filling for the dolmades. Drain and rinse the soaked wild rice. Transfer to a large pot and cover with about 3 times its volume in water. Bring to the boil, cover, reduce to a simmer and cook for 25-30 minutes, until soft but still nice and chewy. Rinse under cold water, drain and transfer to a large mixing bowl.

Meanwhile, dice the onion finely, chop the mushrooms into small pieces and use the flat of a chef's knife to crush the walnuts. Coat the base of a medium pot with olive oil and place over a medium heat. Add the onion, cover and reduce to a low heat to sweat for 10 minutes. Next, add the cumin and paprika to the onions and sweat for a further 3 minutes, stirring regularly to prevent the spices sticking and burning. Add the spiced onions to the mixing bowl.

Now coat a large frying pan with olive oil and place over a relatively high heat. Add half of the mushrooms and a little salt and pepper and sauté until soft and the pan is almost dry. Repeat with the second batch of mushrooms. Add them and the chopped walnuts to the mixing bowl and stir to incorporate. Season with salt and pepper and set aside to cool.

Now make the garlic cream. Chop the shallots finely. Coat the base of a small pot generously with olive oil and place over a medium heat. Add the shallots, reduce to a low heat and sauté gently for 5 minutes.

Next, add the white wine, bring to a simmer and reduce until almost no liquid remains. Then add the cream and simmer for a further 10 minutes. Finally, squeeze all the flesh out of the roasted garlic and add it to the pot. Remove from the heat and use a stick blender to blend to a smooth consistency. Season with salt and pepper and a fresh grating of nutmeg and set aside.

Bring a large pot of salted water to the boil and blanch the savoy cabbage leaves for 5 minutes. Drain and refresh in cold water immediately. Now, using a small sharp knife, pare away the thickest part of the central stem, making the entire leaf a single thickness. Take great care to keep the leaf intact.

Now it's time for some fun: rolling the dolmades. Using the illustration as a guideline, lay one cabbage leaf on a flat work surface and spoon about ⅛ of the rice mixture into the centre. Fold the left and right sides toward the centre.

 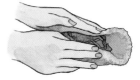

Then, starting with the part of the leaf nearest you, roll into a neat cylinder. Transfer to a baking dish, sealed side down, and repeat until all the leaves have been stuffed and rolled.

Now ladle a small amount of vegetable stock (or boiling water with bouillon) over each dolmade, to prevent them drying out in the oven. Cover the baking dish with foil and bake in the oven for 20 minutes.

While the dolmades are baking, make the pepper purée. Peel the skins off the roasted red peppers. In a suitable container, use a stick blender to blend the peppers, tarragon, dill, 75ml of olive oil and a squeeze of lemon and some salt and pepper. If the purée seems a little too thick to drizzle, add a little vegetable stock from the dolmades.

When the dolmades are nearly ready, reheat the garlic cream sauce very gently and stir in the knob of butter. Place one dolmade on each plate. Spoon over some garlic cream and then drizzle decoratively with red pepper purée.

Cook's notes

Filo pastry

Filo is an anglicised version of '*phyllo*', which means 'leaf' in Greek, thus named because it is an extremely delicate, paper-thin kind of pastry. Working with filo, the following tips may be useful:

·   Filo is usually bought frozen. It needs to be defrosted in the fridge overnight before using. It should never be thawed at room temperature, as the sheets will stick together and tear when you try to separate them.
·   Once exposed to the air, filo rapidly begins to dry and become brittle
·   and unworkable.
·   For best results, don't open the packet until you are ready to start layering/rolling the filo immediately. Have your filling prepared and the butter melted (or olive oil ready).
·   Unravel the pastry, remove the number of sheets you require, reroll the remainder, wrap in clingfilm and return to the fridge, where it can be stored for up to two weeks. If you work quite slowly, place a damp tea towel over the sheets that are waiting to be used.
·   When folding filo (see next recipe), make sure your work surface is very dry, to prevent the filo sticking and tearing. You can dust the area with a little plain flour to be cautious.

Spanakopita

This impressive Greek filo pie looks great, smells great, tastes great and is really, really easy to make. Requiring only the most basic of cooking skills and some school art-class-like assembly, this recipe will deliver fantastic results: crisp, flaky, buttery filo and a soft, warm, flavour-packed filling of spinach, crumbly feta cheese and spring onions.

Spanakopita comes from the Greek *spanoki*, meaning spinach and pita (pronounced pee-ta), meaning pie. You can find -pita at the end of a number of Greek dishes, such as tyropita (cheese filo pie), hortopita (mixed green vegetable filo pie) and karidopita (walnut filo pie). A common herb used in spanakopita is dill, but the Cornucopia version opts for mint, which adds an agreeable freshness to the rich filling.

This recipe introduces the most common way of using filo pastry: layering multiple sheets of filo one on top of the other, each one brushed with melted butter, then introducing a filling and topping it off with further layers of buttered filo. When the filo is baked in the oven, the water in the butter turns to steam and puffs the layers apart, while the fat in the butter makes each sheet crispy. Once you have mastered this basic technique, any number of fillings can be sandwiched between the layers of filo, sweet or savoury. The famous Turkish dessert, baklava, is made just like spanakopita. Instead of spinach, it is filled with finely chopped nuts tossed with cinnamon and sugar. It is baked in the oven and, as soon as it emerges crispy and hot, is soaked with a citrus sugar syrup and left to cool.

Incidentally, should you wish to serve this as an hors d'oeuvre, make the filling as described below and then, instead of building a filo pie, use the triangle folding method demonstrated in the next recipe. Cut the filo into suitably slender lengths to create small, cute spinach and feta pockets, perfect as finger food.

2 onions
4 cloves of garlic
1 bunch spring onions
25g *(small bunch)* fresh mint
200g vegetarian feta cheese
500g spinach or baby spinach
Pinch of freshly ground nutmeg
100g butter
4 free-range eggs
1 tsp ground cinnamon
2 tsp cumin seeds
6 sheets of filo pastry *(keep rolled up and covered until just before use)*
Extra-virgin olive oil
Salt and pepper

Preheat your oven to 180°C. Start with some chopping. Dice the onions and garlic very small. Slice the spring onions into thin rounds. Chop the mint finely and the feta cheese into medium cubes.

Coat the base of a large pot generously with olive oil and place it over a medium heat. Add the onions and garlic, stir for a moment and reduce to a low heat. Sprinkle in the cinnamon and cumin seeds, stir again, then cover with a lid and sweat for 15-20 minutes, stirring occasionally, until the onions are soft and translucent. Remove from the heat, stir in the spring onions and set aside to cool.

While the onions are cooling, cook the spinach. If using regular spinach, remove the stalks and drain and rinse thoroughly. Baby spinach generally comes pre-washed. Bring a large pot of water to the boil and plunge the spinach into it for 1 minute. Drain in a colander, squeezing as much excess water out as possible with the back of a spoon. When it is cool enough, chop the spinach roughly (not necessary for baby spinach) and then add to the onions.

When the onions and spinach have cooled (this may take 20 minutes), fold in the mint and feta cheese. Add some pepper, and salt if required. As feta is naturally quite salty, the mix may not require further salt. Whisk the eggs in a separate bowl and then stir them into the mix. It is important to let the mix cool before adding the feta and eggs, to prevent the feta melting and the eggs starting to cook.

Select a large rectangular or square baking dish. Melt the butter and brush the inside of the dish with it. Lay the 6 filo sheets out flat on your work surface (no need to separate them yet). Cut them in half widthways and stack them on top of each other, creating 12 rectangles. Lay one sheet into the base of the oven dish, allowing the edges to rise up the sides of the dish. Brush with some melted butter. Lay another sheet of filo on top; again, brush with butter. Repeat until six sheets of filo have been used. Now, spoon all of the onion and spinach mix into the dish and distribute evenly. Don't worry that the mix appears quite moist, as the eggs will set when it is cooked. Lay the remaining 6 sheets of filo on top of the filling, brushing each sheet with butter, including the top sheet, so it turns a lovely golden brown in the oven. Cover the dish with foil. Bake on the middle shelf of the oven for 30-35 minutes.

Allow to rest for 5 minutes before slicing and serving. Use a lifter to transfer each portion to the plate. Serve with some tomatoes, halved, brushed with olive oil, seasoned and baked in the oven for 15 minutes.

Wild mushroom, leek & spinach filo parcels
ef (vegan if desired)

This recipe is a celebration of the wild mushroom – a crispy filo pocket bursting with creamy leeks and spinach and whatever wonderful wild mushrooms you can get your hands on, be it from a gourmet supermarket, from your local farmers' market, or from your own trug (wooden basket) of freshly picked specimens, hunted that morning in the woodlands over yonder.

The Irish wild mushroom season is only about six weeks long, from roughly the end of August to the beginning of October. During that period, the fields, woods and forests of Ireland play host to a remarkable array of edible and inedible mushrooms, which quite literally sprout up overnight. There are 3,000 known varieties of mushrooms in Ireland, of which 120 are edible, many more are inedible and several are lethally poisonous. During high season, dedicated mycophagists (those who like to gather and eat mushrooms) stalk the hills and vales for fungal treasures, often returning to secret nooks and crannies where they've reaped tasty rewards in previous years. Amateur gatherers can join groups led by experienced gatherers, who provide guidance in finding and identifying edible mushrooms. A lovely walk in the countryside, basket in hand, could yield a hearty harvest of ceps, chanterelles, wood blewits, honey fungus, parasols, puffballs, shaggy inkcaps, hedgehog mushrooms, cauliflower fungus and birch boleti, to name but a few.

When you get your harvested, bartered or purchased mushrooms home, don't store them in plastic or a sealed bag. Place them uncovered in the fridge with as much airflow around them as possible. As is the general rule for all mushrooms, these wild gems should not be washed but, rather, wiped with a damp cloth to avoid their spongy flesh absorbing too much water. Whilst wild mushrooms are an affordable (or free) treat during high season, they are quite expensive over the rest of the year. If they are priced outside your range, mix a few colourful wild mushrooms (nice orangey chanterelles perhaps) with an equal quantity of Portobello or field mushrooms.

To incorporate your delicious creamy filo pockets into a fine autumn dinner, serve with buttered baby potatoes and carrot batons and green beans, lightly blanched and tossed in French pistou – a herb condiment made by blending fresh basil, cloves of garlic, salt and a little olive oil.

For a lighter plate, serve the filo with a salad of mixed leaves dressed with olive oil, lemon and garlic and scattered with some toasted breadcrumbs.

Note: for tips on handling filo pastry, see page 284.

2 shallots *(or 1 onion)*

3 cloves of garlic

3 leeks

300g wild mushrooms *(or, when not in season, a mix of wild mushrooms & Portobello mushrooms)*

400g spinach or baby spinach

100-150ml cream *(or soy cream if vegan version)*

3 bay leaves

Few sprigs of fresh thyme

25g *(small bunch)* fresh tarragon *(or 1 tsp of dry tarragon if fresh unavailable)*

Pinch of freshly grated nutmeg

6 sheets of filo pastry *(keep rolled up and covered until just before use)*

100ml vegetarian white wine

Extra-virgin olive oil

Salt and pepper

Preheat your oven to 180°C.

Start by preparing the vegetables and herbs. Dice the shallots and garlic small. Slice the leeks lengthways, then chop them crossways into 1cm pieces. Wash them in a big sink of water and set aside to drain fully. Remove the stalks from the fresh tarragon and chop very finely. Tap the wild mushrooms free of any bits of grit and use a damp cloth or sheet of kitchen paper to wipe them clean, if necessary. If using regular (not baby) spinach, remove the stalks and rinse and drain it thoroughly. Baby spinach is usually sold pre-washed.

Coat the bottom of a small pot with olive oil and place over a medium heat. Add the shallots, garlic, thyme and one bay leaf. Stir briefly, reduce to a low heat, cover with a lid and sweat for 15 minutes, until the shallots are soft. Remove the bay and thyme and transfer to a large mixing bowl. Meanwhile, coat the base of a frying pan sparsely with olive oil and place over a medium heat. Throw in half of the wild mushrooms and a little salt and pepper. Stirring regularly, sauté until soft. Repeat with the second batch of mushrooms or, if you have two frying pans, cook two batches simultaneously. Add the cooked mushrooms to the mixing bowl. Next, coat the pan a little more liberally with olive oil and, over a medium heat, add half of the leeks, with salt, pepper, a bay leaf and a grating of nutmeg. When the leeks are hot, add half of the white wine. Cook the leeks until they are soft and most of the liquid has evaporated from the pan. Repeat with the second batch of leeks and the rest of the wine. Transfer

Cook's notes

the cooked leeks to the mixing bowl. Finally, coat the pan sparsely with olive oil and increase to a high heat. Add half of the spinach and wilt until it is soft and most of the moisture has evaporated from the pan. Repeat with the second batch of spinach. When cool enough to handle, chop the spinach roughly and add it also to the mixing bowl. Gently fold all the vegetables in the bowl together.

Add the chopped tarragon and 100ml of cream (or soy cream) and incorporate. If you think the mix could do with a little more cream, add a further 50ml, but don't make it too runny. Season with salt and pepper if required.

Now to assemble the parcels. You need to clear a large work surface for this. Unfold the 6 sheets of filo (no need to separate them yet). Cut them in half lengthways, making 12 very long, thin strips. Lay out 6 of these strips and brush them with olive oil. Place a second sheet on top of each, and brush again with olive oil. Spoon one sixth of the mushroom mix onto the bottom end of each of the double layers of filo. It may be easier to use the diagram for guidance, as the following description is rather unwieldy. Fold the bottom right corner of the strip diagonally to meet the left side of the strip, forming a triangle. Then

take the bottom left corner and fold it over and up, staying on the left side of the strip. Use your hands to encourage all the mix to remain inside the triangular pocket.

Now repeat the process, but from left to right (i.e. take the bottom left corner of the now shorter, fatter strip and fold it diagonally to meet the right side of the strip). Then take the bottom right corner and fold it over and up, staying on the right. Keep folding until all the filo is wrapped

Filo pockets

The filo folding technique introduced in this recipe is a handy method of encasing your favourite filling into a crisp, flaky filo pocket. By cutting the strips of pastry lengthways in three, or even four, rather than in two, you can make smaller triangles suitable for starters or hors d'oeuvres. If you feel like experimenting, here are some other filo fillings to try:

around a neat, triangular parcel.

Roll all the filo parcels (possibly with increasing skill!) and place on an oiled baking tray. Brush the outside of the parcels with a little more olive oil and transfer immediately to the oven. Bake for 20 minutes, until appetisingly golden and crispy.

Roast Mediterranean vegetables in tomato sauce
Oven-roast a variety of peppers, aubergines, courgettes, etc and stir into a well-reduced rich tomato sauce (see page 187).

Creamy leek & potato
Pan-fry some finely-diced potatoes (blanched first), then some chopped leeks and stir into a strong vegetarian cheddar béchamel sauce (see page 186).

Couscous-filled aubergine halves with roasted cherry tomato sauce   *v* *yf* ♡ *(cs)* *cn*

An early version of stuffed aubergine, still popular today, is the Turkish dish imam bayildi, which means 'the imam fainted'. Legend remains divided as to whether the venerable church leader in question swooned at the sheer deliciousness of the dish or dropped unconscious from shock at the quantity of precious olive oil it required, for the cooking technique involved stuffing the aubergine halves with onions, garlic and tomatoes and then simmering them, semi-submerged in a bath of olive oil, spooning hot oil over the filling to soften.

In these more fat-conscious times, we might be inclined to wonder if the imam didn't actually faint, but had a mini-coronary resulting from a lifelong penchant for oil-drenched cooking. Certainly the recipe for stuffed aubergine below poses no threat to the health of your heart – it is an oven-baked aubergine, filled with a light, fresh pea and spinach couscous and brought alive by a spiced (but not spicy), chunky tomato sauce – all delightfully low in fat, but no less fit for an imam!

The tomato sauce to accompany these aubergines deserves a special mention, as it is no ordinary tomato sauce. It is made in two stages: roasting ripe cherry tomatoes in the oven and reducing tinned tomatoes on the stove. By roasting the cherry tomatoes, their flavour is intensified and they become soft and jammy and can be stirred into the sauce rather than being blended, adding wonderful depth of favour and texture to it. On the stove, onions fried with warm, Middle-Eastern spices and blended tomatoes are invigorated by orange zest and mint. And when the two stages are stirred together, none of the individual tastes are lost but rather play together harmoniously.

When making stuffed aubergines, the question arises as to what to do with the scooped-out flesh, so as not to waste it. As the oven is on anyway, toss the pulp in a little olive oil and seasoning, cover with foil and roast until cooked. It can now be blended into a soup to add extra body and flavour or turned into a dip, as described in the recipe for baba ghanoush overleaf.

Preheat your oven to 200°C. Start by making the tomato sauce. Chop the cherry tomatoes in half. Toss them in olive oil, salt and pepper and place them in a baking tray. Roast in the oven until really soft and jammy, 25-30 minutes.

Meanwhile, prepare the sauce. If you are using fresh plum tomatoes, they must first be deskinned. Cut an X into the skin of each, place

For the sauce
800g cherry tomatoes
1 onion
2 cloves of garlic
½ tsp unrefined brown sugar *(or
    1 tsp apple concentrate)*
1 heaped tsp ground cinnamon
Pinch of ground cardamom
½ tsp ground ginger
½ tsp ground coriander
1x400g tin plum tomatoes
    (organic if possible)
    or 500g ripe plum tomatoes
Zest of half an orange
25g *(small bunch)* fresh mint
Extra-virgin olive oil
Salt and pepper

For the aubergines
3 large aubergines *(or 4
    medium) — this will make 6
    or 8 portions*
250g couscous
100g flaked almonds
1 onion
3 cloves of garlic
2 bay leaves
400g baby spinach — *washed
    and drained if not prewashed*
25g *(small bunch)* fresh
    coriander
200g frozen peas
Extra-virgin olive oil
Salt and pepper

them in a suitable bowl and pour boiling water over them. After one minute, drain the tomatoes and the skins can now be removed with ease. Chop them in quarters.

Dice the onion and garlic really small. Blend the freshly skinned tomatoes (in which case add 100ml water) or tinned tomatoes until smooth. Coat the base of a large pot with olive oil and place over a medium heat. Add the onion, garlic and teaspoon of brown sugar (or apple concentrate). Cover with a lid, reduce to a low heat and sweat for 10 minutes. Now add the spices (cinnamon, cardamom, ginger and coriander) and fry for a further 3 minutes, stirring constantly. Next, pour in the blended tomatoes, grate in the zest of half an orange, add a little salt and pepper and simmer for 10 minutes. Finally, stir the soft, roasted cherry tomatoes into the tomato sauce, check the seasoning and set aside. The fresh mint will be added later.

Halve the aubergines lengthways and use a spoon to scoop out most of the flesh, leaving about ¾cm thickness around the edge. Brush the inside and outside of the aubergine halves with olive oil and roast in the oven for 15 minutes, until starting to soften. Don't discard the scooped-out flesh (see introduction for suggestions). When the aubergines are done, reduce the oven to 180°C.

While the aubergines are roasting, start making the stuffing. Place the dry couscous in a bowl, add a pinch of salt, pour 300ml of boiling water over and leave for 10 minutes, fluffing up with a fork once or twice. Spread the flaked almonds onto a baking tray and toast in the oven until golden,

about 5 minutes, tossing once or twice. Chop the onion and garlic finely. Coat the base of a small pot with olive oil, add the onion, garlic and bay leaves, cover with a lid and fry until soft. Remove the bay leaves and set aside.

Lastly, coat the base of a frying pan sparsely with olive oil, place over a high heat and add half of the baby spinach. Cook until soft, stirring regularly, until most of the moisture has evaporated from the pan. Repeat with the second batch of spinach. Now combine all the elements of the stuffing in a large mixing bowl: couscous, toasted almonds, frozen peas, wilted spinach, onion and garlic. Chop the fresh coriander, stir it into the mix and season with salt and pepper.

Fill each of the aubergine halves with stuffing and return to the baking tray. Don't press the stuffing in too firmly; the couscous should stay light and fluffy. Cover the tray with foil and bake in the oven for 25 minutes. When the aubergines are almost ready, bring the chunky tomato sauce back to a gentle simmer. Chop the fresh mint finely and stir it into the sauce. To serve, heat the dinner plates, spoon a generous portion of tomato sauce onto each and place an aubergine in the centre of the sauce. Garnish with a sprig of mint.

Cook's notes

Baba ghanoush (roast aubergine dip)
v gf wf yf

Baba ghanoush could be described as aubergine hummus — the flavourings are similar, with roasted aubergine replacing chickpeas as the main ingredient. It is delicious as a dip or a spread.

For the dip
500g aubergine *(scooped out flesh from the stuffed aubergine recipe opposite, or whole aubergines)*
2 cloves of garlic
4-5 sprigs of fresh parsley
2-3 tbsp lemon juice
1½ tbsp light tahini
2 tbsp extra-virgin olive oil
Salt and pepper

To garnish
1 lemon cut into wedges
Parsley

Preheat oven to 200°C.

If using scooped-out pulp, toss in olive oil, salt and pepper and roast until soft. If using whole aubergine(s), pierce the skin a few times with a fork and roast whole for 40 minutes, allow to cool, then cut in half and scoop out all the flesh, discarding the skin.

When the roasted aubergine is completely cool, blend all the ingredients together in a food processor until almost smooth. Season with salt and pepper. Refrigerate until ready to serve, then place in a suitable bowl and drizzle with olive oil. Garnish with some lemon wedges and sprigs of parsley. Serve with warm pita bread or a selection of crudités: raw chilled carrot, celery, cucumber, red pepper and florets of broccoli (see page 195).

Quiche

Cornucopia has been serving quiche since the dawn of time, or, at least, since the conversion of Dr Shoe dry cleaners and shoe repair shop into a wholefood shop and deli in 1986. Deirdre, our proprietor, recalls that back then, when vegetarian food was still extremely rare and, for some, a bit scary, the quiche was a recognisable food that some of the more nervous customers felt safe ordering. The 'real men don't eat quiche' phenomenon never made it to Cornucopia, where hearty slices of this versatile eggy bake have been enjoyed by both sexes for over twenty years.

This quiche section includes two recipes for popular Cornucopia quiche combinations. However, first of all, it outlines the basic method for putting together a quiche from scratch: your own crisp, buttery pastry case, a rich creamy egg custard and an open invitation to fill the quiche with whatever vegetables, cheeses and flavourings your heart desires.

Making a basic quiche
Note: this recipe is suitable for a 30cm fluted tart case.

Making the pastry

350g plain flour
175g butter
Pinch of salt

- To make it by hand, sift the flour into a mixing bowl, add a pinch of salt and combine. Grate the cold butter coarsely (or chop it into small cubes) and add to the bowl. Use the tips of your fingers to rub the butter into the flour until it is evenly distributed and the mix resembles fine breadcrumbs. Now add very cold water drop by drop, just enough to bring the ingredients together into a soft dough. Push it together into a ball.
- To make the pastry using a food processor, place the flour and salt into the food processor and pulse to combine. Add the butter and blitz until it is evenly distributed and the mix resembles fine breadcrumbs. Now add very cold water bit by bit and pulse until the ingredients come together into a ball.
- Whether you've made your pastry by hand or with a machine, it now needs to rest clingwrapped in the fridge for half an hour to allow the gluten to relax. This makes the dough less elastic and means that, when you roll it out and place it in a tart case, it is less likely to shrink away from the sides as it cooks.

For an interesting twist on this basic pastry recipe, try the following:

- Blend a handful of basil with 30ml extra-virgin olive oil until smooth. Stir this into the flour and butter mix just before adding the water. Use about 30g less butter to balance out the olive oil.
- Roast 50g of hazelnuts and chop them finely or blitz them in a food processor. Stir them into the flour and butter mix just before adding the water.

Rolling the pastry

When the pastry has rested for half an hour, place it on a well-floured flat surface and roll it out to about 3 millimetres thick. Take a 30cm loose-bottom fluted tart case and transfer the pastry onto it. A handy tip is to roll the pastry loosely around the rolling pin to help transport it without tearing it (see illustration). Press it gently into place and trim the edges. Use the trimmings to plug any gaps or cracks that may have occurred when moving the pastry. Hang onto a tiny 'repair kit' ball of trimmings in case you need them later. Place the rolled pastry case in the fridge to rest for half an hour. Meanwhile, preheat the oven to 180°C.

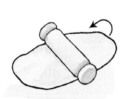 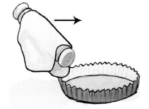 

Par baking the pastry

When the pastry has rested, cut a circle of parchment paper about 50cm in diameter, place it onto the rolled tart case and fill it with a layer of beans – these can be any dried beans (kidney beans, chickpeas, butter beans, cannellini beans) or specially manufactured ceramic beans. Bake in the oven for 15 minutes, then remove the beans and parchment paper and bake for a further 5-10 minutes, until the base is golden brown, dry and slightly crisp. If any cracks or fissures occurred during baking, use your 'repair kit' of raw pastry to fill them. Retain the baking beans, as they can be used over and over again. The tart case is now ready to be filled with ingredients of your choice and topped up with egg custard.

Assembling the quiche

For the egg custard:
4 free-range eggs
125ml cream
125ml milk
Pinch of freshly grated nutmeg
Salt and pepper

Whisk all the egg custard ingredients together in a bowl or large jug. Arrange fillings of your choice (see below) in the pre-baked tart case. Pour egg custard into the case, right up to the top, and transfer the quiche to the oven. If you have a shaky hand or a long distance from work surface to oven, place the quiche onto the oven shelf first and then top up with egg custard. Bake for 30 minutes on the middle shelf, or until the egg in the centre of the tart is set. As the quiche will have puffed up in the heat, allow it to settle back down for 5 minutes before removing it from the ring, slicing and serving.

Some popular quiches
Other than the two recipes that follow, here are some popular quiche combinations on the Cornucopia menu:

Broccoli, strong cheddar & almond
Blanched broccoli, grated vegetarian strong cheddar, flaked almonds

Red pepper, goat's cheese & spinach
Roasted strips of red pepper, vegetarian goat's cheese sliced into half moons, pan-wilted baby spinach

Tomato, spring onion & smoked cheese
Thinly sliced tomatoes, finely chopped spring onions, grated vegetarian smoked cheese

Leek, mushroom & blue cheese
Roasted or pan-fried leeks and mushrooms, finely cubed vegetarian blue cheese

Potato, feta, red onion & rosemary
Baby potatoes halved and roasted with finely chopped rosemary, roasted slices of red onion, crumbled vegetarian feta cheese

Courgette, sweet potato & smoked cheese
Roasted courgette rounds and cubes of sweet potato, grated vegetarian smoked cheese

Courgette, blue cheese & pine nut quiche

cn

Pine nuts, though a little expensive, are a real treat. In this quiche, their slightly sweet flavour and delicate texture contrast beautifully with the blue cheese. As pine nuts are susceptible to decay, once opened, store them in the fridge. Alternatively, turn them immediately into a fabulous pesto, as described opposite.

In Cornucopia, we use Cashel Blue cheese – the first Irish farmhouse blue cheese, produced by a husband and wife team on a dairy farm in County Tipperary. It is a creamy, crumbly vegetarian blue cheese, available in supermarkets and delicatessens all over Ireland and in some specialist food stores around the world.

If serving this quiche with a side salad, try lightly dressed rocket leaves, as their peppery tang holds its own in the company of the salty and flavourful blue cheese.

For the pastry
350g plain flour
175g butter
Pinch of salt

For the custard
4 free-range eggs
125ml cream
125ml milk
Pinch of freshly grated nutmeg
Salt and pepper

For the filling
2 courgettes
150g vegetarian blue cheese
A few sprigs of fresh dill
50g pine nuts
Extra-virgin olive oil
Salt and pepper

30cm loose-bottom
fluted tart case

Preheat your oven to 200°C.

Start by making the pastry, by hand or in a food processor, as described on page 300. Clingwrap and place in the fridge for half an hour.

Next, prepare the filling for the tart. Chop the dill as finely as you can. Dice the blue cheese into small cubes. Slice the courgettes into ½cm-thick rounds. Coat a pan sparsely with olive oil and place over a medium heat. Pan-fry the courgettes until tender and light-brown on both sides.

Meanwhile, make the custard. Whisk together the eggs, milk and cream, along with a pinch of freshly grated nutmeg, a pinch of salt and a twist of pepper.

Remove the pastry from the fridge and roll, rest and par bake it as described on page 301. When the tart case has been baked, spread half of the courgette rounds evenly over the base. Next, scatter with dill, blue cheese and pine nuts. Top with the rest of the courgettes, in a nice pattern. Finally, fill the case with egg custard to the top of the pastry shell and bake for 30 minutes, or until the egg in the centre of the tart is set. Rest for 5 minutes before removing it from the ring and cutting into slices. Serve with a salad, perhaps dressed with the pine nut pesto described below.

Basil pesto

Pesto is a real luxury item and homemade fresh pesto even more so. Stir it through hot spaghetti for a simple pasta dish. Toss baby potatoes or lightly cooked green beans in it. Dip fresh, crusty artisan bread in it. Place a spoon of it into your soup or over your salad. Although 'classic' Italian pesto requires pine nuts, cashew nuts or flaked almonds can also be used to replace part or all of the pine nuts.

Note: commercial pestos, unless otherwise stated, are made with Parmesan cheese, which is not vegetarian.

50g pine nuts *(or cashews, flaked almonds)*
50g *(big bunch)* fresh basil
75g vegetarian regato cheese
2 cloves of garlic
200ml extra-virgin olive oil
Pinch of pepper
Salt — maybe

Toast the nuts in a medium oven for 6-8 minutes, until golden. Set aside to cool. Grate the regato cheese. Then blend all the ingredients in a food processor. Taste the pesto before adding salt, as it's probable that none will be necessary, depending on the saltiness of the regato. Don't over-blend the pesto; try to retain a pleasant element of texture. Pesto can be stored in the fridge for up to one week.

Cherry tomato, feta, spinach & olive quiche

This quiche looks so pretty when assembled: red tomatoes, white feta, black olives and green spinach. I favour spreading the spinach evenly across the bottom of the tart case, evenly sprinkling the feta and black olives on top and then carefully arranging the roasted cherry tomatoes halves, all facing up, in an attractive pattern. Not only does the quiche look delightful when it emerges from the oven, but each slice is vibrant with colourful layers.

An interesting variation on this would be to leave out the spinach and make basil pastry instead of a regular pastry, instructions for which can be found on page 301. You can also replace the roasted cherry tomatoes with thin slices of fresh vine tomatoes for a slightly lighter quiche. If doing so, place the tomatoes in a sieve after slicing and sprinkle with a little salt to draw out the moisture. This will encourage some of the excess juices to drain off, preventing the pastry becoming too moist.

Quiche can be served cold for lunch boxes or picnics. If you are cooking it as finger food, rather than for a hot meal, you might like to bake it in a square baking tray rather than a round tart case, so it can be sliced into little squares, which will pack better and also be easier to pick up than big wedges.

Preheat your oven to 180°C. Start by making the pastry, by hand or in a food processor, as described on page 300. Clingwrap and place in the fridge for half an hour.

Next, prepare the filling for the tart. Slice the cherry tomatoes in half, toss them in a little olive oil, salt and pepper, transfer to a baking tray and roast for about 20 minutes, turning once or twice. Meanwhile, coat the base of a frying pan sparsely with olive oil and place over a high heat. When the pan is hot, add the baby spinach and fry for a few minutes, until it is soft and most of the moisture has evaporated off the pan. Chop the feta cheese into small cubes. Remove the pits from the black olives (if necessary) and slice them in half.

Remove the pastry from the fridge and roll, rest and par bake it as described on page 301. While

For the pastry
350g plain flour
175g butter
Pinch of salt

For the custard
4 free-range eggs
125ml cream
125ml milk
Pinch of freshly grated nutmeg
Salt and pepper

For the filling
200g cherry tomatoes
200g baby spinach — *washed &*
    drained if not pre-washed
100g vegetarian feta cheese
75g black olives
Extra-virgin olive oil
Salt and pepper

Cook's notes

the case is baking, make the egg custard by whisking together all the ingredients. When the tart case is ready, arrange the cherry tomatoes, spinach, feta cheese and olives neatly inside, making sure that the spinach is evenly distributed, not clumped together.

Finally, fill the case with egg custard to the top of the pastry shell and bake for 30 minutes, or until the egg in the centre of the tart is set. Rest for 5 minutes before removing from the ring and cutting into slices.

Sweet potato, spinach & hazelnut en croûte on parsnip mash with red wine & juniper gravy   *cn*

The en croûte is a crisp and delicate flaky pastry filled with delicious herb and onion stuffing, rich spinach and hazelnut purée and caramelised batons of sweet potato. When it emerges golden and fragrant from the oven, it is carved into slices, two of which are placed on a generous mound of creamy potato and parsnip mash, and surrounded by a rich, deeply flavoured red wine and juniper berry gravy. Serve this dish as a wonderful vegetarian Christmas dinner, or as an impressive winter dinner party centrepiece, a sumptuous treat for vegetarians and non-vegetarians alike.

This imaginative and challenging dish was created by head chef Tony Keogh and head pastry chef Claire McCormick for a gourmet vegetarian cooking demonstration hosted by Farmleigh House in the Phoenix Park. The en croûte (which literally means 'in a crust') was suggested as a main course, whilst the dolmades (stuffed cabbage leaves) on page 278 were featured as a starter.

Before you embark on the en croûte journey, bear in mind that it is quite a complex dish with many elements, which will require several hours (4-6) of preparation and a broad range of ingredients, so give yourself plenty of time for both shopping and cooking. You will be rewarded for all your efforts with an exceptionally fantastic festive feast. The recipe has been written so that each individual element of the dish can be made separately, allowing you to make some of the bits in advance, to save yourself being under a lot of pressure just before the mealtime. You could, for example, make the pastry, gravy and fillings one evening, which would leave just the assembly of the en croûte and the potato and parsnip mash for the next day, enabling you to serve your meal at lunchtime or dinnertime without so much as breaking a sweat!

The pastry in this recipe is called flaky pastry, which falls somewhere between shortcrust and puff pastry. To achieve a melt-in-the-mouth flaky crust, the pastry-making process should be both brief and cool. Heat stretches the gluten in the flour, making for a dense, chewy pastry rather than a short, light crust. To prevent this, frozen butter is grated into flour, ice-cold water and a drop of lemon is used to bring it together, without the gluten stretching. The ingredients should be brought together as quickly as possible and then refrigerated immediately. After half an hour, it is rolled out and folded over several times to encourage layers of butter to form in the flour, which, in the heat of the oven, will puff out the pastry and make it crispy all the way through.

Juniper berries are available from gourmet supermarkets and Asian supply shops. They add a pleasantly sharp, tangy note to the deeply flavoured red wine gravy. Juniper berries are not actually berries, but the cones of the juniper tree. The young green cones are the keynote flavour in making gin, which actually comes from the French word *genièvre*, which means juniper. For cooking, however, the mature, resinous red cones are favoured.

Finally, a word of advice about making the en croûte. Read the recipe from start to finish so that you are familiar with all the processes that will be involved. Make a shopping list based on all the separately listed ingredients. Map out a time schedule for making the dish from start to finish, so that you do not find yourself racing against the clock on what is likely to be a special day. Try to include in your schedule a momentary break from the kitchen for yourself towards the end of cooking. Having put so much energy into producing a meal fit for kings, you deserve to enjoy it just as much as the other hungry guests. If you have the mash and gravy ready to be reheated and the herbs for garnish chopped and set aside, as well as the table laid, then as soon as the en croûte goes into the oven, you should have time for a breath of fresh air, a quick change of attire or a relaxing glass of wine before you return to serve up your feast.

Flaky pastry
250g plain flour
½ tsp salt
150g butter *(frozen for half an hour before use)*
1 tbsp lemon juice
125ml ice-cold water

Parsnip mash
5 parsnips — *about 800g*
5 medium floury potatoes *(such as roosters) — about 1.3kg*
75g butter
100ml warm milk
Pinch of freshly grated nutmeg
Salt and pepper

Red wine & juniper gravy
1 large onion
2 carrots
Leaves of a head of celery
1 leek
3 field mushrooms

For the pastry
Place the butter in the freezer for half an hour before using. Sift the flour into a large bowl and stir in the salt. Using the course side of your grater, grate in the frozen butter (no need to rub it into the flour) and add the lemon juice and water. Mixing quickly, bring all the ingredients together into a ball. Knead briefly to a pastry dough consistency then wrap in clingwrap and refrigerate for half an hour.

Remove the dough from the fridge and roll it into an oblong shape. With the back of a knife, mark two lines to divide the dough in thirds lengthways. Fold one end towards the centre and fold the other end over it. Roll again into an oblong and repeat the folding process. This will create layers of butter in the pastry, which, when heated, will allow it to puff out slightly in the oven. Again, wrap the dough in clingwrap and refrigerate for at least half an hour before use.

For the mash
Peel the parsnips and chop them into medium chunks. Place them in a large pot and cover with

2 cloves of garlic

2 bay leaves

10 juniper berries

2 tbsp plain flour

A few stalks of thyme

A few stalks of sage

1 tbsp *(heaped)* tomato purée

50ml shoyu/good quality
    soy sauce

1 heaped tbsp unrefined brown
sugar

200ml vegetarian red wine

Salt and pepper

Extra-virgin olive oil

500ml water

En croûte filling

3 medium sweet potatoes — *about
    500g*

400g hazelnuts

2 bulbs of garlic

Extra-virgin olive oil

25g *(small bunch)* each of fresh
    sage, fresh thyme and fresh
    parsley

600g red onions *(divided into 2
    batches of 300g)*

125ml vegetarian red wine

80g breadcrumbs

250g baby spinach — *washed and
    rinsed if not pre-washed*

¾ clove freshly grated nutmeg

2 free-range eggs

Salt and pepper

plenty of water and a pinch of salt. Bring to the boil, cover with a lid and simmer until soft, about 15 minutes. Drain and set aside.

Meanwhile, peel and quarter the potatoes. Place them in a large pot of salted water and bring to the boil. Reduce to a low heat, cover with a lid and simmer until soft. Drain in a colander, and then return the potatoes to the same pot over a very low heat to release as much excess moisture as possible. Remove from the ring.

Mash the potatoes in their pot. Add in the parsnip, butter, nutmeg and milk. Mash all the ingredients together until the mix is smooth. Season to taste and set aside, to be reheated before dinner. Alternatively, make the mash while the en croûte is baking, so it is ready just as the pastry emerges hot from the oven.

For the gravy
Start by preparing the vegetables for the gravy stock. Roughly chop the onion, carrots, celery leaves, leek, mushrooms and garlic. Rinse the chopped leek under cold water to remove any traces of soil and then drain thoroughly. Now cover the base of a large pot with a generous splash of olive oil and place over a medium heat. Add all the chopped vegetables, as well as the bay leaves and juniper berries. Stir briefly to coat with oil, cover with a lid, reduce to a low heat and leave to sweat for 30 minutes, stirring occasionally to ensure nothing sticks and burns.

When the stock has fully sweated, rain in the flour and cook over a really low heat for five minutes, stirring continuously. If the mixture begins to stick to the base of the pot, add a little water and continue stirring. Next, add the thyme, sage, tomato purée, shoyu/soy sauce, water and a good twist of black pepper. Cook gently for 30 minutes stirring occasionally.

While the gravy stock is cooking, take a medium pot and gently melt the sugar over a very low heat. Next, pour the wine over the melted sugar. It will make a dramatic crackling sound and the sugar will immediately crystallise into blocks, but it will melt again presently. Simmer the sweetened wine for 10 minutes to burn off any alcohol, and then set aside.

Place a fine sieve over the wine/sugar pot and pour the liquid contents of the stock pot into it. Using the back of a ladle, press as much liquid as possible through the mesh. Now remove the sieve and discard the remaining solid vegetable matter. Whisk the contents of the pot over a low simmer to form a smooth gravy. Season to taste and set aside. When you are ready to serve, simply return to a gentle simmer. Add a splash of water if you prefer a slightly thinner gravy.

For the en croûte filling
Preheat your oven to 180°C. Puncture the skin of the sweet potatoes once or twice with a knife. Place them on a baking tray (or wrap them in foil) and roast in the oven until soft, about 45-50 minutes. Set aside to cool, then remove the skins and slice them lengthways into quarters.

Meanwhile, place the hazelnuts on a tray and toast them in the oven for 8 minutes. Set aside to cool, then rub vigorously to remove the loose skins. At the same time, roast the garlic. Slice the top off both bulbs. Toss in a little olive oil, salt and pepper and stand them, cut side up, in a tray. Pour a little more olive oil into the opening at the top, so that the cloves inside are coated with oil. Roast them in the oven until soft, about 30 minutes. Set aside to cool.

When cool, squeeze the soft flesh out through the cut end of the bulbs. Discard the skins.

Chop the fresh herbs very finely and thinly slice the red onions. Set 300g of the onions to one side. Cover the base of a large pot with olive oil and place over a medium heat. Add 300g onions, stir briefly to coat with oil and then cover with a lid and reduce to a low heat to sweat for 15 minutes, stirring occasionally. Next add the red wine to the pot and reduce over a low heat for five minutes to burn off any alcohol. Remove from the heat and stir in the breadcrumbs and most of the finely chopped herbs, keeping a small handful for garnishing at the finish. Season the onion stuffing to taste and set aside.

Next, coat a frying pan sparsely with olive oil, place over a high heat and add half of the baby spinach. Add some salt and pepper and wilt until the spinach is soft and no moisture remains in the pan. Repeat with the second batch of baby spinach. In a food processor, grind the remaining 300g of (still raw) red onions, the flesh of the roast garlic, the wilted spinach and freshly ground nutmeg. Add one egg and half of the toasted hazelnuts. Blend for one minute. Add the second egg and blend for a further minute until completely smooth. Add the remaining hazelnuts and pulse for a few seconds until just roughly chopped. Season to taste.

To assemble
1 free-range egg
Pinch of salt
Cracked black pepper
(or freshly ground)

Large baking tray of at least 25x35cm

To assemble

When you are ready to assemble your en croûte, preheat your oven to 180°C and prepare some egg wash by whisking 1 free-range egg with a small drop of cold water and a pinch of salt. On a lightly floured surface, roll the pastry into a 34 x26cm rectangle, with the longest side facing you.

Transfer the rolled pastry to a large baking tray, with part of the side furthest from you (about 8cm of it) flopped over the edge of the tray. This is the side that will eventually fold over

the filling. Leaving a border of 3cm on the length nearest you, as well as the two short ends, cover 15cm of the pastry with herb and onion stuffing (leaving the pastry on the other side uncovered). On top of the onions, place half of the spinach and hazelnut mixture. Nestle the sweet potato batons lengthways into the centre and cover with the remaining spinach mixture.

Brush a little egg wash along the two short sides, as well as along the edge of the side furthest from you. Lifting up the 3cm border nearest you, carefully fold the length furthest from you over the filling to overlap the pastry nearest you. Roll the en croûte over slightly, so that the seal is carefully secured underneath. Seal the open ends of the en croûte by folding over the 3cm borders and pressing them together. Brush egg wash all over the whole pastry and sprinkle some roughly cracked black pepper over the top. Bake in the oven for 40 minutes, until golden brown all over. Leave to sit for at least 10 minutes before slicing and serving.

To serve

While the en croûte is relaxing, reheat the potato and parsnip mash if necessary and bring the juniper gravy to a gentle simmer. Pop the dinner plates in the still-warm oven to heat. To serve, spoon a mound of parsnip mash in the centre of each plate. Surround this with a moat of juniper gravy, place two slices of en croûte leaning against the side of the mash and sprinkle with some of the remaining chopped herbs.

Alternative assembly: *Wellington option*

This is another way to assemble the en croûte,

To assemble
1 free-range egg
Pinch of salt
Cracked black pepper
    (or freshly ground)

Kitchen scissors
Large baking tray of at
    least 25x35cm

which looks rather wonderful when it is baked. Preheat your oven to 180°C and prepare some egg wash by whisking 1 free-range egg with a small drop of cold water. Set aside, ready for when you need it.

Roll the pastry into a 42x33cm rectangle, with the long side facing you. Carefully transfer it to a baking tray, centred. Unless you have an enormous tray, at this stage pastry will be flopping over all four sides. Leaving a 3cm border at either short end of the pastry, cover the central ⅓ of the length with herb and onion stuffing. Top that with half of the spinach and hazelnut mix. Nestle the batons of sweet potato along the very middle and then top with the other half of the spinach and hazelnut mix.

Use a kitchen scissors to cut the uncovered pastry on either side of the filling into 1cm strips, cutting from the outer edge towards the centre of the en croûte. Now wrap the pastry strips over the filling, taking one strip from the side nearest you, then one strip from the far side and so on. Fold them over at a very slight angle and make sure they overlap with each other in the centre, forming a pattern rather like a plait. Use the extra pastry at the two short ends of the en croûte to close over the two open ends. Brush the whole thing with egg wash and sprinkle with some roughly cracked black pepper.

Bake in the oven for 40 minutes, until golden brown all over. Let sit for ten minutes before slicing and serving. To serve, follow the directions exactly as for the main recipe.

Breads

Introduction to breads

Backstage in Cornucopia, at regular intervals a flour-dusted baker can be seen ascending from the basement kitchen bearing a large tray of bread tins filled with puffed-up loaves, proved to perfection, heading towards the main kitchen ovens. An hour later they may be heard leaving the upstairs kitchen clutching a tower of empty tins, bellowing 'Hot tins, coming through, watch your backs!' — all part of the continuous cycle of bread-in, bread-out that takes place over the course of a day in Cornucopia.

Front of stage at Cornucopia, there is a permanent installation next to the cash desk called the 'bread tray', which is filled daily with a selection of the flour-dusted baker's wares: wholemeal soda bread, multiseed spelt bread, granary bread and a daily special. In front of the bread tray sit two wicker baskets containing the savoury scones, one vegan and one cheesy. They arrive on the counter at noon, just in time for lunchtime service, still a little warm, having emerged from the oven no earlier than 11.30am. And sitting atop the coffee machine next to the bread tray (at time of writing, we're still a bit tight for space!), far from the crumbs and flour particles that might contaminate it, is a basket of individually wrapped slices of gluten-free bread, a staple for many bread-loving coeliacs.

You can wow customers with stunningly original salads, tempt them with a steaming casserole full of the best of seasonal, organic vegetables or distract them with devilishly yummy cakes, but sometimes what a person really wants is a good old slice of bread, plain and simple — with a cup of tea or a drop of soup or a generous scraping of butter. I think if I was down to my last 70c in this world (prices correct to May 2008!), I'd probably be quite happy to spend it on a doorstep of Cornucopia soda bread; it would fill me up with both carbohydrates and good memories and stave off impoverishment for a few hours yet.

We really are a nation of bread-eaters — toast for breakfast, sandwiches for lunch, scones for tea. There was a bit of a gloomy time for bread not so long ago, when many people had stopped baking bread at home and the emergence of freshly baked, gourmet and artisan breads had not yet taken off, a time when bread came almost exclusively to mean sliced pan in many households. Which is one reason why, in 1992, when Cornucopia introduced its own homemade, wholefood breads to the menu, they enjoyed such instant popularity, so real and hearty did they taste in comparison to the often insipid supermarket selection. The first bread recipes were introduced by Pamela Windsor, the then restaurant manager and head chef (an almost inconceivable combination of responsibilities in our now much busier restaurant). Many of the original recipes have remained the same to this day, though the gluten-free bread was refined along the way and the spelt bread was added in recent years.

Serving slice upon slice for year upon year to Cornucopia customers, we are privy to so many delightful quirks of human nature, observing the broad spectrum of bread behaviour from one person to the next. Some people butter their bread patiently and evenly and then slice it carefully into four or six identical pieces, before carefully dipping them one by one into their bowl of soup. Others bypass the butter, rip up the whole slice, plunge all the irregular hunks into the bowl at once and then eat them with a spoon. Some people eat every morsel right up to the very edge, but then staunchly ignore the crusts. Others specifically ask if we have any heels out the back, so much do they love their crusts. Some people request the same type of bread every day, and decline a replacement should their regular choice be sold out. Others enquire with raised eyebrow and a hint of anticipation 'What's the special bread today?' and take it regardless, variety being the spice of life. One (relatively middle-aged) lady always insisted that staff butter her bread for her because first her mother, and then her husband had always done it for her. Another lady, every time she drops by, buys one of each scone, because she simply cannot bear to choose between them. Another real dote comes in every day and orders two slices of soda and two butters to take away, and as he heads off to enjoy his elevenses, he never fails to assure us that he 'loves his soda bread'. In a decidedly exotic twist, Mediterranean customers rarely accept a side plate for their bread, they always pop it on top of their meal and, when later observed, use it to mop up every last morsel of juice and dressing. Each to their own where bread is concerned.

A good slice of bread really can put a smile on the faces of many. One crucial factor in good bread is freshness. Time is not kind to bread. Many commercial breads are pumped full of preservatives to combat the ravages of time spent in transit, on the shop shelf and in your bread bin, chemicals which themselves diminish the quality of the bread. The best natural, fresh, delicious bread is made and consumed within 24 hours, and where better to verify this than under your own roof, where not only do you get to tuck into slices of great bread, but you also get to enjoy the heavenly aromas that waft from your oven, the satisfaction of a job well done and the fulfilling sense that you are continuing a centuries-long tradition of home-baking. And what a precious tradition it is. My granny used to make scones every Sunday for teatime. Usually two batches — one brown, one white — served warm from the oven with butter, cheddar cheese and homemade jam from the plum tree and raspberry bushes in the garden. When I smell fresh scones, I smell my granny's. But I bet when my mother smells fresh scones, she smells something more deeply Proustian — she probably smells childhood, belonging, the bitter-sweetness of home, siblings, all sorts of fuzzy, half-remembered things that wrap themselves around her. And when my granny smells scones, I'm sure she is occasionally transported back to the hearth of her homestead in Drumlish, County Longford, where she learned the art of baking from her mother. Each of them, growing up in homes regularly filled with freshly baked bread and scones, assimilated the know-how naturally and can turn their hand to baking as easily as breathing in and out. That, unfortunately, is where our family's female-to-female baking legacy ends. Although my mother made a mean banana and walnut square when I was a child, as well as the best almond cookies I've ever tasted, she also worked full time, so I, like most of my peers, grew up predominantly on shop bread, and most of the baking knowledge I have gained is from books and professional kitchens. Our current 'foodie' generation, though we may possess several different kits for hand-rolling cucumber and avocado sushi, have completed an intermediate course in Thai cooking in Chiang Mai and can whip up a low GI tofu, asparagus and green bean buckwheat noodle stir-fry, is on the whole rather unsure of the basics of baking.

But it's not too late! Walk past an oven with a batch of bread in it, and experience the overpowering physical reaction — our bodies instinctively know that smell means something good, something comforting, something maternal, something ancient. The appreciation of homemade bread is buried somewhere deep within us, and can be re-ignited by a half-decent oven, a good recipe and a few bags of flour (which, incidentally, cost next to nothing). Hone your skills, develop tricks of the trade, figure out how baking bread can fit into your schedule. And you may never look at a sliced pan in the same way again.

Breads: some basic information

Bread tins

All the bread recipes in this chapter can be baked in a 2lb (900g) loaf tin, which is quite a standard tin, used all around the world. Although the precise shape may vary, its metric measurements are approximately 25x13x7cm. If you do not have a 2lb loaf tin, options for free-form loaves and plaits and mini rolls have also been described (page 332), all of which can be baked on a flat baking sheet.

Most bread tins available in kitchen shops are of the non-stick variety. If you are buying a loaf tin, invest in the heaviest-weight one you can find — it will last much longer and is less likely to buckle over time. When you wash your tin, don't use any abrasive scrubbers or pads, as they will strip away the non-stick coating and leave an uneven surface that bread will cling to. Just use a soft cloth to wipe away any debris. Make sure to dry the tin thoroughly before putting it away, or turn it upside down in the oven if it is still a little warm.

Note: Teflon used to make non-stick pans has been inconclusively linked to certain health hazards. As a result, some cooks choose not to use them. Should you be concerned, use stainless steel bakeware lined with parchment paper.

Removing the bread from the tin

It is absolutely heart-breaking to put your time and energy into baking a loaf of bread, only to have it come apart as you try to take it out of the tin. This is more likely to happen with soda breads and baking powder breads than yeast bread, as the stretchy, elastic dough of the yeast bread doesn't tend to cling to the side of the tin and is strong enough to withstand any tapping or shaking you employ to help it out of the tin. To avoid the disaster of the broken loaf, all tins, non-stick or not, should be well greased before baking bread in them. This, in theory at least, will allow the cooked loaf to slide effortlessly out of the tin. In reality, running a knife around the edge of the bread before turning it out should help the more stubborn loaves to emerge. And if you are using a rather old tin, it is advisable both to grease the tin and line it with parchment paper. Measure the internal dimensions of the base of your tin. Draw a rectangle of those dimensions on your parchment paper. Extend each side by slightly more than the height of the tin and cut it out (see diagram opposite). If you use the tin regularly, you might as well cut out a cardboard template for future use, or cut several linings at once.

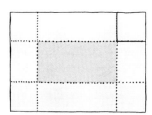
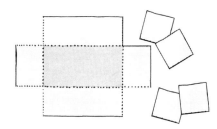

The hollow bread test

This is not to be confused with the 'Why is there a hole in my bread?' conundrum. The reason for the latter, incidentally, is often improperly knocked-back yeast dough – where not all the carbon dioxide bubbles have been punched out and an uneven pocket of air grows during the second proving – so make sure you give your yeast loaves a good pummelling between provings. Back to the hollow bread test, however, which is a way of finding out if your bread is cooked. When the bread has been in the oven for the advised length of time and it seems well risen and browned on top, remove it from the oven and turn it out onto a wire rack. Tap the centre of the underside of the loaf. If the bread is cooked through, it will feel firm and make a hollow sound. If, on the other hand, it feels soft, moist or spongy and makes no sound, or a very dull sound, when tapped, return it to the oven for another 5-10 minutes. The same test applies to scones. If you discover they are undercooked, turn them all upside down and return to the oven for 3-5 minutes.

'Sweaty' bread & crusty bread

When bread emerges from the oven, it lets off steam. For this reason, you should never leave the loaf to cool in the tin, as the vapour becomes trapped, turns to water and your lovely bread ends up sitting in a puddle of its own condensation. For exactly the same reason, never wrap fresh bread in an airtight bag or container until it is completely cool, or it will rain moisture on itself and end up soggy and damp. As the moisture evaporates from the bread, the outside of the loaf becomes quite dry, which leads to a crispy crust, much loved by many for dipping in soup and mopping up vinaigrette. If you prefer a softer crust, particularly in the case of soda bread or spelt bread, which can be quite difficult to cut if the crust is too tough, turn the loaf onto a wire rack and cover it with a tea towel. This allows the steam to evaporate, but prevents the crust from hardening.

Cutting bread

It is a difficult challenge to resist hacking into a fresh loaf of bread only minutes after it emerges from the oven, as the aromas almost demand that you tuck in immediately. However, it is best to wait a while. Cutting hot bread is nearly impossible; the dough just clumps around the knife and you end up with balls of bread rather than slices. Also, any of the loaf that you don't cut will go stale almost instantaneously when the hot dough is exposed to cold air. And another reason, all your efforts will taste so much better if left to cool a bit. Whereas bread straight from oven tastes predominantly of heat and dough, bread that has settled for an hour has had time to establish its flavours and textures, as well as slicing beautifully and not going prematurely stale. If you like warm bread, make little single-portion rolls from yeast bread; they don't need to be sliced and can be devoured in their entirety. Follow any of the recipes for yeast bread in this chapter. After the dough is knocked back, divide it into eight mini rolls on a baking tray, prove again and bake for about 15 minutes. After 5 minutes on a wire rack, they're ready to hit the table.

Shelf life

Homemade bread contains none of the preservatives and stabilisers used by a lot of commercial bakeries to give their products an extended shelf life. Another factor that increases the shelf life of bread is the quantity of oils or fats in the recipe. French baguettes, for example, have no fat content and, as a result, go stale within a day. French brioche, on the other hand, contains a lot of butter and stays fresh for several days. In Cornucopia we keep the fat content of our breads very low.

As a result, all the breads in this chapter are most delicious eaten fresh within 24 hours of baking or toasted within 48 hours of baking. Scones should ideally be eaten on the day they are baked. The next day they can be revived by 5 minutes in a medium oven. Gluten-free bread, as explained before that recipe, has exceptionally short 'keep-ability', as the protein gluten, which helps keep most breads moist, is absent, so the bread dries out really quickly. In both the case of scones and gluten-free bread, it has been suggested in the recipes to freeze whatever won't be consumed immediately and defrost it as required. Best-case scenario, however, with all homemade breads and scones is a willing and hungry audience waiting to devour your wares, rendering the question of shelf life redundant.

Timescale

As an indication of the time required between starting baking and serving up fresh bread, the chart below tracks each of the recipes in this chapter from mixing bowl to mouth.

Timescale	Prep. work	Mixing time	First prove	Second prove	Baking time	Cooling time	Total time
Basic yeast bread	add flavour	15 mins	90 mins	30 mins	60 mins	60 mins	4 h 15 mins
Granary		15 mins	90 mins	30 mins	60 mins	60 mins	4 h 15 mins
Poppy seed		15 mins	90 mins	30 mins	60 mins	60 mins	4 h 20 mins
Basil	5 mins	15 mins	90 mins	30 mins	60 mins	60 mins	4 h 20 mins
Sun-dried tomato	20 mins	15 mins	90 mins	30 mins	60 mins	60 mins	4 h 35 mins
Soda		15 mins			75 mins	60 mins	2 h 50 mins
Spelt		15 mins			60 mins	60 mins	2 h 15 mins
Gluten-free		15 mins			105 mins	120 mins	4 hours
Plain scones		15 mins			25 mins	20 mins	1 hour
Tomato scones	10 mins	15 mins			25 mins	20 mins	1 h 10 mins
Squash scones	45 mins (incl. veg roasting time)	15 mins			25 mins	20 mins	1 h 45 mins

Yeast breads

The four recipes that follow, along with the myriad suggested variations that you can try, are all yeast breads: breads in which the raising agent is fermenting yeast, as opposed to the bread soda and baking powder-based recipes towards the end of this chapter.

The most common baker's yeast available to the home cook, and the yeast used in these recipes, is active dry yeast, which comes in the form of dry granules. These granules are stirred into warm water. Awakened from a long hibernation by immersion in water, the yeast fizzes with delight, forming a thick layer of froth on the surface of the water. Having whetted the appetite of the yeast with a warm water aperitif, you can now stir it into the flour mix, where it will quickly realise that dinner has been served. The yeast tucks ravenously into the carbohydrates in the flour — and, not unlike a human being who has just had a large and rather rapidly consumed dinner, possibly washed down by a pint of beer — a by-product of the yeast's feast is the emission of carbon dioxide gas. As the yeast feeds, it constantly reproduces itself by budding, thus increasing the amount of activity in the dough. So proving the dough for 1½ hours actually means allowing the yeast to feed on the carbohydrates in the flour, all the time releasing tiny bubbles of carbon dioxide, which cause the dough to expand to double its original size.

The dough is then knocked back — that is, completely punctured of air by punching and kneading — shaped into a loaf, and left to double in size again, this time in a tin. The first proving may seem pointless — why let the yeast create all that bubbly carbon dioxide and then simply punch it out? The reason is that the more the gluten in the dough is stretched and puffed, the lighter and more even the final texture of the bread will be. Also, the more comprehensively the molecules in the flour are broken down by the yeast, the more depth of flavour is released into the bread. Dough that was proved only once in the tin and then baked would be tough and bland, whereas bread that has proved twice will be light and flavourful. When the loaf is finally placed in the oven, the surge of temperature stimulates the yeast to have one final feeding frenzy before it dies happy, full to the gills and surrounded by carbon dioxide bubbles of its own creation.

Yeast is quite a reliable friend, once you adhere to two precautions: care with the temperature of the water and patience in relation to proving. Unlike the use of baking powder and bread soda, a little extra or a little too little yeast will not result in total bread disaster (the bread will simply prove slightly more slowly, in which case you'll have to wait a little longer, or more quickly, which is sometimes desirable, for example in pizza dough or focaccia breads). However, scalding the yeast or rushing it through its paces will have adverse effects on its ability to leaven your bread. The optimum temperature in which yeast ferments (converts sugar to carbon dioxide) is 30-37°C. This is why you are advised to use body temperature water to bring the granules to life. Water that is below this temperature will simply slow down the activation process, but water above this temperature will damage the yeast. In temperatures of 40°C, the yeast becomes stressed and less effective and in temperatures of 50°C it dies completely – and the resultant bread will be useful only to the building trade. So err on the side of caution when preparing your starter water.

It was also mentioned that yeast must not be rushed. Proving the dough can seem to require a tedious amount of waiting, but it is all necessary to produce a light, airy loaf. Firstly, ensure that the yeast has formed a good thick layer of foam on the surface of the water when it is activated, before pouring it into the dry mix. Secondly, ensure that your dough has doubled in size before knocking back at the end of the first proving. The recommended time is 90 minutes, but if your dough is in a cool room this may take slightly longer. And finally, allow the shaped loaf to rise splendidly in the tin before transferring it to the oven; the yeast will die shortly after entering the heat, so there is limited scope for further rising once baking begins. If you stave off hunger, impatience and the pressures of modern life long enough to afford your dough all this time to do its thing, 50 minutes after placing it in the oven you will be rewarded with a light, chewy and incomparably fresh loaf of bread.

The four yeast recipes over the next few pages are all built upon the following simple recipe, using part wholemeal and part strong white flour (in the case of granary bread, the wholemeal is replaced with granary flour). Using these ingredients as your basic framework, you can add whatever herbs, spices, nuts, seeds and vegetables your taste buds command.

Basic yeast bread

375g strong white baker's flour*
125g fine wholemeal flour*
1 heaped tsp salt
70ml unrefined sunflower oil
1½ tsp active dried yeast
250-280ml warm water
    (body temperature)

*2lb (900g) loaf tin
    or flat baking sheet*

** For a more wholefoody loaf, use
250g strong white & 250g fine
wholemeal*

Add the yeast to the warm water and stir it once. Leave for 15 minutes in a warm place until it has formed a thick frothy layer on top. While the yeast activates, sift the two flours into a large bowl and mix in the salt. Stir in the oil evenly. If you are flavouring the bread, add your ingredients of choice now (see page 336 for suggestions). Form a well in the centre of the mix and, when the yeast is ready, pour it into the well. Use your hands to combine the wet and dry ingredients into a ball of dough. It should be soft and malleable, but not sticky. If it seems a little dry, add a drop of cold water. If it seems sticky, add a little extra flour.

Turn the dough out onto a lightly floured work surface and knead for 10 minutes. Return to the mixing bowl, cover it with a damp cloth and set aside in a warm place for at least 1½ hours, until it has doubled in size.

For a loaf tin
Knock back the dough by punching it and kneading it to its original size. Oil the bread tin and shape the dough into an oblong. Place it in the tin to prove again for ½ hour in a warm place.

For a free-form loaf
Knock back the dough by punching it and kneading it to its original size. Oil the baking sheet and shape the dough into a free-form roll. Use a knife to make three incisions across the top of the loaf and dust with a little flour. Place the dough on the baking sheet and prove again for ½ hour in a warm place.

As soon as the bread starts this second proving, turn your oven on to 180°C to preheat. After ½

Cook's notes

an hour, transfer the bread to the oven and bake for 50-60 minutes, until evenly browned. Turn it out of the tin and tap the base with your fingers. If it makes a hollow sound, the bread is cooked. Cool on a wire rack.

Shapes of yeast bread

All of the yeast bread recipes that follow can be baked in several different shapes, according to preference, sense of adventure and bakeware available.

Loaf tin
This is the simplest bread shape. It requires a 2lb (900g) loaf tin. After the first proving, knock back the dough and then form it into a loaf shape and prove again for ½ hour in the tin. Bake for 50-60 minutes. This shape is good for sandwiches and toast.

Free-form loaf
This is, as described, a more free shape than the loaf bread. It is baked on a flat baking sheet. After the first proving, knock back the dough and then form it into a neat oblong. Use a knife to make three incisions across the top of the loaf and dust with a little flour for a nice rustic effect. Prove again for an hour before baking for 40-50 minutes.

Mini rolls
Mini rolls are useful if you don't want to wait for your loaf to cool before slicing it. They need much less time in the oven and can be eaten almost immediately. They do not keep well, so should be eaten within a couple of hours of baking.

They are baked on a flat baking sheet. After the first proving, knock back the dough and then divide it into eight even portions. Form each portion into a small round and cut a single incision along the top of each. Transfer to an oiled baking sheet and prove again for ½ hour. Bake in the oven for 20-25 minutes. Cool for 5 minutes and then serve.

Plait

This is a rather impressive loaf, suitable for dinner parties or posh lunches. It is baked on a flat baking sheet. After the first proving, knock back the dough and then divide it into thirds. On a lightly floured surface, roll each third into a long strand, of equal lengths. Press the three

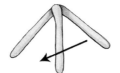

strands together at one end and gently plait them together. When you reach the far end, press the three strands together again. Transfer to a baking sheet and prove again for ½ hour. The plait will require 40-45 minutes in the oven.

Some of the more interesting breads
we have made over the years

In Cornucopia we have four standard daily breads: soda, spelt, granary and gluten-free. The fifth bread is called the special bread, which is the baker's choice of yeast bread, his or her chance at spontaneity. There are, of course, some reliable favourites — which have been included in this book. There have also been some more unusual experiments, some of which caused ripples of intrigue amongst our more daring customers. Although they may not be everyone's cup of tea, they do serve to illustrate just how adventurous bread-making can be. There is, I hasten to add, a lot to be said for a nice loaf of plain bread!

Yellow bread — add 1 dessertspoon each of turmeric and toasted cumin seeds for a bread that will glow in the dark.

Carrot & coriander bread — add 1 large raw carrot grated and 1 dessertspoon of toasted coriander seeds.

Sweet potato & rosemary bread — add 2 small or 1 large sweet potato baked and mashed and a few sprigs of finely chopped rosemary (reduce water slightly).

Cheddar & mustard bread — add 150g grated vegetarian cheddar and 1 dessertspoon of wholegrain mustard.

Roast Mediterranean vegetable bread — add 1 red pepper, ½ courgette, ½ aubergine diced into tiny cubes and roasted and 1 dessertspoon of tomato purée. Use olive oil in the dry mix.

Potato & chive bread — add 2 small or 1 large potato, baked and mashed, and a good handful of finely chopped fresh chives (reduce water slightly).

Chilli & olive — one handful pitted black olives chopped roughly, 1 tbsp cumin, 1 tbsp paprika, 2 cloves garlic chopped finely, 1 red chilli pepper chopped finely. Use olive oil in the dry mix.

St Patrick's Day bread — divide the dry mix evenly into three bowls. Leave 1 plain. Add 1 small carrot, boiled and mashed to another. Add 100g baby spinach, blanched and puréed to the third. Divide the yeast water between the three batches and knead each one. Keep them separate for the first proving. Twist them together into a loaf shape for the second proving, or form three strands and weave them together into a plait (see page 334). An Irish flag tricolour bread of green, white and orange will result.

Granary bread

v ♡

We've been asked for this recipe so many times over the years – the Cornucopia granary bread holds a certain fascination for a particular genre of bread-eater. It may be that it comes close enough to what some people might term normal bread (soft, light, white), but with all sorts of interesting knobbly bits that taste healthy without tasting too austere. It is, indeed, a delicious version of granary bread, textured not only by the malted wheat grains in the flour, but also by a generous handful of oats and sunflower seeds. This is the bread that we use for toast in the Cornucopia breakfast menu. Exposed to the heat of the toaster, the seeds and malted flakes crisp and sweeten, making a delightfully crunchy slice of toast. The granary bread also makes for a fantastic ploughman's lunch sandwich, with strong cheddar, pickles and a scraping of mustard.

Granary flour is actually a brand name, rather than a type of flour. It is produced by Rank Hovis in the UK, used extensively in the UK and Ireland and exported to specialist shops around the world. It is a mix of wholewheat brown flour and malted wheat grains. These malted grains are made by soaking wholewheat grains in water for two days, thus starting the sprouting process. They are then drained and laid out on tile floors to continue sprouting for three days. During this time the starch, once dormant in the grain, converts to maltose (sugar) to feed the shoot. The grains are subsequently piled up into heaps to intensify the heat produced by germination, speeding up the conversion of starch to maltose. The malted grains are then rolled (just like oats) to crack them and form them into flakes. The flakes are slow-roasted for two days to arrest germination and caramelise the maltose. The end product, deliciously crunchy, sweet grains, is blended with wholegrain flour to create the granary mix.

Other companies producing a similar kind of flour call it malthouse flour – this will give approximately the same results as the trademark 'Granary' flour in your bread.

In a suitable sized container, add the yeast to the warm water and stir it very gently just once. Leave for 15 minutes until it has formed a thick frothy layer on top.

While the yeast is coming alive, measure the flours (sift them), seeds, oats and salt into a large mixing bowl and combine well. Next, stir in the oil. When the yeasty water is ready,

250g granary flour *(or malthouse flour)*
250g strong white baker's flour
55g sunflower seeds
55g pinhead *(nibbed/kibbled)* oats — *use regular oats if unavailable*
1 heaped tsp salt
70ml unrefined sunflower oil
1½ tsp active dried yeast
280ml warm water *(body temperature)*

2lb (900g) loaf tin or a flat baking sheet

form a well in the centre of the flours and pour it in. Use your hands to combine the wet and dry ingredients into a ball of dough. It should be soft and malleable, but not sticky. If it seems a little dry, add a drop of cold water. If it seems sticky, rain in a little extra flour. Turn the dough out onto a lightly floured work surface and knead for 10 minutes, until stretchy and light.

Once well kneaded, return the dough to the mixing bowl and set aside in a warm place for 1½ hours to prove. Cover it with a damp cloth to prevent a skin forming on the surface. It will double in size.

When it has finished its first proving, beat back the dough by punching the air out and kneading it briefly. Oil the bread tin/baking sheet and shape the dough into a loaf/free-form (see page 333). Now leave it to prove in the tin/on the baking sheet for another ½ hour in a warm place. As soon as the bread starts this second proving, turn your oven on to 180°C to preheat. After half an hour, transfer the bread to the oven and bake for 50-60 minutes (loaf) or 40-50 minutes (free-form), until evenly browned. Turn it out of the tin and tap the base with your fingers. If it makes a hollow sound, the bread is cooked.

Set the granary bread on a wire rack to cool completely before cutting. For a crusty loaf, expose it to the air and, for a softer crust, cover with a tea towel while it's cooling.

Poppy seed bread

v ♡

Poppy seed bread is one of our most popular yeast breads – simple yet distinguished, it lends itself successfully to sweet or savoury flavours, be it coated with butter and jam (apricot jam in particular), dipped in a bowl of pumpkin soup or used to mop up a nice spicy curry. A particular favourite is toasted poppy seed bread covered with runny honey, an almost perfect combination of sweetness and nuttiness.

This poppy seed bread can be reworked as sesame seed bread or multiseed bread, using a similar quantity of whatever seeds are available in your kitchen. A rather unusual but delicious version is to add one red pepper, diced very finely, at the same time as you add the poppy seeds; it makes for a slightly moister bread with dramatic colouration.

Poppy seeds are a welcome addition to the kitchen cupboard, as their bluish-grey dottiness can bring visual and textural enhancement to all sorts of sweet and savoury creations. Sprinkle them on top of any kinds of breads, rolls, bagels or biscuits before baking for a lovely crunchy crust. Mix them through breadcrumbs as a nutty topping for gratins. In sweet baking, lemon and poppy seed is a classic combination. Add the zest of two lemons and 50g of poppy seeds to either the basic muffin recipe on page 404 or the basic rice cookie recipe on page 436 . Poppy seeds are also used as a pastry or bun filling in Central and Eastern Europe. Overleaf is a lovely recipe for sweet bread, traditional in Jewish kosher baking, using boiled ground poppy seeds.

375g strong white baker's flour*
125g fine wholemeal flour*
75g poppy seeds
1 heaped tsp salt
70ml unrefined sunflower oil
1½ tsp active dried yeast
280ml warm water
   (body temperature)

2lb (900g) loaf tin
   or flat baking sheet

* For a more wholefoody loaf, use 250g strong white & 250g fine wholemeal

In a suitable sized container, add the yeast to the warm water and stir it very gently just once. Leave for 15 minutes until it has formed a thick frothy layer on top.

While the yeast activates, combine the two flours (sift them), poppy seeds and salt in a large bowl and mix well. Next, stir in the oil and distribute evenly. When the yeast is ready, form a well in the centre of the flours and pour it in. Use your hands to combine the wet and dry ingredients into a ball of dough. It should be soft and malleable, but not sticky. If it seems a little dry, add a drop of cold water. If it seems sticky, rain in a little extra flour. Turn the dough out onto a lightly floured work surface and knead for 10 minutes. Once well kneaded, return the dough to the mixing bowl, cover it with a damp cloth and set aside in a warm place for 1½ hours to prove. It should double in size.

When the poppy seed dough has proved for 1½ hours, knock it back by punching it and kneading it into its original size. Oil the bread tin/baking sheet and shape the dough into a loaf/free-form (see page 333). Place it in the tin/onto the baking sheet to prove again for ½ hour in a warm place. As soon as the bread starts this second proving, turn your oven on to 180°C to preheat. After half an hour, transfer the bread to the oven and bake for 50-60 minutes (loaf) or 40-50 minutes (free-form), until evenly browned. Turn it out of the tin and tap the base with your fingers. If it makes a hollow sound, the bread is cooked.

Set the loaf of poppy seed bread on a wire rack to cool completely before cutting. For a crusty loaf, expose it to the air and, for a softer crust, cover with a tea towel while it is cooling.

Cook's notes

Hamentaschen (poppy seed sweet breads)

This is another lovely way to use poppy seeds. These rustic, triangular sweets are traditionally made for the Jewish holiday of Purim, which celebrates the delivery of the Jewish people from Haman's plot to annihilate them in ancient Persia. It takes place on the 14th day of Adar, a Hebrew month which falls around February/March on the Gregorian calendar.

For the poppy seed filling
150g poppy seeds
125ml milk
150g *(3 tbsp)* **runny honey**
    (organic if possible)
Zest of 2 lemons
100g raisins/sultanas

For the dough
400g plain flour
2 tsp *(heaped)* **baking powder**
1 tsp salt
125g caster sugar
1 free-range egg
    (plus extra for egg wash)
200ml milk
75g melted butter

2 flat baking trays

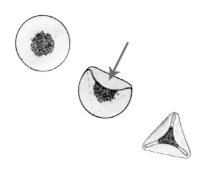

To make the poppy seed filling, grind the poppy seeds as thoroughly as possible in a coffee grinder (or using the rather more laborious pestle and mortar method). Place the ground seeds, milk and runny honey in a small pot over a very low heat and cook gently until thickened (about 15 minutes). Remove from the ring and stir in the lemon zest and raisins. Set aside to cool.

Turn your oven on to 180°C and grease the baking trays. Into a large mixing bowl, sift the flour and baking powder for the dough, then add the salt and sugar and stir to combine. Form a well in the centre of the mix. In a jug, whisk the egg and milk together and then add the melted butter. Pour this into the well in the flour and use your fingers to bring all the ingredients together into a soft dough. Turn this out onto a floured work surface and roll it to about ½cm thick. Using a cookie-cutter or tumbler, cut it into rounds of 7.5cm (3in) in diameter. Press each round to flatten slightly and form a small hollow in the centre. Spoon some poppy seed filling into this hollow and fold three sides towards the centre, forming a triangular pocket with filling still visible in the centre. Squeeze the sides together, then brush all over with egg wash. Bake for 20-25 minutes until well-risen and golden. Cool on a wire rack. Eat still a little warm or cold.

Basil bread

v ♡

Never, ever put a loaf of basil bread in the oven and head into town for the afternoon to run a few errands, leaving a friend or relative in charge of taking it out of the oven in your absence. There are two overriding reasons for this cautionary measure. Firstly, having gone to all the trouble of measuring, sifting, blending, kneading and proving your loaf, it really is not fair that you miss out on part one of the payback: the wonderfully transporting aroma that wafts from the oven as your basil bread cooks. It is an indisputable advertisement for home-cooking, that your home be filled from kitchen to rafters with perfumes of such promise. The second reason you had better not abandon your loaf to the care of others is that you may well discover, upon return, that all that remains of your hard work are a few guilty crumbs scattered about the worktop – it's hard to resist tearing open a fresh loaf of basil bread. It's one of those breads that requires no butter, no filling, no soup, no dressing to mop up; it's delicious just the way it is, with tones of olive oil, a hint of garlic and that heady flavour generated by generous quantities of fresh basil. Turn your back at your peril! Incidentally, the herby greenness of basil dough also makes for an impressive bread plait (see page 334).

This recipe can be used for any kind of herbed bread, or, indeed, a mixture of fresh herbs. Try rosemary, thyme, sage, oregano, chive, dill, tarragon or marjoram, following the instructions exactly as with basil bread. Note that, whilst the basil recipe calls for a large bunch of basil, you should adapt the quantity of herb based on its pungency; for example, rosemary, thyme and sage will require only a few sprigs to produce an aromatic loaf. You might like to try some of the following combinations:

Rosemary bread: 4-5 sprigs of rosemary and a good twist of freshly ground black pepper (use olive oil)
Sage & onion bread: 15 sage leaves with a finely diced red onion (use sunflower oil)
Garden herb bread: 25g (small bunch) chives, 4 sprigs thyme and 25g (small bunch) marjoram (use sunflower oil)
Yoghurt & dill bread: 4 tbsp natural yoghurt, 50g dill (medium bunch) and 1 heaped tsp unrefined brown sugar, (use 50ml less water to balance out the liquid in the yoghurt)

In a suitable sized container, add the yeast to the warm water and stir it very gently just once. Leave for 15 minutes to ferment. It will form a thick frothy layer on top. While the yeast ferments, place the olive oil, garlic and fresh basil into a food processor and blend until smooth. Sift the brown

375g strong white baker's flour*
125g fine wholemeal flour*
1 heaped tsp salt
100g *(big bunch)* fresh basil
2 cloves garlic
70ml extra-virgin olive oil
1½ tsp active dried yeast
250ml warm water
    (body temperature)

2lb (900g) loaf tin or
    a flat baking sheet

* *For a more wholefoody loaf,
use 250g strong white and 250g
fine wholemeal*

and white flours into a large mixing bowl and add the salt. Combine thoroughly. Now, add the basil oil to the mix and stir to distribute evenly.

When the yeast is ready, form a well in the centre of the mixing bowl and pour it in. Use your hands to integrate the wet and dry ingredients into a ball of dough. It should be soft and malleable, but not sticky. If it seems a little dry, add a drop of cold water. If it seems sticky, rain in a little extra flour. Turn the dough out onto a lightly floured work surface and knead for 10 minutes. It will be light and stretchy.

Now return the dough to the mixing bowl, cover it with a damp cloth to prevent a skin forming on the surface and set aside in a warm place for 1½ hours to prove. It should double in size.

When the basil dough has proved for 1½ hours, knock it back by punching all the air out of it and kneading it back to its original size. Oil the bread tin/baking sheet and shape the dough into a loaf/ free-form (see page 333). Place it in the tin/on the baking sheet to prove for another ½ hour, once again in a warm place. As soon as the bread starts this second proving, turn your oven on to 180°C to preheat.

After half an hour, transfer the bread to the oven and bake for 50-60 minutes (loaf), 40-50 minutes (free-form). Don't open and close the oven door during cooking. Turn it out of the tin and tap the base with your fingers. If it makes a hollow sound, the bread is cooked. Place bread on a wire rack to cool completely before cutting.

Sun-dried tomato bread

v ♡

This bread will really impress whoever you serve it to (yourself included). It has a great big flavour and, if you manage it, a really impressive bright red swirl or marbling effect running right through the loaf. This is quite easily, if a little messily, achieved. Rather than integrating all the sun-dried tomato paste into the bread mix, you add just a little of it to the main ingredients and retain most of it to roll into the dough after kneading. There is no scientific method for this. Basically, wrap the dough around the sun-dried tomato paste in whatever manner works, tucking, rolling, pushing, prodding. Just make sure you don't knead it in so much that it becomes part of the dough; you want lines of tomato running through a plainish dough. When cut, this loaf not only looks fantastic, but is also a pleasure to eat as you experience both the intense flavour of the sun-dried tomatoes and the chewy olive oil flavoured bread.

This bread makes a wonderful starter, served with some antipasto such as olives and slices of tasty cheese. You can also use it to whip up a gourmet toasted cheese sandwich. Cut a hearty slice of sun-dried tomato bread, toast it on one side, then layer some roasted or chargrilled aubergines onto the other side. Top with a mix of grated regato and cheddar and toast until golden and bubbling. Finish with a drizzle of olive oil and a couple of torn basil leaves and serve with some zingy rocket salad. Another nice variation is to make mini bread rolls instead of cooking a whole loaf. When you knock back the bread dough after the first proving, divide it into eight equal parts and shape them into balls or oblongs or whatever you fancy. Place them on a greased oven tray to prove for 30 minutes and then cook them for 15-18 minutes, significantly less time than is needed for a large loaf. Sit them on a wire rack for 5 minutes and then serve hot with soup or salad. These mini rolls should be eaten within a few hours.

Note: You may notice that this recipe requires slightly less salt than the other yeast bread recipes in this book. This is to balance out the saltiness of the sun-dried tomatoes.

Immerse the sun-dried tomatoes in boiling water and set aside for 15 minutes to plump up. Add the yeast to the warm water, stir once and leave for 15 minutes until it has formed a thick, frothy layer on top. While the yeast is fermenting in the warm water, make the tomato paste. Drain the now rehydrated sun-dried tomatoes. Destalk a few sprigs of oregano (or herb of your

375g strong white baker's flour*
125g fine wholemeal flour*
1 level tsp salt
75g dry-stored sun-dried
    tomatoes
70ml extra-virgin olive oil
    (used in two lots)
A few sprigs of fresh oregano
1½ tsp active dried yeast
250ml warm water
    (body temperature)

2lb (900g) loaf tin
    or a flat baking sheet

* For a more wholefoody loaf,
use 250g strong white & 250g
fine wholemeal

Cook's notes

choice). Place the tomatoes and herbs into a food processor, add about 40ml of olive oil and blend until smooth. Next, sift the brown and white flours into a large mixing bowl and mix in the salt. Add the remaining 30ml of olive oil, as well as about ⅓ of the tomato paste, and mix through until evenly distributed.

When the yeast is ready, form a well in the centre of the mixing bowl and pour it in. Use your hands to integrate the wet and dry ingredients into a ball of dough. It should be soft and malleable, but not sticky. If it seems a little dry, add a drop of cold water. If it seems sticky, rain in a little extra flour. Turn the dough out onto a lightly floured work surface and knead for 10 minutes. It will be light and stretchy.

Press the dough into a big flat disc. Spread the remainder of the tomato paste all over it. Now roll the dough up from one side to the other, pushing any escaping tomato paste back in. Tuck the ends in — it will all seem quite messy and falling apart-ish. But never fear! Return the dough to the mixing bowl, cover it with a damp cloth to prevent a skin forming on the surface and set aside in a warm place for 1½ hours to prove. It should double in size.

When the dough has proved for 1½ hours, knock it back by punching the air out of it and kneading it once or twice into its original size. Oil the bread tin/baking sheet and gently shape the dough into a loaf/free-form (see page 333), trying not to knead it too much, to prevent the sun-dried tomato paste swirls getting lost. Don't worry if the dough seems a little fragile and gooey — it will all come together in the oven. Now, place the loaf in the tin/on the baking sheet to prove for another ½ hour, once again in a warm place. As soon as the bread starts this second proving, turn your oven on to 180°C to preheat.

After half an hour, transfer the bread to the oven and bake for 50-60 minutes (loaf) or 40-50 minutes (free-form). Turn it out of the tin and tap the base with your fingers. If it makes a hollow sound, the bread is cooked. Place bread on a wire rack to cool completely before cutting.

Non-yeast breads

Breads that are leavened (risen) by methods other than yeast are sometimes called quick breads, as they do not require the hours of proving time necessary for yeast breads. The most common non-yeast leavening technique is to introduce a chemical reaction between alkaline and acidic ingredients in the recipe, causing bubbles of carbon dioxide to be released into the dough. It is believed that the native Americans were the first to utilise this chemical reaction in baking to make corn breads and flat breads. They used wood ash as their alkaline ingredient, procured from juniper, hickory or chamiso bushes. This soda ash was combined with an acidic ingredient to leaven the dough.

In the 19th century scientists developed more convenient products to replace wood ash in baking – bicarbonate of soda and cream of tartar began to become popular amongst home cooks and professionals alike. Bicarbonate of soda (or bread soda) is a dry alkaline compound, cream of tartar a dry acid compound. When they are combined in a liquid environment, they cause immediate effervescing – carbon-dioxide fizzing. During the 1850s baking powder became available, a product which combined soda and cream of tartar in suitable ratio, along with corn starch or wheat starch to absorb any damp, thus preventing the chemicals from reacting prematurely.

Baking powder has since been refined into a more sophisticated product. Cream of tartar, as the acid ingredient, has been replaced by other acids. The most common baking powder available these days is double-acting baking powder, which contains two acids, one of which reacts with soda at room temperature (i.e. as the bread/cake is mixed) and the second of which reacts with the soda at a higher temperature (i.e. when the bread/cake is baking in the oven, making for beautifully risen loaves).

Not all quick bread recipes use pre-mixed baking powder. Soda bread, for example, is leavened by the reaction between bread soda and the lactic acid in buttermilk. Irish soda bread was developed in the 1840s, when bicarbonate of soda was first introduced to Ireland. The kind of wheat that grows in Ireland is soft wheat (a result of a mild climate with no extremes of temperature), which is far more suited to chemical aeration than yeast leavening. Soda bread quickly became the nation's favourite bread – a simple recipe that originally contained just four ingredients: brown flour, buttermilk, bread soda and salt. Of the non-yeast recipes in the section that follows, soda bread uses soda and acidified liquid as a raising agent, spelt bread and scones rely on baking powder and gluten-free bread uses a combination of both techniques.

Wholemeal soda bread

yf   (vegan if desired, see below)

There are a million and one recipes out there for traditional Irish soda bread – brown, white, with dried fruit, with treacle and so on. For many Irish people, there is a soda bread recipe in the family that has been passed on from generation to generation which is considered 'the nicest soda bread in the world' – and that it absolutely is, for the taste of familiarity, imbued as it is with deep undertones of memory and home, is something that no earthly ingredient can imitate. If you are in possession of such a recipe and the associations that go with it, hang on tightly to it, keep it alive for one more generation, bake it, smell it, taste it and let it transport you to times gone by. Let the recipe below be nothing more than interesting reading, or an occasional alternative.

For anyone who does not have an unbreachable ancestral link to a soda bread recipe, here is the Cornucopia one. It is a nice simple brown bread, textured by oats and baked in a loaf tin or, alternatively, a more typical criss-crossed round. It comes in both a buttermilk version and a vegan soymilk version. If you bake it in the evening, leave it to cool overnight with a tea towel over it and start the day with a delicious slice of brown bread with butter and good-quality marmalade, or stick two slices together with butter and make everyone at work jealous when you whip it out for your elevenses. If you bake it during the day, make sure to let it cool before slicing, as it will crumble apart if you slice it warm. Dunk a hunk of it in steaming soup or serve it for tea with slices of cheese or homemade raspberry jam.

Traditional Irish soda bread uses buttermilk, which is a sour-tasting cow's milk. It is called buttermilk because it was originally the liquid left over from churning butter – only the high-fat cream solidifies into butter and any low-fat milk runs off. This unpasteurised milk naturally developed lactic acid because it was left to sit for quite some time before churning. The buttermilk we buy in the shops today is low-fat pasteurised milk that has had lactic acid added to it. The acidity of the buttermilk is important, as it chemically reacts with the alkaline bread soda and releases carbon dioxide, which is what makes soda bread rise.

To make vegan soda bread, you need to recreate this chemical reaction using soymilk. By simply adding a drop of lemon juice to curdle the soymilk, it will react with the bread soda in exactly the same manner as buttermilk – producing a nicely risen, traditional-tasting dark-brown bread without dairy or eggs.

Preheat your oven to 180°C. Brush the bread tin with oil or line it with baking parchment as described on pages 326-327. If using a baking tray, just brush it with oil. Into a large mixing bowl, sift

400g fine wholemeal flour
130g plain white flour
50g wheatgerm
30g pinhead *(nibbed/kibbled)*
    oats — *use more jumbo oats*
    if unavailable
30g jumbo oats
1tsp bread soda *(heaped)*
1tsp salt *(heaped)*
70ml unrefined sunflower oil
600ml buttermilk *(for vegan*
    version, see below*)
A handful of topping:
    oats/pinhead oats/pumpkin
    seeds/sesame seeds

2lb (900g) loaf tin
    or a flat baking tray

*For vegan soda bread, replace
the buttermilk with 300ml water
& 300ml soymilk curdled with a
squeeze of lemon juice

the brown and white flour and the bread soda. Add the wheatgerm, nibbed oats, jumbo oats and salt and combine thoroughly. Next, stir in the oil, distributing it evenly.

For a loaf tin
Now make a well in the centre of the dry mix. If using buttermilk, pour it into the well. If using soymilk, first curdle the milk with lemon juice and then pour it, along with the water, into the well. Use your hand to gently fold the milk into the flour. It is important not to over-mix your soda bread, so use as little mixing as possible to

bring everything together. It will be of quite a sloppy consistency.

Still using your hand, transfer the wet mix to the oiled bread tin. Press it down smoothly and sprinkle it with a topping of your choice, be it oats, seeds, or simply a dusting of wholemeal flour. Bake in the centre of the oven for about 1 hour 15 minutes, until well-risen and browned on top. Run a knife around the edge of the loaf and turn it out onto a wire rack. Tap the base of the loaf with your fingers. If it makes a hollow sound, the loaf is cooked. Cover with a tea towel and leave on the rack to cool fully before slicing.

For a criss-crossed round
Follow the instructions as per 'for a loaf tin' above, but add a little less liquid (550ml) so that you have a slightly stiffer consistency.

Turn the dough out onto a floured surface and gently knead it into a round loaf. Use a knife to score a criss-cross shape across the top of the bread. Transfer to the flat baking tray and dust with a little flour. Bake in the centre of the oven for 45-60 minutes, until well-risen and browned on top. Turn it out onto a wire rack. Tap the base of the loaf with your fingers. If it makes a hollow sound, the loaf is cooked. Cover with a tea towel and leave on the rack to cool fully before slicing, quarter by quarter.

Spelt bread

v   cs   free of regular wheat   ♡

Spelt bread was introduced to Cornucopia in 2005 as an experiment, to see if it would appeal to the customers. Claire, our pastry chef at the time, created a magical recipe that gave spelt the jump-start it needed. Her bread experienced nothing short of instant success, with full loaves being ordered almost daily by customers who simply couldn't get enough of the stuff. It has a massive following, and fans can be seen peering enquiringly at the bread tray from halfway down the restaurant to see if they've arrived in time to secure a slice!

Spelt flour is increasingly popular these days as an alternative to wheat flour, both for taste purposes and also for nutritional purposes, especially as an alternative for people with wheat intolerance. From a taste point of view, spelt flour is less bland than regular flour – it has a deeper, nuttier flavour that can bring interesting dimensions to baking and cooking. Nutritionally, spelt is higher in protein and B vitamins than regular wheat, and is a good source of dietary fibre. Although spelt does contain gluten and is therefore not suitable for coeliacs, it can be enjoyed by many people who cannot eat wheat: it appears to be more easily digested and less likely to cause adverse reactions typical of regular wheat such as bloating and discomfort. Many spelt products such as pasta, muesli, crackers and biscuits are now available in health food shops.

Spelt is a distant cousin of wheat that can be traced back at least 8,000 years and has remained pretty much unchanged over the course of its existence. The industrialisation of food production never latched onto spelt in the way it did to wheat – spelt was a less attractive grain, as it had a different kind of gluten from wheat, which was weaker in terms of holding its structure in cooking. Thus spelt was pretty much left alone by the big boys of agriculture, whilst wheat was improved over and over through breeding to create the perfect commercial grain. The wheat that dominates the food industry today is far removed from its original, natural state. Spelt, on the other hand, is an heirloom grain – one which has not been adapted by mankind but exists as nature created it, which makes it very attractive in terms of the wholefood industry and very worthy of support in terms of protecting crop diversification within agriculture.

This recipe for spelt bread is certainly likely to convert any doubters to the merits of spelt. It has a satisfyingly deep flavour and chewy texture, slightly sweetened and darkened by molasses and bursting with seeds. It is a real slice of healthy energy and is particularly delicious toasted, as the seeds release their flavours even more when exposed to the heat of the grill.

Molasses is also known as treacle. It is a by-product of turning sugarcane into sugar. If you have reason to avoid sugar in your diet, omit the molasses for a lighter-coloured, but equally more-ish bread.

425g spelt flour
40g *(3 tbsp)* sesame seeds*
40g *(3 tbsp)* sunflower seeds*
40g *(3 tbsp)* pumpkin seeds*
15g *(1 tbsp)* poppy seeds*
15g *(1 tbsp)* linseeds*
2 tsp baking powder
1 tsp salt *(heaped)*
550ml water
1 tbsp treacle *(blackstrap
        molasses) — optional*

2lb (900g) loaf tin

** If you do not want to invest in
five different seeds, make up a
total of 150g of mixed seeds with
what you have available*

Cook's notes

Preheat the oven to 180°C and brush the bread tin with oil or line it with baking parchment, as described on pages 326-327. Sift the flour and baking powder into a large mixing bowl. Add the salt and all the seeds and combine thoroughly. Form a well in the centre of the mix.

In a jug, combine the water and treacle, stir well and then pour it into the well in the centre of the dry mix. Use a spoon or your hand to bring all the ingredients together evenly. Make sure that the treacle is evenly distributed, not clumped in sticky pockets. Use as little mixing as possible to achieve an even mix. It should be of a very sloppy consistency.

Transfer the mix to the oiled tin and press down evenly. Bake in the centre of the oven for about 60 minutes, until well risen and evenly browned. Run a knife around the edge of the loaf, turn out onto a wire rack and tap the base with your finger. If it makes a hollow sound, the bread is cooked. Cover with a tea towel and leave to cool completely on the rack before cutting.

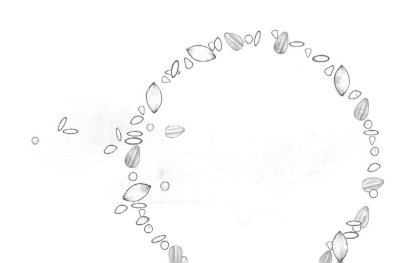

Gluten-free bread

v gf wf yf

The prevalence of coeliac disease in Ireland is thought to be approximately 1 person in every 100-200, one of the highest rates in the world. For a nation that loves its bread, where a doorstep is not an elevated block of concrete but a thickly cut wedge of mother's finest, that's a lot of people who can't grab a slice of granary to fill the gap or throw a sandwich together for school or pop two slices of wholemeal in the toaster to dip in their boiled egg. There are plenty of top-quality gluten-free replacement products on the market. A nice gluten-free bread, however, a good ole slice of arán, is difficult to find — as those sold in supermarkets and health food shops tend to be disappointingly dry and cardboardy as well as containing a lot of additives. The key to a decent loaf of gluten-free bread is to make it and eat it on the same day — fresh and moist — which is exactly what we do in Cornucopia and exactly why our gluten-free bread is known amongst coeliacs as being well worth making a detour to pick up.

If you are a lone gluten-free-er in a household of wheat-munchers, what to do with the bit of the loaf you don't manage to eat on the day of baking? Rather than watch it turn dry and inedible the next day, freeze it. Let the bread cool completely before slicing (this is particularly important with gluten-free bread, as it tends to crumble into little mounds if cut when warm). Individually wrap the slices that you are not going to eat immediately in clingwrap and place them in the freezer. Defrost them one by one as desired and, just before eating, revive them in a warm oven for five minutes (or simply toast them).

Note: if you have any concerns about the safety of wrapping food directly in clingwrap, then first wrap each slice in a square of parchment paper (which can be reused several times) and then place clingwrap around the outside.

This recipe is for plain gluten-free bread. If you would like some variety of flavour, try some of the following:

Poppy seed: add 50g poppy seeds and sprinkle some on top
Sesame seed: add 50g sesame seeds and sprinkle some on top
Herb: destalk and very finely chop a few sprigs of thyme or rosemary
Tomato & fennel: add 1 heaped dessertspoon of tomato purée
    and 2 teaspoons of toasted fennel seeds

100g potato flour
100g rice flour
175g maize flour
150g soya flour
1 heaped tsp gluten-free baking
    powder *(e.g. Royal Baking
    Powder)*
½ tsp bread soda
1 tsp salt
Pinch of pepper
125ml unrefined sunflower oil
600ml soymilk *(or buttermilk if
    not required to be vegan)*
Squeeze of lemon

2lb (900g) loaf tin

Preheat the oven to 150°C (quite cool). Brush the loaf tin thoroughly with oil. As gluten-free bread has a tendency to stick, line the tin with parchment paper, as illustrated on pages 326-327.

Into a large mixing bowl, sift all the flours as well as the gluten-free baking powder and the bread soda. Add the salt and pepper and mix to combine. Next add the oil and stir to distribute it evenly. Make a well in the centre of the flours.

Measure out the soymilk and then stir in a squeeze of lemon juice to curdle it. Pour the soymilk into the well in the dry mix and stir vigorously with a wooden spoon to achieve an even consistency. The mix should be really sloppy – almost the consistency of a batter. This is because the soy flour will absorb a lot of the moisture during cooking. If it seems a little dry, add about 100ml more soymilk or water. There is no fear of over-mixing, as these flours do not contain gluten, so stir as much as you like!

Transfer the mix to the oiled loaf tin and bake in the centre of the oven for 1 hour 45 minutes (the oven temperature is quite low). Remove from the oven, run a knife around the edge of the loaf and turn it out onto a wire rack. Tap the base of the loaf and if it sounds hollow, it is cooked. Cover with a tea towel and leave to dry completely on the rack before slicing. Consume fresh on the day of baking or toasted the next day. Alternatively, freeze individual clingwrapped slices and defrost as required.

Savoury scones

A tray of golden scones emerging from the oven to cool a little before serving for tea —
what an absolute treat. Presuming you have the basic ingredients in your home, a batch of
mouth-watering savoury scones is easily achievable in the space of an hour — half an hour
to make them, half an hour to bake them — and before you know it, you're congratulating
yourself on not taking the 'easy option' of clambering into the car and joining rush-hour
traffic to pick up whatever far inferior baked goods remain in the nearest supermarket.
And your only real challenge is deciding what flavour scones to create.

Now, this is an area where you simply must let your imagination run riot. We make
two batches of scones every day in Cornucopia, one vegan and one cheesy. Every day,
just before noon, the baker arrives up with his or her baskets of fresh scones and informs
the waiting staff what today's delights are. We have a set of laminated cards in the corner
behind the counter to label all the cakes and baked goods, so that customers know what
they are looking at. If new or unusual items arrive, we hand-write a fresh card, as no
laminated one exists. It is no surprise that we have never bothered to laminate our scone
labels. There's no point — such is the variety of ingredients that find their way into them,
almost every batch of scones is unique.

And so the two scone recipes on the next few pages are intended merely as a starting
point, a doorway into the world of savoury scones, inspiration to create your own
delicious combinations. Below are laid out the basic ingredients for a large batch and a
medium batch of scones, which just await the addition of flavours of your choice, be it
cheese, seeds, nuts, herbs, spices, vegetables or fruits. Also included is a list of some of the
favourite scones of the Cornucopia staff, just to show how versatile savoury scones can be.

Some favourite scone recipes of Cornucopia staff

Cheesy ones (ensure all cheeses are vegetarian)
> *Strong cheddar, wholegrain mustard*
>   *& chive*
> *Goat's cheese & roasted red pepper*
> *Blue cheese & walnut*
> *Smoked cheddar & apple*
> *Goat's cheese, (grated) courgette*
>   *& pumpkin seed*
> *Cheddar & roasted red onion*
> *Feta, black olive & basil*

Uncheesy ones
> *Roasted sweet potato, red onion & sage*
> *Tomato & spring onion*
> *Three seed (poppy seed, linseed*
>   *& sunflower seed)*
> *Hazelnut, thyme & sun-dried tomato*
> *Cashew nut & wholegrain mustard*
> *Roasted aubergine & sun-dried tomato*

For 12 scones
450g plain white flour
230g wholemeal brown flour
1½ tsp baking powder *(heaped)*
1½ tsp salt*
Pinch of pepper
225g vegan margarine *(or butter if not required to be vegan)*
150ml milk *(buttermilk or soymilk)*

For 8 scones
300g plain white flour
150g wholemeal brown flour
1tsp baking powder *(heaped)*
1 tsp salt*
Pinch of pepper
150g vegan margarine *(or butter if not required to be vegan)*
100ml milk *(buttermilk or soymilk)*

* Note: if you are using a very salty ingredient to flavour your scones, such as olives, feta cheese, blue cheese or sun-dried tomatoes, reduce the amount of salt by about ⅓

Preheat your oven to 180°C and grease a flat baking tray.

Sift the flours and baking powder into a mixing bowl and stir in the salt and pepper. Use your fingers to rub the butter/margarine into the flours until no lumps remain and the mix resembles breadcrumbs. Add your flavours of choice and make a pool in the centre of the mix. Pour in the milk and stir. Use your fingers to form a soft dough. Turn it out onto a floured work surface and flatten to about 4cm in height. Use a 6-7cm scone cutter or straight-sided tumbler to cut the scones, dipping it into a mound of flour between each cutting to stop it sticking.

Transfer to the greased baking tray and glaze the tops with milk, soymilk or eggwash. Bake in the middle of the oven for 25-30 minutes, keeping the door closed throughout. Tap the base of a scone; if it makes a hollow sound, it is cooked. Transfer to a baking rack and serve warm or cold.

Tomato, feta & basil scones

yf   ef (if glazed with milk)   Makes 12

This is a lovely, fresh scone – the juiciness of the tomatoes makes for a really moist texture and their sharpness contrasts beautifully with the saltiness of the feta cheese. The basil creates a wonderful aroma that fills the room as soon as these beauties emerge from the oven.

After adding the tomato, feta and basil to the flours, try to handle the dough as little and as gently as possible, to keep the tomatoes, and more particularly the crumbs of feta, intact, rather than creamed into the mix.

This scone is appealing enough to be enjoyed on its own, with just a cup of tea to wash it down, although no self-respecting bowl of soup would refuse its company, nor would it be out of place with a crunchy salad with balsamic vinaigrette.

Note: this recipe contains just a little less salt than the 'standard' recipe quoted on previous pages; this is to balance out the saltiness of the feta cheese.

5 tomatoes
200g vegetarian feta cheese
50g *(medium bunch)* fresh basil
450g plain white flour
230g wholemeal brown flour
1½ tsp baking powder
1 tsp salt
Pinch of pepper
225g butter *(or vegan margarine)*
150ml milk *(or buttermilk)*

Preheat the oven to 180°C and brush a baking tray with oil. Dice the tomatoes quite small, season them with a little salt and pepper and sit them in a sieve to allow some of the juices to drain off. Chop the feta into tiny cubes or simply break it into chunky crumbs using your fingers. Chop the basil finely.

Sift the white and brown flours, as well as the baking powder, into a large mixing bowl and stir in the salt and pepper. Spoon knobs of butter/ margarine into the flour mix, until it has all been added. Now use your fingers to rub the fat into the flour, until no lumps remain and the mix resembles breadcrumbs.

Next, add the tomato, feta and basil to the flour mix and stir gently to distribute evenly. Form a well in the centre of the mix and pour in the milk. Use your fingers to bring the mix together into a firm dough. If it seems too dry to incorporate all the dry mix, add a tiny splash of milk. If it seems too sticky to handle, rain in a little more flour.

Turn the scone dough out onto a well-floured work surface and press it flat until it is about 4cm high. Use a 6-7cm scone cutter, or a straight-sided tumbler of similar diameter to cut the scones. First, dip the scone cutter (tumbler) into a small mound of plain flour. Then, starting at the edge rather than in the middle, cut about 12 scones, dipping the cutter into flour between each one to stop it sticking.

Transfer the scones to the oiled baking tray, leaving space between them so they cook evenly. Brush the tops with a little milk. For an even shinier glaze, brush each one with some whisked egg. Bake in the centre of the oven for 25-30 minutes, until the scones are well-risen and golden brown. Don't open and close the oven door repeatedly to check on them, especially at the start, the scones won't rise properly. Tap the base of one and, if it makes a hollow sound, the scones are cooked. Transfer them to a wire rack to cool slightly.

Serve still a little warm or allow to cool completely. Eat within 24 hours, or freeze some of them and refresh for 5 minutes in the oven after defrosting.

Cook's notes

Butternut squash, pumpkin seed & rosemary scones

v   yf   Makes 12

This is one of my all-time favourite scones. Wave a half-used butternut squash inquisitively at me and I am likely to reply 'savoury scones' without a moment's hesitation. I have to confess, when I made these scones in Cornucopia, I always took the easy end of the squash (i.e. the straight end), leaving the rounded, seeded, more cumbersome end for the prep chef, who, I reasoned, was far more versed than I in the art of squash-cutting. This was probably unfair and I'm not recommending it as a course of action, but it's so much easier to get really even tiny cubes from the straight end!

When winter pumpkins are in season, use an equivalent weight of pumpkin flesh. And rosemary can happily be alternated with thyme. The pumpkins seeds are not an absolute necessity, but add an interesting crunch to an otherwise uniformly soft scone. You could also use sunflower seeds or pine nuts.

These particular scones marry wonderfully well with a nice simple blended soup: carrot soup, tomato soup, leek soup … Serve them still slightly warm, as the squash is tastiest when it still has a little heat in it. Alternatively, bung them in a warm oven for 5 minutes just before bringing to the table.

½ **butternut squash** *(400-500g)*
Extra-virgin olive oil
5 sprigs of rosemary
50g pumpkin seeds
450g plain white flour
230g wholemeal brown flour
1½ tsp baking powder
1½ tsp salt
Pinch of pepper
225g vegan margarine *(or butter if not required to be vegan)*
150ml soymilk *(or milk/ buttermilk if not required to be vegan)*

Preheat the oven to 180°C and brush a baking tray with oil. Firstly, roast the butternut squash and rosemary. Chop the squash into tiny ½cm cubes. Destalk the rosemary and chop the leaves as finely as possible. In a bowl, toss the squash and rosemary in a little olive oil, salt and pepper and transfer to a baking tray. Roast in the oven until soft, about 20-25 minutes, turning once to cook evenly. Set aside to cool before mixing into the scones.

Meanwhile, sift the white and brown flours, as well as the baking powder, into a large mixing bowl and stir in the salt. Spoon knobs of margarine into the flour mix, until it has all been added. Now use your fingers to rub the margarine into the flour until no lumps remain and the mix resembles breadcrumbs.

When the roast squash has cooled almost completely, add it, as well as ½ of the pumpkin seeds, to the flour mix and stir very gently to distribute evenly, trying to keep the squares of squash intact. Form a well in the centre of the mix and pour in the soymilk (or regular milk, if using). Use your fingers to bring the mix together into a firm dough. If it seems too dry to incorporate all the flour mix, add a tiny splash of milk. If it seems too sticky to handle, rain in a little more flour.

Turn the scone dough out onto a well-floured work surface and press it into a flat round of about 4cm high. Use a 6-7cm scone cutter, or a straight-sided tumbler of similar diameter to cut the scones. First, dip the scone cutter (tumbler) into a small mound of plain flour. Starting at the edge rather than in the middle, cut about 12 scones, dipping the cutter in flour between each one to stop it sticking.

Transfer the scones to the oiled baking tray, leaving space between each so they cook evenly. Brush the tops with a little soymilk (or milk/egg if not vegan). Sprinkle a few of the remaining pumpkin seeds onto each glazed scone and press slightly to secure. Bake in the centre of the oven for 25-30 minutes, until the scones are well risen and golden brown. Don't open and close the oven door repeatedly to check on them, especially at the start, or the scones won't rise properly. Tap the base of one, and if it makes a hollow sound, the scones are cooked. Transfer them to a wire rack to cool slightly. Serve still a little warm or allow to cool completely. Scones are best eaten within 24 hours of baking. Alternatively, freeze some of them to take out one by one. After defrosting, refresh in a warm oven for 5 minutes.

Desserts

Introduction to desserts

There is nothing quite like a homemade cake. It fills the house with sweet smells and happy anticipation of the treat to come. It might be a tray of cookies made with the kids for afternoon tea. Or a hot apple crumble for an after-dinner treat on a cold winter's evening. Or a tray of date squares, one of which you are going to tuck into your lunchbox every day for the rest of the week. Or a baked chocolate cake, upon which you are going to attempt to inscribe the words 'Happy Birthday Buddy' before presenting it to your best friend on his special day. Part of the joy of baking is that it is not part of the daily grind; it is associated with good times – with special occasions, weekends, summer holidays or with finding oneself with a few unexpected hours off some rainy afternoon. Baking is a luxury, a treat and a direct route to winning the hearts of those around you!

In Cornucopia, the baker works downstairs. Fortunately for all the other staff, the baker's area is on the way to the stockroom and the coldroom. So there is no shortage of excuses for making occasional appearances down there – 'Just collecting some apples from the coldroom', 'Just refilling this salad bowl', 'Just getting some lentils', 'Just checking if we've enough pasta in stock' and so on. The great magnetic attraction of the baking area, aside from the yummy smells that constantly exude from the oven down there, is the infamous baker's tray. This is a 25x35cm plastic white tray upon which the baker places any corners, scraps, broken bits, extra bits or experimental pieces of desserts. It is never an aesthetically well-considered tray. It is, however, full of delicious bits and pieces that the staff are invited to graze upon. It is a major site of culinary interest on the various walking routes around the restaurant, from which people return with a revived skip in their step.

It is occasionally heard muttered 'What are all those cakes doing in a health food restaurant?' Following a wholefood vegetarian diet does not rule out enjoying a nice cake now and again. First of all, as a vegetarian in a non-vegetarian society, the world of desserts is far more open than the world of savoury cooking, whereas typical Western savoury cooking is predominantly meat-based. And from a wholefood perspective, many delicious desserts are made with good-quality, wholesome ingredients, full of both nutrition and energy. So we make no excuses for serving desserts. Enjoyed in moderation, they form an optional part of a healthy and happy lifestyle.

In fact it is often to the cake counter that we turn as a panacea for the many events that occur over a day's work in Cornucopia. Someone receives a spot of bad news on their break time — feed them a cake. Someone receives great news on their break time — insist they have a cake. It's someone's birthday and we haven't yet organised their present from the staff — get the ball rolling with a slice of cake. Someone falls off their bike and arrives at work in shock — sit them down with tea and a cookie. It's someone's last day at work before they return home from whence they came — naturally, they may have their choice of cake from the counter. People feel cared for and looked after when they are given sweet things. Perhaps it dates back to childhood, or perhaps it is a purely chemical emotion, but whatever the psychology or science behind it, a sweet treat is something to look forward to, relish and smile about.

Cornucopia specialises in providing such indulgences for all customers, including people who are regularly excluded from desserts due to their special dietary needs. As so much of traditional baking is structured around eggs, flour, butter and sugar, people with egg allergy, wheat intolerance, sugar intolerance, coeliac disease, or those who are vegan need to be specially catered for. Equally, customers who would rather choose wholefood cakes over more processed goods will find suitably wholesome desserts in Cornucopia. Some of our recipes are our own diet-specific adaptations of classic favourites, and some of them are original creations based on the bakers' experiments, staff fantasies and customer requests.

Central to our desserts is the use of quality ingredients — fresh free-range eggs, unbleached organic flours and gluten-free flours, raw cane sugar, high cocoa content chocolate, real vanilla pods, local and seasonal fruit, as well as a smattering of less traditional ingredients which have added new flavours to the traditional palate and facilitated a broader range of special diet desserts. All are offered with a choice of thick Greek-style natural yoghurt or whipped cream as well as the delicious dairy-free alternatives that are soy yoghurt and soy cream (available from health food shops).

A couple of years ago a favourite customer of mine asked me a favour. She proposed that, if she brought an ovenproof dish from home, I should fill it with an uncooked apple crumble and charge her accordingly. She had a date and wanted to wow him by removing a hot, bubbling apple crumble from her oven as a fabulous finale to the meal she was cooking for him. I offered to jot down the recipe instead, to save her paying restaurant prices for something she could whip up at home for next to nothing. She was reluctant. I told her just how easy our apple crumble is to make. Still she declined, convinced that there was no way she could create something as delicious as the dessert she so enjoyed regularly in the restaurant. So I could do nothing but agree to make her an apple crumble, all the time remarking to myself that it really was time that we put together a recipe book to encourage people to try some of our recipes in their own homes, where they can enjoy the process, drift away on the aromas and take pride in their own creations. And here it finally is. So if you are a cake lover looking for new inspiration, an oat bar muncher desperate to know the secret of Cornucopia's most enduring dessert or someone with a special dietary requirement who's itching for a sweet snack, delve into this selection of Cornucopia staples for a suitable delight.

Information about yeast-free diets

Many of the desserts in this section do not contain any fermented products such as vinegar, yeast or alcohol, which are generally avoided by people adhering to a yeast-free diet. We have nevertheless chosen not to mark any recipes that contain sugar as yeast-free. This is because sugar, though not a fermented product, does contribute to yeast infections in the body by providing an easy source of yeast's favourite food: simple carbohydrates.

The only dessert that we have marked yeast-free is the fig and banana tart on page 432, as it contains neither fermented goods nor refined sugar. It varies from person to person as to whether natural fruit sugars are acceptable on a yeast-free diet.

If you adhere to a yeast-free diet but do not mind eating sugar, the only desserts that you should avoid are: chocolate orange silken torte if Tia Maria is added, coconut, chocolate and brandy petits fours and the sugar-free date and orange squares (which contain vinegar).

Desserts: some basic information

As with all cooking, investing in really good ingredients will optimise the quality, flavour and joy of baking.

Sugar

The vast majority of recipes in this chapter use unrefined brown sugar, or offer the option of using brown sugar or white sugar. A few recipes – those for sweet pastry, frangipane and cream cheese icing – all work better with caster sugar, so we've stuck with that. In Cornucopia we use organic dark Muscovado sugar, which is available in most supermarkets, but any raw cane sugar will do. Unrefined brown sugar makes for a deeper, more caramelly flavour in baking, as it still contains the molasses (treacle) that is removed to make white sugar. A lot of products on the market marked 'brown sugar' are actually made of refined white sugar with molasses added back in, so, when choosing a sugar, look for the words 'unrefined' or 'raw cane'.

Note: other sweeteners used in the restaurant are organic honey, apple concentrate and blackstrap molasses.

Eggs

When a recipe calls for eggs, always choose free-range eggs and, if possible, organic, for flavour, nutrition and animal welfare.

Why free-range?
As elaborated in the introduction of this book, free-range chickens are given daytime access to outdoor enclosures. They are free to come and go from the henhouse to the yard to stretch their legs and scratch for food, which means they are infinitely better treated than chickens that spend their entire lives in cages with slanted floors. They experience fresh air, natural exercise and a diet varied by the fruits of their own scratching, all of which contribute to the flavour of their eggs.

Why organic?
However, non-organically raised free-range chickens may be fed low-level antibiotics throughout their lives to stave off illness. They are fed hormone-enhanced foodstuffs, foodstuffs which may originate from GM crops sprayed with pesticides.

Their feed may also be treated with artificial food colouring to enhance the yellowness of the yolk and the brownness of the shell. Organically raised chickens, on the other hand, are fed on chemical-free, non-GM crops. They are allowed free access to the outdoors, into pastures that are also pesticide-free. The colour of the egg yolk will be affected, not by food colouring, but by the type of grubs the hens scratch from the earth and the type of greenery in their environment. Organic, free-range eggs are lower in fat, higher in vitamin A and higher in essential Omega-3 fatty acids. The taste difference is also quite noticeable: organic, free-range eggs have a deep-tasting, almost sweet yolk with a dense texture.

Flour

All of our recipes use plain flour or plain wholemeal flour. Try to use unbleached, organic flour.

Why unbleached?

When the wheat grain is first milled to produce flour, it is yellowish, due to the presence of natural carotenoid pigments. The flour is then matured. Natural maturation involves exposing it to air over a period of time. Oxygen in the air both bleaches the flour and changes the structure of the gluten, making it stronger and more elastic and therefore suitable for baking. The finished flour still retains a slightly golden hue. The problem for mass production has always been that this process is slow and takes up a lot of space. So chemical processes that bleach and oxidise the flour in a matter of minutes were developed. Chemically bleached flour is both cheaper and whiter and therefore more attractive to the consumer. However, as a result, unnecessary chemicals are present in both the flour and the environment, so both health advocates and environmentalists recommend unbleached flour over bleached.

Why organic?

By choosing to buy organic flour, you are choosing to pay a little more in support of responsible, chemical-free farming: farming that uses crop rotation and natural fertilisers over chemical fertilisers to enrich the soil, that employs fieldwork rather than weed killers and pesticides to support the crops and that balances business and profit with eco-friendly policies. Your flour will be free of unwanted chemicals and you will be contributing to a more holistic, sustainable approach to farming.

Plain flour

A lot of high street supposedly plain flours actually contain a small amount of raising agent, which can upset the balance of a recipe or, where making pastry is concerned, corrupt the final result quite significantly. Plain flour purchased in health food shops is generally free from any raising agents, as are some the of the supermarket flours. Check the ingredients before purchasing.

Overworking the flour

Many recipes warn you not to overwork the dough or the cake mix. This essentially means, not to stir it for too long or too vigorously. Ideally, once the wet ingredients are added to the dry ingredients, you should use as little movement as possible to bring the mix together into an even enough consistency. The reason for this is to prevent the gluten in the flour from stretching too much, which will result in a tough, heavy product, as opposed to a short, or light and crumbly one.

Note: this does not apply to yeast buns and yeast breads in which the gluten is intentionally stretched.

Chocolate

In recent years, dark chocolate has been revealed to contain powerful anti-oxidants, as well as lowering blood pressure. It is, of course, also high in calories, so should be consumed in delightful moderation! For baking purposes, always use good-quality, dark chocolate with at least 55% cocoa content. Try to source organic, fairtrade chocolate.

Why fairtrade?

All of the world's cocoa beans originate in Africa and South America, in countries where there are large populations of people living in poverty and without proper education. With these disempowered communities at its disposal, the cocoa trade is renowned for its association with improper treatment of its workers. Chocolate which has earned the fairtrade seal of approval ensures that workers in the cocoa business are neither children nor forced workers, work a legal number of hours per week and are paid fairly for their labour.

Why organic?

The huge profits possible in selling cocoa to the Western world have resulted in whole eco-systems being damaged in order to clear land for cocoa production, which is also second only to cotton in the high use of pesticides. As organic farming represents a holistic approach to farming, which looks, not only at the profitable production of a particular product, but also at the soil life, plants, animals and human beings that will be affected by it, organic cocoa farming is carried out on small, shaded plots that are designed to complement the local environment rather than destroy it, and foster the habitats of wildlife and migratory birds rather than eliminate them.

Note: some chocolate and chocolate products contain whey, a by-product of cheese-making, which commonly uses non-vegetarian coagulating agents (usually rennet). Check the packaging to avoid. Most high-quality dark chocolate does not contain whey.

How to melt chocolate

When melting chocolate, place it in a glass bowl over a pan of simmering water (called a bain marie), ensuring that the bottom of the bowl does not come into contact with the water. Do not stir excessively, as you risk integrating steam into the chocolate, which causes it to fudge (go lumpy); just leave it to do its thing. When just melted, remove it from the heat and set aside; it will continue melting in its own heat. Make sure no water accidentally splashes into the melting chocolate, as that too will cause it to fudge.

Parchment piping bags

While we're on the subject of chocolate, one of the easiest ways to decorate a dessert or to pipe a message on a birthday cake is to make a parchment piping bag and fill it with chocolate. One of the greatest lessons a pastry chef once taught me was, whether I needed one or not, always make a parchment piping bag and fill it with any melted chocolate leftover from baking. It's a great way to avoid wasting (or eating!) the scraps. You can use it immediately or let it set and leave it to one side (see overleaf for diagram). When you discover the need to decorate a cake, sit the prepared parchment piping bag on top of a warm surface (not too hot, or it will burn), for example near the oven or on top of the kettle. It will melt within minutes and you'll be ready to start your artwork.

- Cut a square of parchment paper of approximately 23cm.
- Fold it in half to make a double-sided triangle and cut it along the fold. Each triangle will become a parchment bag.
- Fold over one triangle, forming two smaller triangles, press along the fold and then open it again. There is now a creased line running through the centre of your triangle, which will serve as a guide.
- Fold one of the corners opposite the crease and align it with the crease.
- Wrap the opposite corner around it, forming a cone shape.
- Use your hands to hollow out the cone and fold the little protruding pointed edge downwards into the cone, to secure the bag.
- Now fill the bag with chocolate, leaving enough empty space at the top to seal it.
- To seal, flatten out the top of the bag and fold it over twice, as you might do a paper lunch bag. Tuck the two protruding corners backwards to secure.
- Use immediately by snipping a tiny hole in the point of the conical bag.
- Alternatively, leave the bag to set and, when ready to use, put it in a warm place to melt, snip the top and get piping.

Get to know your oven

All ovens have a personality of their own. It might not be evident from the moment you first buy it, but it will emerge over the course of time and use. Temperatures quoted in recipes don't take into account the quirks and foibles that your oven may have developed in its lifetime. Therefore, it is advisable to get to know your own oven intimately. For instance, the domestic oven that we used to test the recipes for this book had a somewhat worse-for-wear overhead element, which hung down lower on the front right, so everything in that part of the oven cooked more quickly than the rest. The solution with cookies was to keep rotating the tray, so that each corner had its time in the heat. The solution for cakes that don't appreciate the oven door being opened and closed, was to cook them on a lower shelf, thus minimising the effect of the low-riding element, but perhaps increasing the cooking time by a few minutes. The point is, no cookbook knows your oven like you know your oven, so monitor its behaviour and, rather than cursing its eccentricities, work with them, factor them into your baking and be rewarded with a long and loyal relationship.

Bakeware

We have used very standard, readily available bakeware throughout this chapter, many of which you may already have in your kitchen. The only items that will require going to a specialist kitchen shop are the tartlet cases.

For baked goods in general
1x25x40cm wire rack

For traybakes
23x23x5cm square baking tray (you can also use a 20x25x5cm rectangular baking tray, which has the same capacity)

For cookies
2 flat baking trays

For muffins
12-hole muffin tray (plus muffin cases)

For tofu silken tortes
10in (25cm) springform tin

For fig and banana tart
11in (28cm) loose-bottom fluted tart case

Baking beans
Either regular dry beans or ceramic beans from cooking shops

For bakewell tartlets
8x9.5cm (4in) loose-bottom fluted tartlet cases

Electric equipment

The two items of electric equipment used in this chapter are:

Electric whisk (hand-held or mixer)
For creaming butter, sugar and eggs together (this can also be done by hand)

Food processor
For mixing all the ingredients for the tofu silken tortes (this cannot be done by hand)

Lining with parchment paper

Obviously flat baking trays require nothing more than a suitably sized square or rectangle of parchment paper. For deeper trays, draw a square/rectangle to fit the internal dimensions of the base of the tray and then extend each side by a little more than the height of the tray. Always grease the tray before inserting the baking parchment, to hold the paper in place.

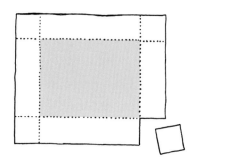 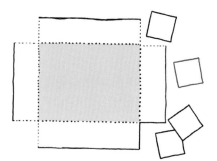

To line a springform tin, trace the circumference of the tin on parchment paper. Draw a second circle outside of the first circle, about 2cm larger all around. Cut out the larger circle. Now cut small incisions all around the circle of parchment in as far as the inner circle. This will allow the parchment to rise up the inside of the tin. Grease the springform. Cut a long strip of parchment, as wide as the tin is tall and place it all around the inside wall of the tin. Brush it with a little oil and then insert the frilled circular piece of parchment into the base of the tin, pressing it against the walls of the tin where it rises up.

 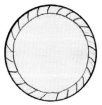  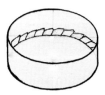

Yoghurt, ice-cream, custard

Many people like to accompany a dessert/pudding with cream, ice-cream, yoghurt or custard. In Cornucopia we offer vegetarian Greek-style natural yoghurt, whipped dairy cream, soy yoghurt and soycream.

Some care should be taken in choosing commercial ice-creams and yoghurt. Certain ice-creams contain E numbers (many of which are not vegetarian) or gelatine. Choose a good-quality, additive-free ice-cream and ensure that, if it contains eggs, they are free-range. Full-fat natural and fruit yoghurt tend to be vegetarian. Watch out for low-fat yoghurts, some of which contain gelatine. As for custard, apart from the fact that homemade is infinitely more delicious than shop bought, many commercial custards contain battery egg derivatives. If buying custard choose a high-quality one that boasts the use of free-range eggs.

Cook's notes

Oats

Oliver Twist was displaying good sense beyond his young years when he asked the cantankerous keeper of his orphanage for some more porridge – with the amount of hard work lined up for poor little Oliver each day, a second bowl of energy-rich oats was exactly what he needed to see him through the morning. Although Oliver probably knew little about the low-GI diet favoured by many nutritionists over the last decade, with its emphasis on slow-release complex carbohydrates, he did know that a decent bowl of porridge would fill him up and stave off hunger pangs for hours to come.

Oats became listed as a health food in the 1980s, when their high water-soluble fibre content was identified as being useful in lowering cholesterol and preventing heart disease. An adult should get 5-10 grams of soluble fibre each day. A bowl of porridge (not instant porridge) provides over 2 grams, a good start. Adding an apple (skin on), banana or handful of dried fruit will double the amount of soluble fibre in the bowl. And by adding a handful of oats to gratin toppings, crumbles, muffins, breads, even soups, you can increase the amount of oat fibre in some of your other meals.

As well as fibre, oats contain more protein than any other grain. Depending on the area of cultivation and the level of processing, they contain between 12% and 24%, useful in maintaining protein levels in a vegetarian diet. They are an excellent source of B-vitamin thiamine and iron and a good source of B-vitamins riboflavin and B6, as well as calcium, magnesium and zinc.

Oats also contain more lipids (fat) than other grains, which makes them a great treat for birds in winter; mixed with some nuts and fruit, they help the birds put on the few extra layers of padding needed to keep warm over the cold months.

In Cornucopia we use jumbo oats, which are whole oat groats (the bit inside the indigestible hull) that have been steamed quickly and then rolled into flakes. They are available from health food shops. As the name suggests, they are larger than the average rolled oat, which is made by cutting the oat groat into two or three pieces and then steaming and rolling it. Jumbo oats make nicely textured porridge, a really robust oat bar and are delightfully chewy when added to cookies or muffins. If you cannot find jumbo oats, regular oats are fine, but not quick-cooking oats, as they have been more processed and have lost some of their nutritional benefits. Although this is the start of the desserts chapter, while we're on the theme of oats, it's a good opportunity to include two popular items from the Cornucopia breakfast menu: porridge with fruit compôte and honey-roasted granola.

Porridge with fig & prune compôte

*v (using soymilk)   **wf   yf   no added sugar***

To cook porridge, place 1 part traditional (not quick-cook) rolled oats into a pot with 2 parts water or a combination of water and milk. Add a pinch of salt. Bring to a gentle boil and reduce to a simmer for 5-10 minutes, depending on desired consistency (add an extra 5 minutes if using jumbo oats). Stir regularly to prevent the porridge sticking to the base of the pot. If you soak your porridge in the required amount of water overnight, the cooking time will be reduced and a more creamy consistency will be achieved.

Add a splash of milk, soymilk or cream and a generous spoonful of compôte to each bowl. You can heat the compôte slightly first or simply allow the hot porridge to take the chill off it. This recipe makes enough compôte for about 20 bowls of porridge. Store in the fridge for up to 2 weeks.

400g dried figs
500g dried prunes
2 cinnamon sticks
½ orange
3 cloves

Remove the feet (stalks) from the figs. Place them in a large pot with the two cinnamon sticks (break them in half) and the half orange studded with three cloves. Cover the figs with water and bring to a very gentle simmer. Cook for 10 minutes.

Now add the prunes, adding a little extra water if necessary to ensure they are covered. Cook for 20 more minutes, stirring occasionally, until all the fruit is really soft and the water has reduced to a small quantity of light syrup. Cool and then remove the cinnamon sticks and orange. Transfer to a container and refrigerate.

Cornucopia honey-roasted granola
df ef wf yf cn   no added sugar

1kg jumbo oats
150g flaked almonds
150g cashew nuts
75g hazelnuts
175g pumpkin seeds
175g sunflower seeds
175g desiccated coconut
3 tsp ground cinnamon
70ml unrefined sunflower oil
2-3 tbsp runny honey
    (organic if possible)*
175g sultanas or raisins

* To make this recipe vegan, you can replace the honey with apple concentrate

Preheat your oven to 180°C.

Mix all the ingredients except the sultanas/raisins in a large container and ensure that the honey and oil are evenly distributed throughout. Transfer the mix to baking trays, only one layer deep at a time. Use several baking trays at once to speed up the process. Toss the contents of the tray once during roasting. Roast until the oat flakes and coconut have turned golden brown and the nuts and seeds are starting to swell. Cool in a large container, stirring regularly. When the last batch has been baked, add the sultanas/raisins and stir to spread evenly.

Store in an airtight container and munch through a bowl daily with regular milk or soymilk. In Cornucopia another popular option is a bowl half-filled with fresh fruit salad, covered with Greek-style natural yoghurt and topped off with a generous sprinkling of this wholesome granola.

Cook's notes

Raspberry & blueberry oat bars

v   wf   cn (coconut)

Oat bars take pride of place at the head of the baking section, as they are, without a doubt, the most enduring Cornucopia dessert. Rarely a day goes by in the restaurant that doesn't see at least one piled-high tray of oat bars arrive up to the counter. Even tucked into the least conspicuous corner of the display fridge, their fans will seek them out, no advertisement necessary!

Our oat bars are essentially a soft flapjack filled with fruit, made with soy margarine rather than butter and soy flour rather than plain flour. This makes them suitable for both vegans and anyone who needs to avoid wheat (but not gluten). There is nothing light, fluffy or wispy about the Cornucopia oat bar: it is a high-energy, chew-and-chew-some-more slice of fuel, delicious and filling and moreish. The top layer of oats is golden brown and just a little crunchy, whilst the juicy tartness of the berries seeps into the base layer of oats, combining beautifully with the brown sugar to give a hint of caramelly fruit syrup.

Beware the addictive quality of the berry oat bars. One of our most recent regular customers at first couldn't resist the allure of a mid-afternoon oat bar, drenched in soy cream washed down with an Americano coffee. Daily he came and daily we provided him with his reliable treat. Subsequently, however, it was more than the oat bars that he couldn't resist: the charms of she-who-served-it also won him over. And they are currently living happily ever after – brought together by the love of an oat bar!

A well-wrapped oat bar makes a perfect mid-hike energy boost, or, served with natural yoghurt, a hearty dessert. If you can source jumbo oats, all the better, as they make for a robust and chunky bar. Fresh berries are preferable when they are in season. If unavailable, however, frozen berries used direct from the freezer (don't defrost) work wonderfully well too.

Preheat your oven to 180°C and line the baking tray with parchment paper (see page 384).

Measure the oats, sugar, coconut and soya flour into a large mixing bowl and combine thoroughly. Form a well in the centre of the mix. Melt the margarine, pour it into the well and stir until it is evenly distributed.

Press half of the oat mixture into the lined baking tray, making sure to fill the corners. Next, scatter

300g jumbo oats
  (or regular oats)
170g unrefined brown sugar
170g desiccated coconut
100g soya flour
300g vegan margarine *(or butter if not required to be vegan)*
300g mixture of raspberries & blueberries *(fresh or frozen)*

23x23x5cm baking tray
  (or 20x25x5cm)

the berries evenly over this base. If you are using frozen fruit, use straight from the freezer. Now cover the layer of berries with the rest of the oat mixture and press down. If you press quite firmly, the oat bars will be firm enough to be lunchbox- or picnic-friendly. If you opt for a light-handed, loose scattering, the bars make a delicious warm dessert with vegetarian natural yoghurt.

Place the oat bars in the oven and bake for 30-35 minutes, until golden brown. Cool in the tray and then cut into 12 or 16 squares. If you have any difficulty lifting the bars from the tray, try the flip trick: place a chopping board over the baking tray and, with one hand on the chopping board and one hand under the tray, flip them upside-down. Now, simply lift off the baking tray and transfer the oat bars to a plate or storage container. Oat bars can be kept for up to 5 days in an airtight container.

Variations
Vary the fruit in the centre of your oat bars to suit the season, the availability of produce and personal taste. Fresh berries of all sorts, jams, stewed apples or purées of dried fruits all produce delicious results.

Apple & blackberry
In autumn, when both blackberries and Irish apples come into season, stew/bake two or three Bramley cooking apples with a little brown sugar. Spread some apple purée onto the base layer of oat mix and then scatter some blackberries on top.

Apple & raspberry
Instead of stewed cooking apples, you can also use fresh eating apples. Peel, core and grate two or three apples, spread over the oat base and top with some fresh raspberries.

Purée of dried fruit
Select from: dried apricots, prunes, figs, dates, sultanas, raisins, etc. Measure 400g of mixed dried fruit into a small pot. Cover the fruit with water and, keeping a lid on the pot, bring to a gentle simmer. Take great care not to let the base burn, stirring regularly and adding a drop extra water if necessary. Cook until all the fruit is soft and plump and most of the water has been absorbed. Purée in a blender and spread over the oat base.

Dried fruit & apple
As above, but instead of using 400g dried fruit, use 200g, stewed and puréed, along with two or three Bramley apples, baked or stewed (or eating apples, peeled, cored and grated).

Chocolate & nut oat bars
Make oat mix as per recipe. Meanwhile toast 200g of hazelnuts, cashew nuts, almonds, Brazil nuts or macadamia nuts for about 8 minutes in a medium oven.
Chop roughly and add to the oat mix, along with 1 tsp ground cinnamon. Press into tray and bake until golden brown. Cool for 20 minutes then spread 250g of melted vegetarian chocolate (dark, if required to be vegan). When the chocolate has set, dip a very sharp knife into boiling water and cut into bars, dipping the knife regularly.

Bramley apples

Before sharing the recipe for Cornucopia's much-loved hot apple crumble, it might be appropriate to write a short eulogy to the wonderful apple without which baking would not be the same: the Bramley cooking apple.

Bramley apples are the only commercially available apples used solely for cooking, and are often referred to simply as cooking apples. They are extolled for their high acidic quality, which balances out the sugar content in cakes and tarts. They also have a unique feature: when baked, they become golden and fluffy, lending a wonderful light texture to baked goods.

The Bramley apple is a relatively recent addition to culinary history. The original Bramley tree grew from an apple seed planted by one Mary Anne Brailsford in her back garden in 1809. She lived in Southwell, England. The tree grew tall and strong and by 1857, when it was noticed by a passing nurseryman, Henry Merryweather, was producing an abundant annual crop. Merryweather propagated from the tree and began exhibiting his results at agricultural shows, naming it Bramley's Seedling, after the garden's then owners. The Bramley apple's illustrious future was sealed when it received great acclaim at the Royal Horticultural Society's annual congress in 1883, after which commercial orchards began springing up all over Britain and, by the early 1900s, all over Ireland. Since then it has become an essential ingredient in apple tart, apple cake and apple crumble and the base for both sweet and savoury apple sauces.

To bake Bramley apples, simply peel, core and chop the apples and then toss them in a little lemon juice to prevent them turning brown. Place them in an ovenproof dish, sprinkle with a little unrefined brown sugar and cover with either foil or a lid. Bake in a medium oven for approximately half and hour, or until soft.

To make stewed Bramley apple, peel, core and chop the apples and toss them in a little lemon juice. Place them in an appropriately sized pot with a tiny splash of water. Cover and heat slowly until the apples have become soft and fluffy. Sweeten to taste with some unrefined brown sugar or honey. Beat in a small knob of butter (optional) and serve hot or cold with ice-cream, Greek-style natural yoghurt or homemade custard (see page 385 for information about dessert accompaniments).

Hot Bramley apple crumble

v   wf

There's something particularly irresistible about hot desserts. Many a customer has been observed to arrive in Cornucopia and squint at the blackboard to choose between the two soups of the day, only to catch a glimpse of a container of hot apple crumble on the hotplate and perform a spontaneous mental u-turn from intentions of carrot soup with brown bread and butter to ordering apple crumble with cream and tea. And walk away from the counter, tray in hand, looking pleased as punch.

Of the many restaurants in Dublin's city centre, offering everything from baked New York cheesecake to Turkish baklava to old-fashioned iced buns, it's rare to find one serving a hot dessert straight from the oven, just like you'd have it at home. Which is probably why every apple crumble that emerges bubbling from the Cornucopia kitchens is greeted with a ripple of interest amongst anyone poised to notice it. And why the lifespan of a dish of apple crumble is unusually short, as customer after customer deem it too extraordinarily yummy to pass by.

Unfortunately the sheer volume of food that our little hotplate has been required to sustain in recent years has sometimes edged the apple crumble out – there is not always space to devote an entire corner of the main food counter to a dessert. As a result, quite a number of crestfallen crumble-hunters have had to be told, 'Not today, I'm afraid', which is never nice for anyone involved. However, the future of the apple crumble has been secured, and it is a bright one: in the design for the new hotplate which will grace the counter of our expanded restaurant in late 2008, there is an entire section specifically assigned to hot desserts, where apple crumble will take pride of place.

Irish-grown Bramley apples are available all year round and are very reasonably priced. Once you've bought packets of seeds for the topping, this dessert can be created with very little expenditure, yet, as it emerges hot and aromatic from the oven, it is as luxurious a sweet treat as any.

Preheat your oven to 180°C. Peel, core and roughly chop the cooking apples. Place them in an ovenproof dish and scatter them with 115g soft brown sugar. Cover with foil or, if the dish has a lid, cover with a lid. Bake in the oven for 25-30 minutes, until soft and juicy.

While the apples are baking, place all the topping ingredients in a bowl and rub together until the margarine is evenly distributed.

Topping
115g pumpkin seeds
115g sunflower seeds
115g jumbo oats
   (or regular oats)
85g unrefined brown sugar
70g vegan margarine *(or regular margarine if not required to be vegan)*
Pinch of ground cinnamon or ground ginger

Filling
900g cooking apples *(Bramley apples)*
125g unrefined brown sugar

When the apples come out of the oven, sprinkle them with all the crumble topping and return to the oven for 20 minutes or until golden brown and crunchy. Serve warm with cream, soycream, yoghurt or ice-cream (see page 385 for vegetarian dessert accompaniments).

Alternatively, you can bake the apple well in advance and refrigerate it. About half an hour before you are ready to serve your crumble, assemble it and place it in the oven, allowing 35 minutes' cooking time, as the apples will have started from cold.

Crumble variations

This delicious hot crumble can be adapted to almost any seasonal local fruit.

Spring

Rhubarb – trim and chop 900g rhubarb. Bake covered in the oven until soft with 125g brown sugar and a thumb-sized knob of peeled fresh ginger, chopped in two or three. Remove the ginger before sprinkling on the crumble topping.

Summer

Apple & raspberry – peel and core 500g of cooking apples. Bake covered with 75g brown sugar. Add 400g fresh raspberries to the baked apple just before the crumble topping goes on. Other summer fruits to try – cherries or blackcurrants.

Autumn

Plum – peel, halve and stone 900g Irish plums. Cover with foil or a lid and bake in the oven until soft and juicy.

Apple & blackberry – peel and core 500g of cooking apples. Bake covered with 75g soft brown sugar. Add 400g blackberries to the baked apple just before the crumble topping goes on.

Apple & elderberry – as above, replacing blackberries with elderberries.

Winter

Apple & cranberry – to introduce a seasonal touch to your apple crumble, add a handful of fresh, frozen or dried cranberries to the raw apples and bake them together.

Dallas cookies with oats, chocolate chips & hazelnuts
cn

Dallas cookies are a satisfying mouthful of oats, nuts and chocolate chips, much favoured for their dotty appearance and their crunchy texture. They are really easy to make and the dough is a sturdy, no-nonsense one that lends itself well to the enthusiastic hands of little children, should they fancy getting involved in a spot of baking. A simplified version of the method has been included for the younger readers. Measure out all the ingredients together in advance and let the mini pastry chef follow steps 1-10. Step 11 might have said 'Eat cookies washed down with a glass of milk', but I thought it an unnecessary instruction!

This recipe makes quite a big batch of cookie dough. Bake off as many cookies as you reckon will be eaten today and tomorrow. Roll the rest of the dough into balls and store in the fridge (up to 5 days) or freezer. When you are ready to bake the next batch of cookies, let the dough soften (or defrost) to room temperature before pressing the balls out onto lined baking trays and baking as normal.

The origin of this recipe is a bit of a tale. A version of it was included in *Delicious Dishes*, a booklet published in 1993 by St Michael's National School in Limerick. The contributor claimed that a friend of a friend of hers had eaten a sumptuous cookie in a restaurant in Dallas the previous year. When she enquired as to the availability of the recipe, she was told that she was welcome to it for a charge of two-fifty. She happily took the recipe home with her and was astonished, when she received her credit card bill the following month, to see that her card had been charged $250 for the recipe. She was assured, when she phoned the restaurant, that no mistake had been made, $250 was indeed the cost of the recipe. In order to get her money's worth, the lady in question vowed to distribute the Dallas cookie recipe to as many people as possible and to encourage them, in turn, to pass it on. Which is how it came to us, all the way from Dallas. Or so the story goes.

Preheat your oven to 180°C and line the baking trays with parchment paper. Place the hazelnuts on a baking tray and toast them for 8 minutes. Set aside to cool and then rub them to remove the loose skins and chop them roughly.

Using an electric whisk or a wooden spoon, cream the butter and sugar together until light and fluffy. Next, beat in the eggs and vanilla extract. Sift the flour, baking powder and bread

240g hazelnuts *(or almonds, macadamias)*
240g butter at room temperature
340g unrefined brown sugar
2 large free-range eggs
1 tsp natural vanilla extract
310g plain flour *(or half plain, half wholemeal)*
1 tsp baking powder
½ tsp bicarbonate of soda *(bread soda)*
310g jumbo oats *(or regular oats)*
½ tsp salt
340g good-quality *(55% or over)* *vegetarian chocolate chips (or crumbled bar)*

2 flat baking trays

soda into a mixing bowl. Add the oats and salt and stir to combine. Add these dry ingredients to the creamed butter and mix thoroughly. Finally, fold in the chocolate chips and chopped nuts. The nuts should be cool, so that they don't start melting the chocolate.

Roll the dough into balls approximately half the size of a golf ball. Press into ½cm-thick rounds on the baking trays, leaving space between each cookie. Bake for 15-20 minutes, or until golden brown. Cool for 5 minutes in the tray, and then transfer carefully to a wire rack. When the cookies have cooled completely, store in an airtight container for up to 3 days. Place any unused cookie dough balls in the fridge or freezer. When you want to bake them, allow the dough to soften at room temperature before pressing into trays.

Dallas cookies for kids

1. Turn oven on to 180°C, line baking trays and measure the ingredients
2. Toast hazelnuts. Cool. Chop (be careful!)
3. Bowl A: cream butter + sugar
4. Bowl A: add eggs + vanilla and mix well
5. Bowl B: sift flour, soda, baking power
6. Bowl B: add oats, salt, chocolate + hazelnuts and mix well
7. Pour bowl B into bowl A and mix
8. Make balls of cookie dough
9. Press onto baking tray
10. Bake for 15-20 minutes

Muffins

cs   (cn)

The first item out of the baker's oven every morning in Cornucopia is a tray of fresh, bulging muffins, the flavour of which is a daily surprise, the baker's opportunity for a spot of early-morning spontaneity. A bit like our savoury scones, there is no list of Cornucopia muffin flavours from which to choose, there is just a basic recipe to which can be added infinite combinations of fresh fruit, dried fruit, zest, chocolate, cocoa, spices, nuts, seeds, oats, honey, even vegetables (carrot, sweet potato). With standard muffins available in most coffee shops and newsagents, part of the charm of the Cornucopia muffin is that it is different and surprising every day.

A plate of still-warm mystery muffins is carried upstairs from the baking area in the basement, dredged with icing sugar, drizzled with chocolate or left plain to show off their knobbledy tops. They often come complete with irregular bulges and protrusions that you just want to pick off and nibble, a true sign of their homemade nature. If the mood is ripe for guessing games, the breakfast staff may make a stab at what might be in today's muffins. If it's a rather less interactive morning, a grunt from the baker will let them know what should be written on the muffin label.

Flexibility with the muffin flavour gives the baker a chance to balance out the cake counter. If the selection for the day is predominantly quite health-conscious, they might go for a lush white chocolate and raspberry muffin. Whereas on a day when more sumptuous cakes prevail, a honeyed banana and bran muffin might be a suitable balancing act. The basic recipe below allows you the same adaptability: you can use white flour, caster sugar and a heap of chocolate chips for a fluffy, sweet, indulgent muffin, or you can opt for half brown flour and all brown sugar with oats and sultanas for a breakfast-style, wholefood-based muffin. The flavours listed on page 406 are popular combinations in Cornucopia, to be chopped and changed and reworked to match your own personal muffin desires.

The wonderful convenience of muffins is that, not only do they cook really quickly, but they are ready to eat/transport shortly after emerging from the oven. And once you have picked off the nice crunchy overhang, and peeled down the paper, they come with their own built-in plate, for effortless and hygienic consumption at your desk, on a train journey or sitting on a park bench in an out-of-nowhere hour of Irish sun. Muffins away!

Firstly, choose your flavour of muffin (see page 406). Preheat the oven to 180°C and line a muffin tray with muffin cases. Sift the flour and baking powder into a mixing bowl. Add the salt, sugar and mixed spice, if using, and mix thoroughly.

700g flour (*plain, or part plain/ part brown*)

2 heaped tsp baking powder

300g sugar (*caster or unrefined brown sugar*)

Pinch salt

1 tsp natural vanilla extract or 2 tsp mixed spice

170g butter

3 free-range eggs

200-300ml milk or buttermilk

Flavouring of your choice

12-hole muffin tray & 12 paper cases

Other flavourings that should be added at this stage are cocoa powder, orange/lemon zest or dry spices such as cinnamon or ginger. Next form a well in the centre of the mix.

Melt the butter. Add the milk and whisked eggs, as well as the vanilla extract, if using, to the well in the centre of the mixing bowl. Start with 200ml milk. Stir briefly to combine. If necessary, add a drop more milk. The mix should be of a spoonable consistency – not too stiff and dry, nor too sloppy.

Flavourings that should be gently folded in at this stage are chocolate chips, nuts, fresh or dried fruit and berries. Take particular care with fresh or frozen berries, folding them in with only two or three stirring motions to prevent them bleeding colour into the dough.

Spoon the mix into the muffin cases and bake in the oven for 25-35 minutes, until well-risen and golden brown all over.

Leave in the tin for 5 minutes and then transfer to a wire rack to cool. Muffins are best eaten on the day of baking, or within 24 hours.

Cook's notes

Flavours to inspire you

Raspberry & white chocolate

· 200g fresh or frozen raspberries. If using frozen, use directly from the freezer. Add as the very last ingredient in the muffins, and stir very briefly so the berries stay intact and don't bleed, turning the whole mix pink
· 125g vegetarian white chocolate (chips, buttons or crumbled bar)
· 1 tsp natural vanilla extract or 2 tsp mixed spice
· When cool, melt a little white chocolate and drizzle it in zigzags over the top of the muffins.

Chocolate orange

· Zest of two oranges
· 2 tbsp cocoa powder
· 175g good-quality vegetarian dark chocolate (chips, buttons or just crumbled bar)
· 1 tsp natural vanilla extract

Banana & walnut

· 3 ripe bananas mashed and added at the same time as the eggs and milk.
   Note: a little less milk will be required, as the bananas will provide some of the liquid necessary to bring the mix together.
· 125g walnuts crushed into chunky crumbs
· 2 tsp mixed spice

Banana & coconut

· As above, but replace 125g walnuts with 125g desiccated coconut

Pear & cinnamon

· 2 ripe, flavourful pears, peeled, cored and chopped into tiny cubes
· 2 tsp ground cinnamon
· 1 tsp natural vanilla extract

Blueberry & almond

· 200g fresh or frozen blueberries. If using frozen, use directly from the freezer. Add as the very last ingredient in the muffins, and stir very briefly so the berries stay intact and don't bleed, turning the whole mix purple
· Replace 100g of the recipe's flour with 100g ground almonds
· Top each muffin with a sprinkling of flaked almonds before baking
· 1 tsp natural vanilla extract or 2 tsp mixed spice

Lemon & poppy seed

· Zest of two lemons
· 75g poppy seeds
· 1 tsp natural vanilla extract

Apple & lemon

· Zest of two lemons
· 2 eating apples, peeled, cored and chopped into tiny cubes
· 1 tsp natural vanilla extract

Sultana & oatmeal

· 100g sultanas (or raisins)
· Replace 100g of flour with 100g jumbo (or regular) oats
· 2 tsp mixed spice

Carrot cake muffins with cream cheese icing

cn

This may be a muffin, but it's so much more too. It's a carrot cake. It's an iced bun. It's spicy, moist, caramelly and rich, and is topped with one of the most irresistible icings known to humankind – whipped and sweetened cream cheese.

We really wanted to include a carrot cake of some description in this book, for it is, after all, one of the most popular cakes of the Western world. We opted for a muffin, rather than a cake or loaf, just to be a little different. Unlike the basic muffin recipe on the previous page, carrot cake muffins use oil rather than melted butter. This is common in carrot cakes, to make them really moist and tender, so we have adhered to tradition. Consider the cream cheese icing optional. Without it, you have a wholesome, tasty muffin, which can be packed in with your lunchbox. With it, you have a more luxurious dessert, with a higher amount of calories from fat, to be enjoyed at a leisurely pace over afternoon tea and perhaps followed by a brisk walk.

The success of carrot cake muffins in Cornucopia was all down to the phenomenon known as Saturday Breakfast. Saturday is by far and away our busiest breakfast morning, with at least double the number of orders of an average weekday, placing both the waiting staff and the breakfast chef under a challenging and sometimes terrifying amount of pressure. On mornings of such mania, a useful distraction technique is to have an irresistibly delicious muffin sitting aloft the counter, which causes a certain number of breakfast customers to abandon notions of boiled egg and toast in favour of carrot cake muffin with cream cheese icing and a cup of coffee. Saturday mornings also attract numerous families to the restaurant. As Mammy and Daddy enjoy their well-earned vegetarian sausages with homemade baked beans and caramelised red onion, their little ones' antics can be temporarily tamed by a good old carrot cake muffin.

Decorating the cream cheese icing can be fun, especially when children are involved. This recipe suggests sprinkling the icing with toasted chopped nuts. A little blob of apricot jam in the centre of the cream cheese also looks great. Or a grating of lemon and orange rind is really colourful. Or for fun make mini carrots: cut a thin sliver of carrot, slice it into carrot-shaped triangles and give it its characteristic feathery green top using a little bit of dill or fennel leaf or, if you have them, real carrot leaves. Your artwork will, however, be short lived. The first thing nine out of ten people do with their muffin is lick off the cream cheese!

Muffins
340g plain flour
340g wholemeal brown flour
2 tsp baking powder *(heaped)*
2 tsp mixed spice *(heaped)*
1 tsp ground cinnamon *(level)*
300g unrefined brown sugar
Pinch of salt
100g desiccated coconut
100g sultanas
3 medium carrots
3 large free-range eggs
125ml unrefined sunflower oil
175ml milk plus splash
    extra if needed

Cream cheese icing
225g vegetarian cream cheese
80g caster sugar *(or 2 tbsp
    runny honey)*
Seeds of one vanilla pod
    or zest of one orange
Handful of toasted & chopped
    nuts *(optional)*

*12-hole muffin tray
    & 12 paper cases*

Preheat the oven to 180°C and line the muffin tray with muffin cases. Sieve the flour, spices and baking powder into a large mixing bowl. Add the sugar, salt, coconut and sultanas and combine thoroughly. Peel the carrots, grate them finely and stir them into the dry mix. Form a well in the centre of the mixing bowl.

Combine the eggs, oil and milk in a separate jug. Pour this wet mix into the centre of the dry mix and fold together. The mix should be of a thick but spoonable consistency. If too stiff, add a little more milk, being careful not to overwork the mix.

Divide the mixture into the muffin cases and bake for 25-35 minutes, or until risen and golden. Leave in the tray for five minutes, and then transfer to a wire rack to cool.

Meanwhile, make the cream cheese icing by beating the cream cheese, sugar and vanilla seeds together until light and smooth. If using orange zest, stir it in at the end. Spoon the icing liberally over the muffins when they are completely cool. Top with toasted nuts if desired. Muffins should be eaten on the day of baking or within 24 hours.

Note: if you use a vanilla pod in the cream cheese icing, place the empty pod in an open bag of sugar, and it will infuse it with a light vanilla flavour and scent.

Joan's scones

The illustrious Joan McGrath was a baker in Cornucopia from 1994 to 2002, before she reluctantly left to put her energies into another kitchen equally worthy of her compassionate cooking and warm-hearted spirit. Joan combined an eye for glorious presentation with an underlying devotion to simple, rustic baking. Some of her famous hits were hearty apple crumble tarts, mouth-watering focaccia bread and fine old-fashioned iced carrot cake. And, of course, her eponymous sweet sultana scones, the recipe for which has been written down for the first time ever in this book.

You can pick up a fruit scone in pretty much any supermarket, deli, petrol station or coffee shop all over the country. They vary in quality from bland and dry to light, crumbly and moreish. But none that I have tasted (and I have tasted many) has quite equalled the Joan scone. When she worked in Cornucopia, a cloud of mystery surrounded the glowing loveliness of Joan's scones. We all used to speculate as to what could make them so delicious. We wondered if, as a rather magical and intuitive earth mother, Joan didn't secretly sprinkle in some invisible enchanted dust that gave her scones sumptuousness above and beyond the sum of their parts.

One thing is certain: everything Joan made, she made with love. And that is one great secret of baking. It is not a process that should be rushed or performed under duress. Baking is about being calm and attentive, touching and appreciating your ingredients, enjoying making a bit of a mess, safe in the knowledge that it'll be cleaned up presently, wafting away on the heady aromas, visualising the end product and, above all, serving your wares with pride to an appreciative audience.

A Joan scone served still a little warm with a knob of butter and a touch of jam is in no danger of lacking that admiring audience. Rich and moist and satisfying, they are a wonderful mid-morning or afternoon tea treat. I know Joan would certainly advocate enjoying them with a big pot of freshly brewed Earl Grey tea. And you can add your own magic dust for that extra-special result!

Preheat your oven to 220°C and grease a baking tray. Sift the flour and baking powder into a large mixing bowl. Add the sugar, salt and ground almonds and mix thoroughly.

Chop the butter into cubes and add it to the mixing bowl. Use your fingers to rub the butter into the dry ingredients, until the mixture resembles course breadcrumbs.

375g plain flour
1½ tsp baking powder
60g caster sugar *(or unrefined brown sugar)*
Pinch of salt
75g ground almonds
100g butter
1 heaped tsp ground cinnamon
150g sultanas
2 free-range eggs
250ml buttermilk

1 flat baking tray

Stir in the sultanas and cinnamon. Form a well in the centre of the bowl.

In a separate bowl, whisk together the eggs and the buttermilk. Pour most of this into the well in the flour mix, reserving about 100ml as egg wash with which to brush the tops of the scones. Use a spoon to bring the ingredients together into a soft dough. If you need to, add a tiny extra drop of buttermilk to incorporate all the dry ingredients, but be careful not to add too much, as the dough should not be in any way sticky.

On a lightly floured surface, roll the dough out to approximately 2cm thick. Dust the top with some more flour. Use a 6-7cm scone cutter (or a straight-sided tumbler of similar dimensions) to stamp out about 12 rounds. Dipping the cutter/tumbler into a small mound of flour between each stamp will stop the dough sticking to the inside.

Transfer the cut scones to the baking tray and brush the tops with a little of the leftover egg and buttermilk mix. Bake in the centre of the oven for 12-14 minutes, until golden and risen. Tap the base of a scone with your hand. If it makes a hollow sound, it is cooked through. Cool slightly on a wire rack. Serve still warm or cold, dusted with icing sugar and with butter and jam available for those who would like it.

Joan's scones are best consumed on the day of baking. You can revive them the following day by placing them in a warm oven for about 5 minutes.

Cook's notes

Vegan cheesecakes

A vegan cheesecake is a cake that looks and tastes quite similar to a traditional cheesecake but is made without cream cheese and eggs. Tofu replaces the cheese and cornflour replaces the setting function of the eggs. Because the natural fat content of the cream cheese and eggs is absent, vegan cheesecakes are often enriched with soy cream, chocolate and, in the case of the marble torte below, tahini.

There follow three recipes for silken tofu cakes – two chocolate and one lemon. They are all very similar in method but entirely different in flavouring. It was a task to choose between them, as each have their loyal supporters, so in the end we included all three.

The recipes include a homemade ginger biscuit, which is crumbed to form the base of the cake. Alternatively, you can use a pack of vegan gingernuts, which also make for a fantastically crunchy, spicy biscuit base. Should gingernuts be unavailable, add one teaspoon of ground ginger to any packet of plain, vegan biscuits. We use a Japanese-origin firm silken tofu, which is available from Asian food stores and most health food stores. If you have a limited range of tofu available to you, any firm tofu will do.

Chocolate marble silken torte

v

This very interesting vegan cheesecake was brought from Canada by Tamarack, one of our former pastry chefs. When she made it first, the vegans on the staff went nuts for it. The proof of this pudding was definitely in the eating. One of the major perks of working in Cornucopia is that we can eat as much soup, salad, bread and main courses as possible on the house. However, because desserts are more limited in supply, they have to be paid for (at a 20% staff discount), which generally serves as a disincentive to eat cake. It is truly the mark of a really exceptional dessert if staff dip into their pockets to purchase a slice for their break time, rather than sticking with free food. This marble torte caused a wave of lavish expenditure when it hit the counter, resulting in several impulsive people taking out advances on their next week's wages!

The ingredient of note in this recipe is tahini, which is to sesame seeds what peanut butter is to peanuts. It is a thick, rich paste used predominantly in Middle-Eastern cooking, most notably in hummus (see page 193) and baba ghanoush (see page 299). Although quite high in fat, tahini is rich in nutrients: it is a good source of calcium, fibre, protein and vitamin B1, as well as essential fatty acids important for good skin. Add to that the fact that dark chocolate contains magnesium, calcium, iron, zinc and a high concentration of anti-oxidant flavonoids, associated with fighting cancer and maintaining a healthy heart. Not to mention tofu, which is a zero-cholesterol, low-fat source of protein and folic acid. So, although this chocolate marble silken torte is a rich indulgence, you are by no means eating a wedge of empty calories – there are benefits galore embedded in its lavish swirls.

Speaking of swirls, that is the visual aesthetic that you are aiming at in making this cake. Half of the mix is plain white sweetened tahini and tofu, the second half of the mix is combined with melted chocolate. The finished cake should display the two different colours weaving and intertwining in a marbled effect. There is no exact science to achieving this – just pour the plain mix in first, pour the chocolate mix all over it and then move the tip of a knife in small, circular motions to mingle the layers, but without stirring them together into one homogenous mass. The result is that every single slice of cake will be totally unique.

For the biscuit base*
200g vegan margarine *(150g and 50g)*
75g soft brown sugar
300g plain flour *(or half fine wholemeal, half plain)*
1 tsp baking powder
2 tsp ground ginger
Pinch of salt

* Alternatively, use one 300g pack of vegan gingernut biscuits

Preheat your oven to 180°C and line the baking tray and springform tin with parchment paper (see page 384).

For the biscuit base
In a mixing bowl, beat the sugar and 150g of the margarine together until light and fluffy. Sift in the flour, baking powder and ginger and add a pinch of salt. Fold together until evenly distributed.

Place the dough onto the lined baking tray, sprinkle it lightly with flour and roll it out (any shape) to about ½cm thick. Bake in the oven for 20 minutes, until golden brown. Set aside to cool.

When completely cool, blitz the enormous cookie in a blender. Melt the remaining 50g of vegan margarine and add it to these crumbs. Press firmly into the base of the lined springform tin and then place in the fridge to set.

For the cake filling
700g *(2 standard packs)* firm
    silken tofu
200ml soy cream
175g tahini
120ml unrefined sunflower oil
200g golden syrup *(or honey*)*
2 tbsp cornflour (cornstarch)
225g good-quality vegan dark
    chocolate (55% or higher)

** If you use honey instead of
golden syrup, the recipe will no
longer be vegan*

*Flat baking tray
    & 10in springform tin*

For the cake filling

Break the chocolate into a bowl and place over a pan of gently simmering water, ensuring the bowl is not touching the water. When just melted, remove from the heat and set to one side.

Drain the tofu. Place it, along with the soy cream, tahini, oil, golden syrup and cornflour, into the food processor and blend until smooth. Pour half of this mix onto the biscuit base. Add the melted chocolate to the second half of the tofu mix, blend again to combine thoroughly and pour into the tin on top of the first layer.

With the tip of a knife, make swirling motions through the two tofu layers to create a marbled effect, making sure to distribute the chocolate mix evenly throughout. Bake for 45-50 minutes or until the centre of the cake is just set. It will still feel a little soft to the touch – the chocolate will set as it cools.

Cool the marble cake in the tin and then refrigerate (also in the tin) for at least two hours before slicing and serving. This cake will keep for three days in the fridge.

Chocolate orange silken torte with optional Tia Maria   *v*

This tofu cheesecake is very similar to the last recipe, only easier, as it does not involve marbling two different mixes together. The rich chocolaty pudding mix is enlivened by the zest of two oranges, a glorious combination.

If you are making a dessert for a really special occasion, this cake can be fancied-up to achieve a high-level wow factor with the addition of a splash of booze and some enthusiastic decorating: chocolate curls and caramelised orange segments. Add two or three capfuls of Tia Maria to the main mix (have a taste – you may like a little more). While the cake is cooking, melt some dark chocolate and, using a palate knife or similar, spread it out as thinly as possible on a clean work surface (if your kitchen is relatively cool) or onto a smooth tray or marble cutting board (if you need to move it to a cooler environment to set). When the chocolate has set, use the sharp edge of a knife or a bench scraper to scrape the chocolate into curls. Different angles and different amounts of pressure will make various kinds of curls. Set them aside in a very cool place, or even the fridge, to keep their shape until you are ready to use them.

To make caramelised orange segments, take one of the oranges that you have zested for the main cake. Peel it and then carefully slice each individual segment out, without any pith. If you have a catering blowtorch, toss the segments in 1 tablespoon of caster sugar, place in a roasting pan and torch them until the sugar has caramelised. If you don't have a blowtorch, heat a dry pan to very hot. Place the orange segments in and cook for one minute, then turn and cook for a further 30 seconds. Now sprinkle one tablespoon of caster sugar into the pan, reduce the heat and cool gently until fully melted, tossing the segments in the caramel. Decorate your chocolate orange silken torte with orange segments around the edge and a great big pile of chocolate curls in the centre.

Which leaves you with one leftover zested orange. This should be halved, juiced, topped with a capful of tia maria and imbibed as you admire your stunning creation!

Preheat the oven to 180°C and line the baking tray and springform tin with parchment paper (see page 384).

For the biscuit base
In a mixing bowl, beat the sugar and 150g of the margarine together until light and fluffy. Sift in the flour, baking powder and ginger and add a pinch of salt. Fold together until evenly distributed.

For the biscuit base*
200g vegan margarine
    (150g & 50g)
75g soft brown sugar
300g plain flour *(or half fine
    wholemeal, half plain)*
1 tsp baking powder
2 tsp ground ginger
Pinch of salt

** Alternatively, use one 300g
pack of vegan gingernut biscuits*

For the cake filling
700g *(2 standard packs)* firm
    silken tofu
250ml soy cream *(1 standard
    mini-carton)*
75ml oil
3 tbsp cocoa powder
200g good-quality vegan dark
    chocolate *(55% or higher)*
4 tbsp cornflour
250g caster sugar *or unrefined
    brown sugar*
Zest 2 oranges
2-3 capfuls of Tia Maria or
    Kahlua *(optional)*

*Flat baking tray
    & 10in springform tin*

Place the cookie dough onto the lined baking tray, sprinkle it lightly with flour and roll it out (into any shape) to about ½cm thick. Bake in the oven for 20 minutes, until golden brown. Set aside to cool.

When completely cool, blitz the enormous cookie in a blender. Melt the remaining 50g of vegan margarine and add it to these crumbs. Press firmly into the base of the lined springform tin and then place in the fridge to set.

For the cake filling
Break the chocolate into a bowl and place over a pan of gently simmering water, ensuring the bowl is not touching the water. When melted, remove from the heat and set to one side.

Now drain the tofu. Place it, along with the soy cream, oil, cocoa, cornflour, caster sugar and orange zest, into a blender and blend until smooth. If you are using a splash of alcohol to enrich the cake, blend it in at this point too.

Pour the chocolate tofu mix onto the gingernut base and bake in the oven for 45-50 minutes, until the centre has just set. It will still feel quite soft — the chocolate will become firmer as it cools.

Cool the cake in the tin, then refrigerate for at least two hours before slicing and serving with a squiggle of soy cream.

Lemon, raspberry & ginger silken torte

v

This lemon vegan cheesecake is a recent addition to the Cornucopia repertoire. It grew out of the chocolate silken tortes described on the previous few pages. We wanted a lighter, zingier version of the torte, more suited to a spring and summer palate. The resulting lemon and raspberry delight has graced the counter regularly since; drizzled with just a little soy cream, it is a luxurious end to a light meal.

The magic ingredient in this recipe is the psyllium husk, which serves as a wonderful replacement in vegetarian cookery for non-vegetarian gelatine. Psyllium husks are available from health food stores.

Psyllium husks are the outer part of the seed of the psyllium plant, a plant cultivated in eastern Europe, the Middle East and the Orient, traditionally as a herbal medicine. It is used in both Eastern and Western medicines to relieve constipation and other digestive tract problems. Psyllium is high in dietary fibre and in more recent years has been added to breakfast cereals and health drinks to boost the cholesterol-reducing fibre content.

For the purposes of cooking and baking, psyllium is valued for its mucilage content. Mucilage is a tasteless, colourless gelling agent. Psyllium husks absorb water and bind to it, expanding by up ten times, making them useful for setting, binding and thickening. They are used in fruit compôtes, sugarless jams, ice-creams and other frozen goods. In this recipe, two tablespoons of psyllium husks are sufficient to set the purée of raspberries, so that it sits soft, but firm, a pleasantly tart topping for the rich lemon torte.

Preheat the oven to 180°C and line the baking tray and springform tin with parchment paper (see page 384).

For the biscuit base
In a mixing bowl, beat 150g of the margarine and sugar together until light and fluffy. Sift in the flour, baking powder and ginger and add a pinch of salt. Fold together until evenly distributed.

Place the cookie dough onto the lined baking tray, sprinkle it lightly with flour and roll it out (in any shape) to about ½cm thick. Bake in the oven for 20 minutes, until golden brown. Set aside to cool.

For the base*
150g vegan margarine
75g soft brown sugar
300g plain flour *(or half fine wholemeal, half plain)*
1 tsp baking powder
2 tsp ground ginger
Pinch of salt

* Alternatively, use one 300g pack of vegan gingernut biscuits

For the cake filling
Zest and juice of 4 lemons
700g *(2 standard packs)* **firm silken tofu**
250ml soy cream *(1 standard mini-carton)*
4 tbsp cornflour
250g caster sugar
150ml unrefined sunflower oil

For the raspberry topping
300g raspberries *(fresh or frozen)*
2 tbsp psyllium husks
1 tbsp caster sugar *(optional)*

Flat baking tray
& 10in springform tin

When completely cool, reduce the enormous cookie to crumbs in a blender. Melt the remaining 50g of vegan margarine and add it to these crumbs. Press firmly into the base of the lined springform tin and then place in the fridge to set.

For the cake filling

Wash, zest and juice the four lemons. Add both zest and juice to a food processor, along with the tofu (drained), soy cream, cornflour, caster sugar and oil. Blend until completely smooth. Pour this mix onto the cookie crumb base and bake in the centre of the oven for 45-50 minutes, or until just set.

For the topping

When the cake is completely cool, place the raspberries and psyllium husks in a food processor and blend until smooth. Taste the mix and, if necessary, sweeten with a little caster sugar. Spread it immediately over the top of the cake. Refrigerate for 1 hour, during which time the topping will set. Remove from the tin, slice and serve.

Coconut, chocolate & brandy petits fours
(aka mutiny on the bounty)   *v gf wf cn (coconut)*

Firstly, a word of explanation about the origin of these gooey balls of delight. There are often lengthy discussions around Cornucopia about what food people really miss since turning vegetarian or since becoming a vegan or since cutting out wheat, and so on. A topic that always raises particular interest is nostalgic descriptions of now eliminated sweets, be it vegetarians reminiscing about innocent days of toasted marshmallows or vegans remembering dipping Twix fingers in tea or coeliacs recalling the pleasure of a slice of moist carrot cake. Part of our job in Cornucopia is to satisfy as best we can the desires of people on special diets, so it's not at all surprising that one such 'sweets I used to eat' conversation led to the creation of these petits fours, known familiarly amongst staff as 'mutiny on the bounty' — inspired by fond, pre-vegan memories of a certain well-known coconut chocolate bar.

Claire, the pastry chef, set her imagination going. Together with her sidekick Jon, kitchen-porter-cum-culinary-adviser, she experimented, tasted, tweaked and perfected and finally presented us with these delicious after-dinner treats, far superior to the chocolate bar that got the whole ball rolling. They are great fun to make too. No oven necessary, just a pot for the syrup and a bain marie for the chocolate. The simplicity of their creation and the messy pleasure of rolling sticky, coconutty balls into a big lake of chocolate is rather like a grown-up's return to playschool. But with alcohol this time.

The recipe uses soya milk powder, which is available from health food shops. However, if you do not require the recipe to be vegan, ordinary milk powder can be substituted. You will also notice the inclusion of one teaspoon of cream of tartar in the recipe. More commonly known as an ingredient in baking powder or used for stabilising and strengthening egg whites in meringues, on this occasion cream of tartar is used to prevent the sugar in the sugar syrup from crystallising, making for a creamier overall texture. Cream of tartar is a natural product obtained from sediment in the winemaking process.

First of all, chop the block of coconut cream into chunks. Next, split open the vanilla pod and scrape out all the seeds. Set them to one side and place the empty vanilla pod into a large pot. Add the water and sugar and place over a low heat. Stirring all the time, bring to a gentle simmer, and then add the cream of tartar. Cook for 5 minutes, still stirring regularly. Now add the

225g caster sugar *or unrefined
    brown sugar*
175ml water
50g soya milk powder *(or
    regular milk powder)*
40ml *(about 3 tbsp)* brandy
1 vanilla pod *(or 1tsp natural
    vanilla extract)*
Pinch of salt
1 tsp cream of tartar
250g coconut cream
    (1 standard block)
450g desiccated coconut
450g good-quality *(55% or
    higher)* vegan dark chocolate

2 cocktail sticks or a 2-prong fork

chunks of coconut cream and continue to cook for 2 minutes. The coconut will melt into the sugar syrup. Remove the pot from the ring and discard the empty vanilla pod. Stir in the brandy, vanilla seeds, salt and milk powder. When well integrated, fold in the desiccated coconut until an even consistency is achieved. If your pot is not large enough, transfer everything to a large mixing bowl. Allow this coconut mixture to cool enough to handle.

Meanwhile, place the chocolate into a bowl over a pan of gently simmering water, ensuring the bowl is not touching the water. When melted, remove from the heat and set to one side. Prepare a wire rack, under which is placed a sheet of parchment paper. Next, roll all the coconut mix into truffle-sized balls. Using two cocktail sticks or a 2-prong fork, immerse each ball in melted chocolate, holding it over the bowl of chocolate for a moment to allow excess chocolate to drip back into the bowl. Then place the ball on the wire rack. Any further drips of chocolate will be caught on the parchment paper and can be added to ice-cream or cookies.

Place the wire rack in a cool place for the chocolate to set (but not a fridge, as the chocolate will turn cloudy). Meanwhile, make a parchment paper piping bag as described on page 382 and fill it with the remaining melted chocolate, or, if there is none left, melt a little more chocolate. When the balls have set, streak some lines of chocolate across the top of each. These mutiny on the bounty, brandy-imbued treasures can be served in mini paper cases as after-dinner petits fours and are delicious with a strong cup of espresso.

Spiced date & orange squares

v   no added sugar

For many years, customers have been requesting sugar-free desserts. For a while honeyed apple and sultana strudels were a hit. However, they contained butter and honey, which made them unsuitable for the vegan and dairy-free audiences. This traybake has become our most popular sugar-free dessert in recent times. It is a spiced vegan wholemeal cake, filled with stewed dates and sweetened with apple concentrate. Apple concentrate is readily available in health food shops. It is also an ingredient in some of the dressings in the salad chapter (glass noodles, sprouted beans, beetroot).

Reasons to avoid sugar or reduce sugar intake are too numerous and too varied to fully elaborate upon here. However, it is doubtlessly true that the average 21st-century Western diet contains more sugar than the human body requires, and often more than the body can comfortably cope with. Sugar in itself is not bad – fruit is full of sugar (fructose), as are many vegetables, such as carrots, sweet potatoes and onions. The problem with processed sugar, brown or white, is that it represents empty calories, food with no nutritional benefits, which is why it should not play a major role in our daily food intake. Moreover, for some people, refined sugar causes immediate adverse physical reactions, be it swelling, headaches, hyperactivity or the worsening of candida symptoms. For others, too much sugar and the resultant sugar highs and sugar lows affect their moods. And in the long-term, too much sugar in our diet is associated with tooth decay, gum disease, ageing of the skin, osteoporosis, arthritis and reduced absorption of nutrients from our foods. A high-sugar diet is also linked to increased risk of certain cancers.

This is not to suggest that everyone should immediately eliminate all traces of sugar from their food, cupboards and life. Unless faced with an immediate and serious health challenge, a small quantity of sugar within a balanced diet represents one of life's great pleasures. A sweet treat can sometimes hit the spot in a way that puts a smile back on your face, which is medicine in itself. Should you have reason to avoid processed sugar completely, this recipe and the one that follows are fine examples of using fruit and fruit concentrate to create a sweet and satisfying cake, without the inclusion of a single grain of sugar. It is a great square to slip into childrens' lunchboxes; they'll be happy to find a little cakey treat and you'll be happy to know they're getting a wholesome snack.

Preheat your oven to 180°C and line the baking tray with parchment paper (see page384). First of all stew the dates. Place them in a small pot and cover them with water. Place over a low heat with a lid on and allow them to simmer very gently

300g plain white flour
300g wholemeal brown flour
2 tsp ground ginger
2 tsp mixed spice
1 tsp *(level)* bicarbonate of soda
 (baking soda)
1½ tsp baking powder
Pinch salt
Zest of 2 oranges
Dash of vegetarian vinegar
250ml apple concentrate
250ml oil
400g chopped dates

*23x23x5cm baking tray
 (or 20x25x5cm)*

for about 10 minutes, until they are soft and have absorbed most of the water. Stir regularly to prevent the fruit sticking to the pot and burning. Remove from the ring and set aside to cool.

Sift the plain flour, brown flour, ginger, mixed spice and baking powder into a large mixing bowl. Add a pinch of salt and mix thoroughly. Form a well in the centre of this dry mix.

Measure the oil and apple concentrate into a jug and add the baking soda and vinegar. Stir to create a bubbling effect as the soda reacts with the vinegar. Pour it all into the well in the centre of the mixing bowl and quickly combine all the ingredients. Add a tiny splash of water if necessary to create a thick but spreadable cake mix.

Spoon half of this mix into the base of the baking tray and smooth it over, making sure to fill the corners. Cover it with stewed dates, spreading them as evenly as possible. Now top with the second half of the cake mix. This is easiest done by spooning it on in five or six scoops and then smoothing it out with a spatula or the back of a metal spoon.

Transfer the cake to the oven and bake for 35-40 minutes, until well-risen and golden brown all over. Allow to cool in the tray, and then slice into 12 or 16 squares. Some people like to trim the edges first, so that no single slice has too much crust, but this is a matter of personal preference. This cake is best eaten within 24 hours of baking. You can also freeze individual portions and defrost them as required for lunchboxes or afternoon cups of tea.

Cook's notes

Variations

Should you find you like this sugar-free traybake, there are many ways to vary the ingredients to keep your palate interested:

Spiced apricot & orange square
- Replace the ground ginger with ground cinnamon
- Replace the stewed dates with stewed dried apricots. Either liquidise them or chop them roughly before spreading them into the cake

Blueberry & almond square
- Replace 100g white flour with 100g ground almonds
- Leave out the ground ginger
- Add a dash of natural almond extract (optional)
- Scatter 300g fresh or frozen blueberries into the cake
- Sprinkle flaked almonds over the top layer of the cake

Spiced apple & sultana square
(this has the fruit all through the cake, not sandwiched in the middle)
- Soak 175g sultanas in the apple concentrate before you start
- Replace the ground ginger with ground cinnamon
- Peel, core and grate 2 sweet eating apples into the dry mix
- Slice a third eating apple (unpeeled) into very thin slices and arrange them attractively on the top of the cake before baking

Fig & banana tart
v   yf   no added sugar

This tart is a relic from the old-school vegetarianism of the 1980s. Back in the early days of Cornucopia, when the cooking facilities were more limited, a wonderful cook called Lorna Burrows baked fig and banana tarts at home. She delivered them, as well as her delicious lentil pies, to the restaurant for sale. The fig and banana tart experienced a comeback when Claire, our more recent pastry chef, tried it out on the Cornucopia counter as a sugar-free dessert and it turned out to have considerable appeal for a certain kind of customer. Golden, soft-baked bananas immersed in sweet, sticky figs, encased in crisp wholemeal pastry, enjoyed warm with a dollop of natural yoghurt or soya yoghurt, it has all the charm of a sweet and filling pudding, with rather less of the guilt.

Gourmet cooking, which represents more and more what the Irish consumer considers good food, tends to focus primarily on taste-bud satisfaction and visual appeal, with health and nutrition concerns taking a secondary, and sometimes negligible, place of importance. Which makes for fabulous food, but not necessarily a balanced diet. More old-fashioned cooking worked the other way round. First settle upon the nutritious components of a dish, and then decide how they can be attractively and deliciously presented. This tart falls into that category — it is a simple recipe that combines bananas and figs in a sugar-free pastry base with a dash of spice. That's it. No fancy extras, no fussy decoration. A plain, hearty, rustic tart.

Bananas are rich in dietary fibre, potassium and vitamin C, as well as easily digestible carbohydrate energy. Figs are also a good source of dietary fibre and potassium as well as a significant provider of calcium (even more than milk) and iron. Try not to buy no-soak figs, as they lend themselves less to stewing than regular dried fruit. Figs bought in a health food shop are usually suitable. Considering that wholemeal brown flour is also full of dietary fibre, a sliver of this tart each day could be relied upon to keep the insides regular. Although bananas are an essential ingredient in this tart, for texture and sweetness, the figs can be varied with other dried fruits. Try stewed dried apricots or prunes, or a combination of both.

Pastry preparation
Sift the plain and wholemeal flours into a mixing bowl and stir in a pinch of salt. Use the tips of your fingers to rub in the vegan margarine to achieve an even breadcrumb consistency (if using butter, grate it first, then rub it in). Adding a very small splash of water at a time, bring the mix together into a soft dough. Work the dough as little as

110g wholemeal brown flour
110g plain flour
110g cold vegan margarine
    *(or cold butter if not required
    to be vegan)*
Pinch of salt
Cold water
450g dried figs
700g ripe bananas *(about 6
    medium bananas)*
2 tsp mixed spice

28cm (11in) fluted tart tin

possible – just push it around lightly until it forms a ball. Wrap the dough in clingwrap and place in the fridge for an hour before rolling.

Assembling the tart:
Preheat your oven to 180°C. Destalk the figs and then place them in a suitably sized pot. Cover with water and bring to a very gentle simmer. Cook until the figs are plumped up and completely soft and the water has reduced to a light syrup. If the pot runs dry before the figs are soft, add a little extra water. Remove from the ring and set aside to cool.

Next, remove the pastry from the fridge and roll it out on a lightly floured surface to about 3mm thickness. Transfer to the tart tin, pressing it into place and trimming the edge (see page 301). Cut a large round piece of parchment paper, place it over the pastry and fill it with dried beans or ceramic baking beans. Place it in the oven for 10 minutes, then remove the beans and bake for a further 5 minutes, so that the centre of the tart is just starting to crisp.

When the figs have cooled sufficiently, chop them into quarters and place them in a large mixing bowl along with the mixed spice. Peel the bananas and chop them into 1cm-thick rounds. Fold together the figs, bananas and any syrup left in the pot from cooking the figs. Spoon this mix into the par baked tart case and smooth it over. Bake in the oven for 20-25 minutes, until the bananas have turned a beautiful golden brown. Leave to settle in the tin for at least half an hour, then remove the tart ring and slice. Serve warm or cold with soya or natural yoghurt.

Leftover figs
If you are wondering what to do with any remaining dried figs:

Chopped small
· Add them to cookies, muffins and sweet scones
· Stir them through bulghar wheat/couscous salads or accompaniments
Halved
· Add them to stews such as tagines and curries about 15 minutes before the end of cooking
Stewed and puréed
· Use them as a filling for oat bars (page 392) or sugar-free spiced squares (page 428)
· Spread them on toast
Cooked whole
· Try the fig and prune compôte (page 388) for serving on porridge, Greek-style natural yoghurt or with sweet polenta (page 257)

Gluten-free rice flour desserts

This section comprises a selection of sweets suitable for anyone adhering to a strictly gluten-free diet. They are also suitable for anyone with wheat intolerance, or who would like to reduce the amount of wheat in their diet.

The four recipes that follow are all based on rice flour, one of the key flours for gluten-free baking. It is a neutral-tasting flour, quite grainy in texture, that works best in cookies or in desserts that are designed to be quite intense and moist, rather than in fluffy cakes and buns. Try to source brown rice flour, if possible. Just like the difference between white rice and brown rice, white rice flour lacks many of the nutrients contained in brown rice flour, which is less processed and supplies a good source of B vitamins, iron and fibre. It has a slightly deeper taste and coarser texture.

All the rice flour recipes here include eggs. Without the gelling power of the gluten in wheat, cookies and cakes made with rice flour require a strong binding ingredient, and egg is the most natural choice. Also, without gluten, rice flour is less stretchy than regular flour, and the leavening (raising) agents have to work extra hard to make it rise. Eggs help this process: they integrate little bubbles of air when whisked, they release pockets of expanding moisture when the cake is cooking and they set the risen cake so that it doesn't collapse.

Rice flour is quite sticky – it releases a glutinous (not gluten!) content when cooked, which, in baking terms, means it sticks to tins and trays very easily. Always use parchment paper to line your bakeware for traybakes, loaves or cookies, to prevent the untold disaster of a delicious, but immovable dessert. For a gluten-free dessert that is also vegan turn to page 424 for coconut, chocolate and brandy petits fours.

Gluten-free baking powder

While the main components of regular baking powder are bicarbonate of soda and cream of tartar (or other acid ingredients), which are gluten-free, wheat flour is also added to the mix to strengthen it, making it unsuitable for gluten-free baking. Gluten-free baking powder, available from health food shops, uses potato starch instead of flour as the added ingredient. Although it is not our policy to recommend particular brands, it is worth noting that Royal Baking Powder, a common supermarket brand, uses maize flour rather than wheat flour and is therefore a gluten-free baking powder, significantly cheaper than the specifically marketed health food products.

Rice cookies
gf wf

This is a basic recipe for gluten-free rice cookies, which can be cooked plain or to which you can add your own choice of flavouring. Below are listed some of the many variations that we have served in the restaurant, with chocolate chip being perhaps the most popular. To cook them plain, simply sprinkle them with granulated sugar before they go into the oven for a buttery, crumbly, crunchy shortbread biscuit.

This shortbread-style cookie is very suitable for baking with rice flour as, even when made with regular flour, it is supposed to be a dry, crumbly biscuit, which is exactly what rice flour produces. In fact, a lot of recipes for traditional Scottish shortbread use a small quantity of rice flour mixed through the plain flour to give the shortbread a more melt-in-the-mouth, tender texture. So it is not a far cry from that to bake shortbread entirely with rice flour.

One advantage of a cookie dough made of rice flour is that there is no danger of overworking the flour and stretching the gluten, so it is a perfect recipe to let children help out with. They can push and prod and shape the dough without damaging it in any way. A simplified version of the method has been included for younger readers. First measure out all the ingredients together, and then follow the simple 1-10 guide.

On the flip side, as with most gluten-free baking, once the cookies emerge from the oven, they require very gentle handling. Allow them to cool on the tray for at least 5 minutes before trying to move them. Slide them carefully from the tray to a wire rack using a lifter. When serving, don't stack them one against the other, as they will start to crack, but rather lay them flat on a plate. And when storing, they shouldn't be placed higgledy-piggledy in a cookie jar, or you will return to biscuit bits rather than biscuit rounds. They are best stored flat in an airtight container with a sheet of parchment between each layer or laid flat on a tray wrapped with clingwrap. Unlike most cookies, they store well in the fridge, as it solidifies the butter in them and gives them a bit of extra strength.

Preheat your oven to 180°C and line the baking trays with parchment paper. Place the butter and sugar in a mixing bowl and use an electric whisk or wooden spoon to cream together until light and fluffy. Add the vanilla extract and the eggs and beat again until smooth.

In a separate bowl, mix together the rice flour and whatever flavouring you have decided to add

200g caster sugar
　(or soft brown sugar)
200g butter — *at room
　temperature*
2 free-range eggs
1 tsp natural vanilla extract
450g rice flour
Flavouring of choice *(see below)*

2 flat baking trays

to your cookies. Add this to the butter mix and fold together with a wooden spoon until an even dough has been formed.

For large cookies, divide the cookie dough into 12 equal balls and, for medium cookies, divide it into about 18. Sprinkle a little rice flour onto the baking parchment on the baking trays and press the balls into flat discs of about ½cm thick. Bake in the oven for 20-25 minutes, until golden on top. Reverse the trays half way through cooking, to ensure they cook evenly.

Allow to rest for 5 minutes on the baking trays, and then carefully transfer them to a wire rack using a lifter. Cool completely before storing flat in an airtight container.

Flavour variations
Choose any of the following cookie flavours, or invent your own:

Chocolate chip
· 150g vegetarian chocolate chips (or buttons or crumbled bar) — *use dark chocolate or a mixture of dark chocolate and white chocolate*
· Zest of one orange (optional)

Double chocolate
· 125g vegetarian dark or white chocolate chips
· Replace 50g rice flour with 50g cocoa powder

Coffee, white chocolate & walnut
· 100g vegetarian white chocolate chips (or buttons or crumbled bar)
· 100g walnuts crushed into chunky crumbs
· 2 tsp granulated coffee

Lemon & almond
· Zest of 2 lemons

- Replace 75g recipe rice flour with 75g ground almonds
- Scatter flaked almonds onto each of the pressed-out cookies

Lemon & poppy seed
- Zest of 2 lemons
- 50g poppy seeds

Peanut butter
- Replace ½ of the recipe butter with unsweetened peanut butter (smooth or crunchy) — *cream the smaller quantity of butter with the sugar, and then beat in the peanut butter*
- Press some whole peanuts into the top of each cookie before baking

Sultana & hazelnut
- 100g hazelnuts, toasted for 8 minutes, rubbed to remove skins and chopped into chunky crumbs
- 100g sultanas or raisins

Cranberry & coconut
- 100g finely chopped dried cranberries
- 100g desiccated coconut

Chocolate chip rice cookies for kids

1. Turn the oven on to 180°C, line baking trays and measure ingredients
2. Bowl A: Cream butter + sugar
3. Bowl A: add eggs + vanilla and beat
4. Bowl B: mix rice flour and chocolate chips
5. Pour bowl B into bowl A and mix with wooden spoon
6. Make balls of cookie dough
7. Press them flat on baking tray
8. Bake for 20-25 minutes until golden
9. Leave for 5 minutes on tray
10. Carefully move to wire rack to cool

Bramley apple & cinnamon crumble squares
gf wf

'But it doesn't taste gluten-free!' is a remark often made in reaction to these moist, crumbly squares. For, as any sweet-toothed coeliac will testify, gluten-free cakes are often dry and cardboardy, an austere alternative to more sumptuous gluten-enhanced standard baking. Not so these immensely popular apple gems. Using rice flour rather than wheat flour, a cinnamon shortbread base is covered with tangy Bramley (cooking) apple and topped with crunchy, buttery crumble – the perfect cake for a lazy afternoon tea. You may be a little taken aback at the amount of butter that the recipe requires, but don't be tempted to reduce it, for that will make a brittle biscuit rather than a rich, crumbly base. Instead, embrace the butter and plan a brisk, energetic walk to follow!

Some of the Cornucopia staff particularly like to heat up these squares and top them with lashings of Greek-style natural yoghurt, the tartness of which is a pleasant foil to the sweet shortbread. A tasty boost on a long Saturday shift!

Unlike a lot of gluten-free cakes, these squares actually keep really successfully for up to three days without drying out – but make sure they are very well covered, otherwise every time someone passes them they'll nibble at a piece of crumble and before long your apple squares will be missing their top layer. This is spoken from experience – our cheeky manager Margaret has often sidled past the baking shelves and surreptitiously picked off the biggest, crispiest chunk of still-warm crumble and backed silently away into her office with a triumphant look on her face, leaving a small but significant crater in the middle of the traybake as evidence of her crime.

Preheat your oven to 180°C and line the baking tray with parchment paper (see page 384). Take care when following this recipe to distinguish between the ingredients for the base and the topping, as they are quite similar.

Base
Use a mixer to beat together the butter and sugar for the base until light and fluffy. Add the eggs and vanilla extract and beat again until combined. In a separate bowl, combine the rice flour, cinnamon, gluten-free baking powder and salt. Add half of this to the butter mix and beat together slowly.

Base
200g butter — *softened*
200g unrefined brown sugar
2 large free-range eggs
1 tsp natural vanilla extract
275g rice flour
2 tsp ground cinnamon
1½ tsp gluten-free baking
    powder *(or regular baking*
    powder if not required to be
    gluten-free)
Pinch salt

Topping
200g rice flour
100g unrefined brown sugar
1 tsp natural vanilla extract
Pinch of ground cinnamon
100g cold butter
3 medium cooking apples
    (Bramley apples)

23x23x5cm baking tray
    (or 20x25x5cm)

Now add the second half and beat again. Spread the mixture onto the baking tray and par bake it for 20 minutes until golden brown and slightly risen.

Topping
While the base is cooking, prepare the topping. Stir together the rice flour, sugar, vanilla extract and cinnamon. Cut the cold butter into small cubes and, using the tips of your fingers, rub them into the dry ingredients to achieve a nice crumbly consistency, with a few lumps that will crisp up nicely in the oven.

Now peel, core and grate the cooking apples and spread evenly all over the par baked base. Sprinkle a little brown sugar onto the apple. Press to flatten and cover it all over with the crumble topping. Return to the oven for a further 25 minutes, until golden and crispy all over.

Allow to cool for an hour in the tin, and then slice into 12 or 16 pieces. Serve warm or cold, dusted with icing sugar. Delicious with fresh cream or vegetarian ice-cream. These squares keep for up to 3 days.

Chocolate & hazelnut brownie
gf wf cn

In Cornucopia we consider a really successful gluten-free recipe one that is enjoyed by both coeliac and regular-diet customers alike. Gluten-free cakes, if the recipe and ingredients are chosen expertly, can be moist, delicious and indistinguishable from regular cakes. These brownies are a fine example of such a recipe, where the conversion from plain flour to rice flour actually enhances the original recipe.

The resultant traybake is a moreish, nutty chocolate lover's dream, which is, delightfully for some, gluten-free. Using rice flour and gluten-free baking powder instead of regular flour and baking powder, this classic brownie loses none of its crisp-on-the-outside, gooey-on-the-inside texture, whilst being edible by people whose special dietary requirements often exclude them from such indulgences.

This is one of the simplest recipes in this chapter – it just involves roasting the nuts, combining the dry ingredients in one bowl, melting the butter and chocolate in another bowl, adding the eggs, mixing everything together and pouring it all into a lined baking tray. Decorating the brownies is probably the most fun of all. Don't bother with piping bags for the chocolate, just melt some dark chocolate in one bowl, some white chocolate in another bowl and place a teaspoon in each. Scatter chopped hazelnuts over the traybake and then do some freehand Jackson Pollock-style chocolate art all over it – the messier the better!

Preheat your oven to 180°C.

Place the all the hazelnuts in the baking tray (200g for the cake and 50g for decoration) and toast in the oven for 8 minutes. When cool, rub to remove the loose skins, chop roughly and set to one side, keeping 50g separate for decorating at the end. Now line the baking tray with parchment paper (see page 384).

Place the chocolate and butter into a bowl over a pan of gently simmering water, ensuring the bowl is not touching the water. When just melted, remove from the heat and set to one side.

In a mixing bowl, beat the eggs. Add the sugar and continue beating until light and fluffy.

200g hazelnuts
250g good-quality *(55%*
    or higher) vegetarian dark
    chocolate
250g caster sugar or unrefined
brown sugar
100g rice flour
2 tsp gluten-free baking powder
    (or regular baking powder
    if not required to be
    gluten-free)
Pinch salt
4 free-range eggs
200g butter

To decorate
50g vegetarian dark chocolate
50g vegetarian white chocolate
50g hazelnuts — *toasted*
    & chopped roughly

23x23x5cm baking tray
    (or 20x25x5cm)

Add the rice flour, gluten-free baking powder and salt and combine thoroughly. Form a well in the centre of this mix.

Melt the butter and pour it, along with the melted chocolate, into the well in the centre of the mixing bowl. Beat together until an even consistency is achieved. Finally, stir in 200g of the chopped nuts. Spread the brownie mix evenly into the lined baking tray. Bake for 35-40 minutes until the centre is just set. It will still feel quite soft – the chocolate will become firmer as it cools.

Cool in the tray and slice into 12 or 16 squares. Decorate the brownies before removing them from the tray. Melt the dark and white chocolate separately. Sprinkle a few chopped hazelnuts onto each brownie. Using a teaspoon, streak the hazelnuts first with dark chocolate, then with white chocolate. Then lick the spoon. Allow the chocolate to set before transferring the brownies from the tray. Serve immediately or store for up to 2 days in an airtight container.

Cook's notes

Raspberry bakewell tartlets
gf   wf   cn

The bakewell tart is a classic English dessert, which originated in the town of Bakewell in Derbyshire. In its simplest form, it is a pastry case covered with strawberry jam and topped with an almond-enriched sponge filling called frangipane. It has also taken on many more elaborate forms: chocolate bakewell, iced cherry bakewell and pear bakewell, to name but a few.

For many years we served a bakewell tart almost daily. Then a bit of experimentation by our pastry chefs discovered that, by using a new gluten-free pastry and replacing flour with rice flour in the frangipane, the recipe converted wonderfully well into a gluten-free dessert. As gluten-free pastry does not have the strength of regular pastry, we now serve individual tartlets rather than slices of a large tart, as they hold together better.

This recipe is for raspberry bakewells. The fresh tartness of the raspberries balances beautifully with the almost cloying sweetness of the frangipane. However, as the variations below will suggest, this is a recipe that can be adapted to whatever fruits or jams you have available to you. As it involves quite an amount of work, what with making both pastry and frangipane, the quantities listed are enough to make two batches of 8 tartlets. After cooking one batch, the pastry and frangipane will store in the fridge for up to five days, until you are ready to use them again.

Should tartlet cases be unavailable, these little bakewells can be baked in a muffin tray, in which case the quantities listed will make two batches of 12 tartlets, as each one will be slightly smaller.

The pastry described below is not limited to use in bakewells; it can be used for all sorts of gluten-free tartlets. Prepare the tart shells as described below. For apple crumble tartlets, fill the blind-baked pastry with cooked Bramley apples and cover with a crumble topping (150g rice flour, 100g soft butter, 75g sugar rubbed together into chunky crumbs). Bake at 180°C until golden brown and crispy. For lemon tartlets, fill the blind-baked pastry with lemon custard (4 free-range egg yolks, 300ml cream, 60g sugar, juice and zest of two lemons all whisked together). Bake at 160°C (low oven) for 25-30 minutes until just set.

If you are a coeliac who enjoys baking, you could double the pastry quantities below, bake off 8 tartlets and freeze the rest in three batches, to be taken out as required for different kinds of tarts.

Sweet pastry
125g caster sugar
250g butter — *at room temperature*
2 free-range eggs
500g rice flour
Pinch of salt

Frangipane
250g butter — *at room temperature*
250g icing sugar
250g ground almonds
5 free-range eggs
1 tsp natural vanilla extract *or 1 capful of brandy*
80g rice flour

Filling
300g fresh raspberries
100g flaked almonds

8x9.5cm fluted tartlet cases or a 12-hole muffin tray

Muffin paper cases (required for both tartlet cases & muffin tray)

Start by making the pastry. Using an electric whisk or wooden spoon, beat the butter and sugar together until light and creamy. Whisk the eggs in a separate jug. Now, continuing to beat the butter and sugar, stream the eggs in very slowly (so they don't curdle) until fully combined. Add the rice flour and salt and combine all the ingredients into a smooth paste. Form the pastry into a ball, clingwrap it and place it in the fridge for at least an hour before rolling (or 20 minutes in the freezer).

Next, make the frangipane filling. Cream the butter until light. Measure the ground almonds and icing sugar into a separate bowl and combine. Add this dry mix bit by bit to the creamed butter. If using an electric whisk, start on a very low speed, as icing sugar tends to send puffs of powder everywhere, until it has been integrated into the butter. Next, whisk the eggs in a separate jug and add them, bit by bit, to the butter mix, ensuring each batch is fully combined before adding more. Don't be tempted to pour in all the eggs at once, as the mix may curdle. When all the eggs have been added, stir in the rice flour and vanilla extract/brandy. Refrigerate until ready to use. Remove the pastry from the fridge/freezer.

If using 9.5cm tartlet cases

Take a 55g ball of pastry, roll it in a little rice flour and place it in the centre of a flattened-out muffin case. Press it flat with your fingers until it almost reaches the edge of the muffin case (you can also use a rolling pin). Transfer this disc to a tartlet case and press into place. Repeat for 7 more tartlet cases. This will use about half of your pastry.

Variations

Try the following fillings in your bakewell tartlets (the frangipane topping remains the same)

Other kinds of berries
- fresh or frozen blueberries
- cranberries, stewed with a little sugar until soft
- autumn blackberries or elderberries

Fresh fruit
- pears, peeled and poached with a vanilla pod and a cinnamon stick, then halved; place one half into each tartlet, rounded side up
- ripe summer apricots, halved and stoned; place one in each tartlet, rounded side up, and cut a grid shape on the skin
- ripe autumn plums, halved and stoned; do the same as with apricots

Homemade jams
- if you have a delicious homemade jam, simply fill each tartlet with a generous spoonful

If using a 12-hole muffin tray

As above, but start with a 40g ball of pastry, which, when pressed flat to the edge of the muffin case, will make a thinner disc. Transfer to the muffin tray and press into place. Repeat until the muffin tray is filled. You will have used about half of your pastry.

Place the empty pastry shells in the oven to partially bake for 10 minutes, until the centre has started to dry out. Remove from the oven. If using tartlet cases, place 5 fresh raspberries in each. If using a muffin tray, place 3 fresh raspberries in each. Now fill the case with frangipane to just level with the top. No need to be too fussy about smoothing it over, as that will occur naturally in the heat of the oven. Scatter a few flaked almonds onto the top of the frangipane. When all the pastry cases have been filled, transfer to the middle shelf of the oven for 25 minutes until puffed up and golden brown all over. Let settle for 10 minutes before removing from the tartlet rings or muffin tray. Serve warm or cold with a generous spoon of freshly whipped cream.

Refrigerate the other half of your pastry, frangipane and raspberries until you are ready to make a second batch of bakewells. Alternatively, cook a second batch as soon as the tartlet cases/ muffin tray are free and store in an airtight container for up to 3 days.

⤜ Special diet symbols ⤛

v	vegan	*ef*	egg-free
gf	gluten-free	*cn*	contains nuts
wf	wheat-free	*cs*	contains sugar
yf	yeast-free	♡	low-fat
df	dairy-free		

⤜ Conversion tables ⤛

Weight

Common weight conversions (approximate)

Grams	Ounces
25 g	1 oz
50 g	2 oz
75 g	2½ oz
100 g	3½ oz
150 g	5 oz
200 g	7 oz
250 g	9 oz
300 g	10½ oz
400 g	14 oz
500 g	1 lb 2 oz

Liquid capacity

Common liquid conversions (approximate)

Millilitres	Fl. ounces
25 ml	1 fl oz
50 ml	2 fl oz
75 ml	2½ fl oz
100 ml	3½ fl oz
150 ml	5 fl oz
200 ml	7 fl oz
250 ml	9 fl oz
300 ml	10½ fl oz
400 ml	14 fl oz
500 ml	17½ fl oz
1 litre	35 fl oz
(1 litre	*1¾ pints)*

Oven temperatures

Celsius	Fahrenheit
110°C	225°F
130°C	250°F
140°C	275°F
150°C	300°F
170°C	325°F
180°C	350°F
190°C	375°F
200°C	400°F
220°C	425°F
230°C	450°F
240°C	475°F

Index

(Page numbers in bold refer to illustrations and captions)